THE SETTING
OF SECOND CLEMENT
IN EARLY CHRISTIANITY

SUPPLEMENTS TO
NOVUM TESTAMENTUM

VOLUME XXXVIII

LEIDEN
E. J. BRILL
1974

THE SETTING
OF SECOND CLEMENT IN
EARLY CHRISTIANITY

BY

KARL PAUL DONFRIED

LEIDEN
E. J. BRILL
1974

ISBN 90 04 03895 7

PRINTED IN BELGIUM

GÜNTHER BORNKAMM
† HERMANN BABIST (1939-1966)
HANS PETER REICH

in Dankbarkeit

CONTENTS

PREFACE

The words which follow are intended as a doxology of thanksgiving to all those generous and gracious persons who have given assistance along the path of academic and theological development and in the preparation, either directly or indirectly, of this manuscript. First and foremost I must express my deep and lasting gratitude to my *Doktorvater*, Professor Günther Bornkamm, for his patient and wise counsel, for his unfailing kindness and for his constant example of rigorous and critical exegesis. My thanks are also due to the Theological Faculty of the University of Heidelberg who accepted my dissertation on 2 Clement in 1968, which now appears here in substantially revised form. I am especially indebted to Professors Hans von Campenhausen, the late Gerhard von Rad, Hans Walter Wolff, Ferdinand Hahn and Dieter Georgi, who were on that faculty during my stay in Heidelberg. I must also briefly express my great indebtedness to my earlier teachers who helped lay the foundation for a most profitable academic experience in Heidelberg: at Harvard, Amos Wilder, Krister Stendahl, Helmut Köster and G. Ernest Wright; at Union, John Knox, W. D. Davies and Oscar Cullmann.

This study has profited enormously from the close association I have had with my colleagues in the Columbia University Seminar for New Testament Studies. Many have made good and helpful criticisms; most especially I have appreciated the generous assistance I have received from Harvey McArthur, Abraham Malherbe, Robert Kraft and E. Earle Ellis. Equally valuable have been the solid suggestions of Wilhelm Wuellner, Horst Moehring and other members of the *Studiorum Novi Testamenti Societas*. Obviously all remaining errors of fact or judgment are entirely my own.

Professor Wilhelm van Unnik has kindly accepted this study in the *Supplements to Novum Testamentum* series and Smith College has not only kindly provided me with a sabbatical semester to complete revisions on this manuscript, but also with a generous grant to subsidize a portion of the publication cost. Finally, and most importantly, the biggest "thank you" must go to my wife, Kathy, and to my children, Paul and Karen, for their unfailing support and understanding.

Paris   KARL PAUL DONFRIED
January 12, 1973

ABBREVIATIONS

DLZ	*Deutsche Literaturzeitung*
EvTh	*Evangelische Theologie*
ExpT	*Expository Times*
GGA	*Göttingische Gelehrte Anzeigen*
GP	*Gospel of Philip*
GT	*Gospel of Truth*
HibJ	*Hibbert Journal*
HNT	*Handbuch zum Neuen Testament*
HR	*History of Religions*
HTR	*Harvard Theological Review*
HUCA	*Hebrew Union College Annual*
Int	*Interpretation*
JBL	*Journal of Biblical Literature*
JSJ	*Journal for the Study of Judaism*
NTS	*New Testament Studies*
Phil	*Philologus*
*RGG*³	*Die Religion in Geschichte und Gegenwart*, third edition
ThLZ	*Theologische Literaturzeitung*
ThQ	*Theologische Quartalschrift*
ThRu	*Theologische Rundschau*
TS	*Theological Studies*
TWNT	*Theologisches Wörterbuch zum Neuen Testament*
TZ	*Theologische Zeitschrift*
VC	*Vigiliae Christianae*
ZKG	*Zeitschrift für Kirchengeschichte*
ZNW	*Zeitschrift für die neutestamentliche Wissenschaft und die Kunde der älteren Kirche*
ZTK	*Zeitschrift für Theologie und Kirche*

CHAPTER ONE

LITERARY AND HISTORICAL PROBLEMS

1. The Origin of 2 Clement

1 Clement was written from Rome about 96-98 A.D. to the Corinthian church in the hope of ending a schism which had developed there after some persons had succeeded in removing the presbyters from office. The intervention of 1 Clement was successful and those presbyters who had been removed from office were in all probability reinstated. It is our thesis that shortly after their reinstatement these presbyters wrote a hortatory discourse, known to us as 2 Clement, which one of them read to the Corinthian congregation assembled for worship. Because both 1 and 2 Clement had together averted a severe crisis in the life of this congregation they were preserved together by the Corinthians.

This close connection with 1 Clement would suggest that 2 Clement be dated about 98-100 A.D. Some other factors, which will be explored in greater detail further on, also suggest an earlier date than has been customary in previous studies of 2 Clement. These include the fact that 2 Clement represents a very early stage in the total process which eventually leads to the formation of a New Testament canon. As we will show, 2 Clement is still largely dependent on an oral, as opposed to a written, gospel tradition.[1] Further, 2 Clement shares a number of themes and expressions with Valentinian gnosticism; however, these are clearly a part of a gnosticizing trajectory which lead to Valentinian gnosticism but which are not yet a part of it.[2]

Let us review some of the factors which may support the plausibility of the hypothesis just presented concerning the origin of 2 Clement. There are two clues which 2 Clement itself provides with regard to the city of its origin: 1) its relation to 1 Clement in the tradition and in the manuscripts; 2) the use of $\kappa\alpha\tau\alpha\pi\lambda\acute{\epsilon}\omega$ in chapter 7 and the related athletic imagery. Let us discuss each of these factors.

The close relationship between 1 and 2 Clement in the tradition of

---

[1] See especially pp. 56-82.

[2] See, for example, pp. 123-24.

the early church indicates that they were preserved together.[1] This fact alone gives a certain priority to Rome or Corinth, as opposed to Alexandria, since we know the 1 Clement was a writing from the congregation at Rome to the congregation in Corinth. Thus, it is most likely that 2 Clement was preserved with 1 Clement at either Rome or Corinth. But how does one decide between these two ? Let us visualize the situation for a moment. The church at Corinth, according to 1 Clement, was faced with a serious schism and asked Rome for assistance. The church at Rome,[2] after a number of delays, finally wrote to Corinth in order to help correct this situation. From all reports preserved in the early church, 1 Clement did make an impact, the situation at Corinth was corrected, and 1 Clement continued to be read in the worship services at Corinth. This fact is substantiated by a quotation from Dionysius in Eusebius, to which we will refer shortly,[3] and by a quotation from Hegesippus cited and introduced by Eusebius:

> But it is well to listen to what he said after some remarks about the epistle of Clement to the Corinthians: 'And the church of the Corinthians remained in the true doctrine until Primus was bishop at Corinth, and I conversed with them on my voyage to Rome, and spent some days with the Corinthians during which we were refreshed by the true word.[4]

From this it is clear that 1 Clement was valued and preserved in the Corinthian church. It is only natural that the Corinthians would cherish this letter since it helped solve a severe crisis within the life of their congregation. Since 2 Clement was preserved together with 1 Clement and since we know that 1 Clement was especially valued in Corinth, it seems only logical to deduce that 2 Clement, even if it did not originate in Corinth, was also held in a position of prominence by the Corinthians.

A second factor which points to Corinth is the use of κατα πλέω in 2 Clement 7. 2 Clem. 7:1 reads as follows: "Ωστε οὖν, ἀδελφοί μου, ἀγωνισώμεθα εἰδότες, ὅτι ἐν χερσὶν ὁ ἀγὼν καὶ ὅτι εἰς τοὺς φθαρτοὺς ἀγῶνας καταπλέουσιν πολλοί, ἀλλ' οὐ πάντες στεφανοῦνται, εἰ μὴ οἱ πολλὰ κοπιάσαντες καὶ καλῶς ἀγωνισάμενοι. First Zahn[5] and then

---

[1] See pp. 16-21.

[2] At no point is it stated in 1 Clement that it was written by Clement of Rome, although this is very likely. Concerning the authorship of 2 Clement all that can be said, other than the fact that the author was a presbyter, is that it is anonymous.

[3] See pp. 17-18.

[4] *H.e.* 3.22.1ff.

[5] *GGA* 45 (1876), pp. 1414ff. and 1429ff.

Lightfoot[1] argued that the use of καταπλέω in the context of this chapter suggested Corinth as the place at which 2 Clement originated. Lightfoot succinctly states his viewpoint as follows: "When the preacher refers to the crowds that 'land' to take part in the games ... without any mention of the port, we are naturally led to suppose that the homily was delivered in the neighbourhood of the place where these combatants landed. Otherwise we should expect εἰς τὸν Ἰσθμόν, or εἰς Κόρινθον, or some explanatory addition of the kind."[2] This argument is rejected by Harnack. "Man sagt, ... dass das 7. Cap. auf einen korinthischen Verfasser deute, weil dort von den Wettspielen und von denen, die zu ihnen schiffen, die Rede ist; allein nachdem Paulus dieses Bild in die christliche Sprache eingeführt hat, dürfte die Behauptung, dass es nur in Korinth gebraucht werden konnte, sehr unvorsichtig sein."[3] Harnack's criticism in not convincing. Certainly Paul introduces this example into the Christian world, but he does so specifically in reference to Corinth. Further, the important point for Lightfoot is not simply the athletic imagery, but the athletic imagery in conjunction with the verb καταπλέω, a term which is not found in the extant Pauline letters.[4]

Funk, Bardenhewer and Krüger accept the Corinthian hypothesis of Zahn and they add nothing essentially new.[5] Di Pauli, Knopf and C. Richardson reject it.[6] Di Pauli's criticism is not helpful since he

---

[1] J. B. Lightfoot, *The Apostolic Fathers*, I, 2 (London, 1890), pp. 197ff.

[2] *Ibid.*, p. 197.

[3] Adolf von Harnack, *Die Chronologie der altchristlichen Literatur bis Eusebius*, II, 1 (Leipzig, 1897), p. 441.

[4] Harnack himself does not appear overly confident in his criticism of Zahn and Lightfoot. This is suggested by the footnote he adds to the above sentence: "Will man aber durchaus dem 7. Cap. eine specielle Beziehung zu Korinth geben, so hindert schliesslich nichts, anzunehmen, dass dies Capitel mit besonderer Berücksichtigung der korinthischen Gemeinde nachträglich von den Römern in die Predigt eingestellt ist. Indessen bin ich nicht geneigt, das anzunehmen" (Harnack, *Chronologie*, p. 441-42, n. 4). The integral relation of this chapter to the whole document makes the suggestion of a later gloss unlikely.

[5] F. X. Funk, "Der sogennante zweite Klemensbrief," *ThQ* 84 (1902), pp. 349-64; *idem*, "Der sogennante zweite Klemensbrief," *Kirchengeschichtlichen Abhandlungen und Untersuchungen* 3 (1907), pp. 272-75; Otto Bardenhewer, *Geschichte der altkirchlichen Literatur*, I (Freiburg, 1913), p. 489; G. Krüger, "Bemerkungen zum zweiten Klemensbrief" in *Studies in Early Christianity*, ed. by S. J. Case (New York, 1928), pp. 419-39.

[6] A. Di Pauli, "Zum sogennanten 2. Korintherbrief des Klemens Romanus," *ZNW* 4 (1903), pp. 321-29; R. Knopf, *Die Lehre der zwölf Apostel. Die zwei Clemensbriefe* (Tübin-

refuses to deal with the verbal form καταπλέουσιν in verse 1. His only reference is to καταπλεύσωμεν in verse 3. That καταπλεύσωμεν is used metaphorically here is clear; but that does not invalidate Lightfoot's argument for the meaning of καταπλέω in verse 1. Both Knopf and Richardson make their criticisms of the Corinthian hypothesis contingent on the meaning of the verb καταπλέω. "Das Wort καταπλεῖν bedeutet einfach: von der hohen See zum Lande hinab- oder herabfahren, nicht aber: über See zu uns herfahren, und die Worte müssen nicht für eine Hörerschaft bestimmt sein, die an einem Orte wohnt, wo berühmte Wettspiele stattfinden und zu dem man über See fährt "[1] Knopf has given no evidence for his criticism and his suggested definition of καταπλέω does not really stand in contradiction to the Corinthian hypothesis. Richardson proceeds in a similar direction: "Moreover, the reference to the games in ch. 7 cannot be unduly pressed. The verb katapleō can be used in a derived sense, meaning little more than 'resort to'; and the popularity of the Isthmian games were matched by that of those in other centers. Indeed, there were important games held in Alexandria."[2] Richardson, too, fails to provide evidence for these assertions. For example, we have not been able to find any reference to the fact that important games were held in Alexandria. If there were, we have no information that would suggest that they compare in importance with the Isthmian games in Corinth.[3] Also, we have been unable to find evidence for the use of καταπλέω as "resort to." Even if such a reference were to be found, the overwhelming evidence is against such a meaning, as we shall suggest below. Even before turning to this evidence, it must be pointed out that Richardson is not consistent. While he raises the possibility that καταπλέω may mean simply "resort to," he translates it as "while many come by sea ..." in 7:1 and in 7:3 he translates it as "let many of us sail to it and enter it ...."[4]

It will be necessary to examine briefly the uses of καταπλέω in Greek literature. However, before doing so, it may be helpful to ask which games were the most significant during the first and early second

---

gen, 1920), p. 152; C. Richardson, ed., *Early Christian Fathers* (Philadelphia, 1953), pp. 184-87.

[1] Knopf, *Zwei Clemensbriefe*, p. 163.

[2] Richardson, *Early Christian Fathers*, p. 185.

[3] See Oscar Broneer, "Paul and the Pagan Cults at Isthmia," *HTR* 64 (1971), pp. 169-87.

[4] Richardson, *Early Christian Fathers*, pp. 195-96.

century A.D. This is relevant since καταπλέω is directly connected with the imagery of the athletic contest in 2 Clement. There can be no doubt whatever that the most important games toward the end of the first century were the Isthmian.[1] It was neither in Olympia nor in Athens that the Roman Q. Flamininus proclaimed the freedom of Greece in 196 B.C., but in Corinth. In 67 A.D. Nero once again used the occasion of the Isthmian games to proclaim the freedom of Greece. Corinth became a world gathering place both because of the Isthmian games [2] and because of its strategic location.[3] Because of the city's location, the Corinthian festival was the most central and easily accessible, whether by land or sea. Livy suggests that the Isthmian festival "owed its popularity not only to the national love of witnessing contests of every sort in arts or strength or agility, but especially to the advantageous situation of the Isthmus, which, commanding the resources of the two seas, was the natural meeting-place of the human race, the mart of Greece and Asia."[4]

It is also important to remember that many Romans would come to Corinth at this point in history since athletic events of such proportions were frowned upon in Rome itself. L. Friedländer summarizes this attitude: "Solange die national-römische Abneigung und Opposition gegen Althletentum und griechische Agone in Rom bestand (also mindestens noch am Anfange des 2. Jahrhunderts), bewirkte sie wenigstens so viel, dass die Beteiligung an diesen Schauspielen bei den Männern aus den höheren Ständen sich auf ganz vereinzelte Fälle beschränkte und auch in den unteren Ständen Roms keine sehr verbreitete war."[5] In fact, so many Italians came to the Isthmian games by sea that the port town of Lechaon, twelve stadia from Corinth, was

---

[1] Strabo 8.6.20; Aristides, *Isthm.* 45; see also Broneer, "Paul and the Pagan Cults at Isthmia."

[2] Schneider, in Pauly-Wissowa, *Real-Enzyklopädie der klassischen Altertumswissenschaft* IX. col. 2253-54, writes: "In der Kaiserzeit sah man an den Isthmien Leute von Ionien und Sizilien, von Italien und Libyen, von Marseille und von Borysthenes (Dion von Prusa IX 5)."

[3] Fimmen, in Pauly-Wissowa IX. col. 2258, writes: "Die Bedeutung der I. -Häfen war um so grösser, da die Landenge der kürzesten Verbindung des im Altertum sehr starken Seeverkehrs von Ägäischen zum Ionischen Meer Aufenthalt und Unterbrechung gebot."

[4] Livy 33.32; cited in E. Norman Gardiner, *Greek Athletic Sports and Festivals* (London, 1910), p. 215.

[5] Ludwig Friedländer, *Darstellungen aus der Sittengeschichte Roms*, II (Leipzig, 1922), p. 155.

used just for their ships, while Cenchreae was used primarily for the ships coming from Asia.

A review of the use of the verb καταπλέω in Greek literature reveals a term with a variety of nuances. It can simply mean "to sail from the high sea to land, to put in,"[1] either in the sense of sailing into shore after a battle at sea[2] or sailing in from another location as in Josephus, *Bell.* 1.610: "However as he [Antipater] was entering (κατέπλει) the harbour of Celenderis...." This latter use is similar to 2 Clem. 7:1 where καταπλέουσιν surely means "a coming in by sea." That καταπλέω can definitely be used to describe a movement from one city to another by means of the sea in amply attested. In Herodotus I.2, "They sailed in a long ship to Aea"; I.165, "they first sailed to Phocaea ..."; III.45, "they sailed back to Samos ..."; VIII.109, "let us set sail for the Hellespont and Ionia"; VIII.132, "entreating the Greeks to sail to Ionia"; IX.98 "make sail for the Hellespont;" also Xenophon, *Hell.* V.1.28, "sailing to Athens."[3] In view of these references, Lightfoot's argument makes sense: for 2 Clement καταπλέω is used to mean a coming into shore and the reason it is unnecessary to name the city is because the persons addressed by 2 Clement are in that city. Secondly, if one were a citizen of Celenderis in Cilicia and were referring to Antipater's arrival in some illustration, it would be unnecessary for that person to mention his own city by name and thus belabor the obvious. In the same way it is most probable that the congregation in Corinth clearly understood the reference in question as referring to the Isthmian games in their city and that it was so intended by the author of 2 Clement.[4]

Our investigation leads to the same conclusion as that of the late classical scholar, Rudolf Herzog: "Der Verfasser hat im 6. Kapitel die

---

[1] See H. G. Liddell and R. Scott, *A Greek-English Lexicon* (Oxford, 1961), p. 906.

[2] Xenophon, *Hell.* I.7.29; Herodotus VI.97; VII.195.

[3] We must briefly refer to another, less frequent meaning of καταπλέω: "to sail down stream." This meaning, rather than referring to the larger sense of sailing in from the high sea, is used more narrowly in the sense of sailing down the Nile to Alexandria, for which the verb καταπλέω is regularly used in the papyri. One example from the list cited by Moulton-Milligan is from the third century B.C., P. Lille I.17:7: καταπλεῖ γὰρ εἰς Ἀλεξάνδρεαν φίλων (J. H. Moulton and G. Milligan, *The Vocabulary of the Greek Testament* [London, 1963], p. 331). This sense we might add, would not be foreign to Corinth, since to arrive there from Italy involves a "sailing down." However, the first meaning, "to sail from the high sea to land, to put in," is more adequate given the context of 2 Clement 7.

[4] Not, though, in 7:3 where it is used metaphorically.

beliebte Antithese von den φθαρτά und ἄφθαρτα gebraucht. Die hat ihm I. Kor. 9, 24-27 in die Erinnerung gerufen, wo Paulus zu den Korinthern mit deutlicher Bezugnahme auf die Agone der Isthmier, die für das Leben der Stadt von grosser Bedeutung waren, in Vergleichen aus diesen Agonen redet. Das tut nun der Prediger im 7. Kapitel noch ausführlicher und mit so technischen Ausdrücken, dass die Sache ihm und seinen Hörern ganz geläufig gewesen sein muss. Insbesondere kann man εἰς τοὺς ἀγῶνας καταπλέουσιν πολλοί nur von den Isthmien sagen, denn καταπλεῖν gibt das Ziel der Reise an. Die Antithese φθαρτός — ἄφθαρτος regt den Verfasser sodann zu einem Wortspiel mit dem technischen Ausdruck φθείρειν τὸν ἀγῶνα an, der alle betrügerischen Vergehen gegen die Spielregeln, namentlich solche auf Grund von Bestechungen, Verkauf des Siegs, umfasst. Auch die Strafen dafür gibt er richtig an."[1]

As we turn now to other factors affecting the origin of 2 Clement, let us recall the hypothesis which we are proposing with regard to the *Sitz im Leben* of this document: 2 Clement is a hortatory address written by presbyters at Corinth who had been expelled from office earlier, but who have now been reinstated. It was read shortly after the arrival and successful impact of I Clement and it is a call to the congregation to repent from their past errors. That this exhortation was accepted seems indicated by the fact that Corinth had no further difficulties at least until the time of Primus and, of course, by the very fact that it was preserved. Had the congregation rejected it out of hand, it would be difficult to account for its preservation.

Before we examine the historical connection between 1 and 2 Clement, the background leading to the writing of 1 Clement must be described.[2] The basic problem in Corinth was a revolt against the ruling presbyters.

---

[1] Cited by Krüger, "Bemerkungen," p. 424, as a letter from Herzog to Krüger. There is one other observation which might also suggest that a reference such as the one found in 2 Clem. 7:1 would be understood as referring to Corinth. We have in mind the popular saying of the first and second century which is cited by Strabo 8.378 and 12.559 (ca. 63 B.C. to ca. 21 A.D.) and Aulus Gellius *Att. noct.* 1.8.4 (ca. 123 to ca. 165 A.D.) as proverbial: οὐ παντὸς ἀνδρὸς ἐς Κόρινθον ἐσθ' ὁ πλοῦς ("Not everyone can have the opportunity to sail to Corinth"). This saying refers to the whole complex of activities available at Corinth, including not only the Isthmian games but also its sexual promiscuity. If πλέω can refer proverbially to Corinth, it is entirely possible that one resident in Corinth could easily use the term καταπλέω without having to further specify the referent.

[2] See the study by Karlmann Beyschlag, *Clemens Romanus und der Frühkatholizismus* (Tübingen, 1966) and the literature cited there.

This is suggested by 1 Clem. 3:3 and explicitly stated in 44:6ff.: "But you, we observe, have removed a number of people, despite their good conduct, from a ministry they have fulfilled with honor and integrity. Your contention and rivalry, brothers, thus touches matters that bear on our salvation." Because of this situation the church at Rome dispatched the letter known to us as 1 Clement to the congregation at Corinth together with three delegates, Claudius Ephebus, Valerius Bito and Fortunatus (65:1). There is a wide consensus among scholars that this letter was written either at the end of Domitian's reign or at the beginning of Nerva's, that is, between 96-98 A.D.[1]

What kind of persons stood behind the revolt in Corinth? What were the causative factors in this revolt against the presbyters? Many scholars have described these persons as pneumatics who claimed to have particular spiritual gifts. This position has recently been accepted by such scholars as C. Richardson and G. Bornkamm. "We can recognize fairly clearly," observes Bornkamm, "that the group of younger men who revolted against the office-bearers in the congregation consisted of pneumatics (13:1; 38:1f; 48:5f) and thus were not dissimilar to the opponents of Paul in 2 Corinthians."[2] This conclusion can be supported from the text of 1 Clement at a number of points.

1 Clement 13 and 15-19 can best be understood if one views the opponents as pneumatics who so boasted in their spiritual power that it produced rivalry and dissension within the congregation. This would explain the significance of a whole series of quotations, such as "be rid of all pretentions and arrogance" or "let not the wise man boast of his wisdom ... let him that boasts boast in the Lord ..." (13:1). This theme continues when 1 Clement speaks about the arrogance and rivalry of those "who exalt themselves above the flock" (16:1). The Corinthians are told that the "Lord Jesus Christ did not come with pomp of pride or arrogance, though he could have done so. But he came in humility ..." (16:2). The remainder of 1 Clement 16 is a criticism of the arrogant.[3]

---

[1] For example, Richardson, *Early Christian Fathers*, p. 34, and G. Bornkamm, "The History of the Origin of the So-Called Second Letter to the Corinthians" in *The Authorship and Integrity of the New Testament*, ed. by K. Aland, *et. al.*, (London, 1965), pp. 73-81.

[2] Bornkamm, "History," p. 81.

[3] W. Lütgert, *Amt und Geist im Kampf* (Gütersloh, 1911), p. 68, refers to these chapters in the following way: "Ähnlicher Vorzüge also müssen sich die Führer des Aufruhrs gerühmt haben. Sie nahmen prophetische Begabung, besondere Frömmigkeit und

The practical result of this spiritual superiority is that these persons refuse to obey the presbyters, which is in contrast to their previous behavior when they were obedient to their rulers and presbyters: "You were all humble and without any pretensions, obeying orders rather than issuing them" (1 Clem. 2:1).[1] All of 1 Clement 37 is a discussion about the necessity of discipline. Further, the argument in chapters 42-44 suggests that the opposition of the pneumatics, while possibly including personal elements, was essentially an opposition to the office of the presbyter.[2]

This failure to obey the presbyters is related to worship. As one reads 1 Clement 40-41 it appears as if Clement is trying to correct a false understanding concerning the time and place of worship by referring to the Old Testament. In 1 Clement 40 it is stressed that worship is to be carried out in an "orderly fashion ... not in a careless and disorderly way, but at times and seasons he fixed. Where he wants them performed, and by whom, he himself fixed by his supreme will....' " That differing views on worship created a problem in Corinth is further elaborated by Harnack and Lütgert.[3]

Thus far we have reviewed three topics which the Romans judged significant enough to deal with at some length in their letter to the church at Corinth: a) the failure to obey the presbyters, b) a description of the schismatics, and c) the problem of worship. It may be helpful to inquire whether 2 Clement reflects this same situation and whether its author is responding to it.

Let us begin with the problem of disobedience to the Corinthian presbyters, which is a prominent theme throughout 1 Clement. A characteristic description of the situation is found in 57:1-2: "And that is why you who are responsible for the revolt must submit to the presbyters. You must humble your hearts and be disciplined so that you repent. You must learn obedience, and be done with your proud boasting

---

Gerechtigkeit, ein besonderes Verhältnis zu Gott, Weisheit, Geist, Kraft, Heiligkeit für sich in Anspruch und zwar in einem höheren Masse als die Gemeinde, und erhoben sich damit über die Gemeinde."

[1] See also 1 Clem. 1:3.

[2] Lütgert, *Amt und Geist*, p. 57: "Der Ungehorsam der Gemeinde ist nicht nur ein tatsächlicher, sondern ein grundsätzlicher. Sie verweigern den Presbytern den Gehorsam prinzipiell. In dieser Aufkündigung des Gehorsams besteht der Aufruhr."

[3] Adolf von Harnack, *Das Schreiben der römischen Kirche an die Korinthische aus der Zeit Domitians (I. Clemensbrief)* (Leipzig, 1929), pp. 88ff.; Lütgert, *Amt und Geist*, p. 62.

and curb your arrogant tongues." Then at the end of the appeal, in 1
Clem. 63:1ff., the Corinthians are exhorted to "bow the neck and adopt
the attitude of obedience," to follow "the plea of our letter for peace
and harmony" and to "rid yourselves of your wicked and passionate
rivalry." When one keeps these and the previous references in mind,
together with the hypothesis that 2 Clement may be an address
exhorting the Corinthians to repentance by their recently reinstated
presbyters, then a number of passages in 2 Clement fall into place.

One of these passages is 2 Clem. 19:1: "For compensation I beg you
to repent with all your heart, granting yourselves salvation and life."
Is this not a strange request on the part of the speaker: $\mu\iota\sigma\theta\grave{o}\nu$ $\gamma\grave{a}\rho$
$a\grave{\iota}\tau\hat{\omega}$ $\acute{\upsilon}\mu\hat{a}\varsigma$ $\kappa\tau\lambda$. ? Why does the presbyter ask for "compensation"?
He asks for compensation precisely because he has been wronged: he has
been removed from his office. Now that the presbyters have been
restored to their former position he, acting on behalf of the other
presbyters, asks the congregation for compensation, viz., to repent
from their disobedience to the presbyters and their faithlessness toward
Jesus Christ.[1]

In 2 Clement 13 the author is urging that the Name, Jesus Christ,
not be blasphemed.[2] He then writes, "How is it scoffed at?" and the
answer is, "By your failing to do what I want." It is this failure to
obey the presbyters which is the basic reason why the name of Jesus
Christ is scoffed at by the heathen. This factor of disobedience against
the presbyters is brought to very clear expression in 2 Clem. 17:5-6
where we have the imagery of the last judgment when the sovereignty of the world is given to Jesus and suddenly "those who were
ungodly among us and who perverted the commands of Jesus Christ"
will say, "Alas for us, for you really existed, and we neither recognized
it nor believed, and *we did not obey the presbyters* who preached to us
our salvation." This relationship of obedience to the presbyters and
salvation is also a theme in 1 Clem. 45:1: "Your contention and rivalry,
brothers, thus touches matters that bear on our salvation." The theological misapprehension of the pneumatics in both 1 and 2 Clement
leads to a basic misunderstanding of Jesus and a failure to obey the
presbyters. These two errors together have a definite bearing on the
theme of salvation. Is not this what 2 Clem. 1:1 is also expressing?

---

[1] See 1 Clem. 1:3; 2:1; 3:3; 9:3; 10:2,7; 19:1; 21:6; 44:5; 47:6; 54:2; 55:4.
[2] See the discussion below, pp. 154-59.

"Brothers, we ought to think of Jesus Christ as we do of God—as the 'judge of the living and the dead.' And we ought not to belittle our salvation." These factors do suggest the possibility of an interrelationship between 1 and 2 Clement; both, in different ways, reflect the unrest in the Corinthian congregation.

The second factor we explored above was the nature of the schismatics who stood behind the revolt in Corinth. That these pneumatics boasted of an elite γνῶσις is stressed not only in 1 Clem. 48:5, but also in 41:4, "You see, brothers, the more knowledge we are given, the greater risks we run"; and in 1:2 we hear that in the past the Corinthians had "a perfect and trustworthy knowledge", the implication being that this is not now the case.[1] In 2 Clement the question of a correct understanding of gnosis also plays an important role. Immediately after the theological section, which we will suggest below reflects a tendency quite similar to that of the pneumatic schismatics in 1 Clement, the ethical section is introduced with a rhetorical question dealing with the matter of the proper gnosis. In fact, one could understand the whole of the ethical section as an explication of what this proper gnosis is. 2 Clem. 3:1a is a summary of the credo in chapter 1: "Seeing, then, that he has had such pity on us, firstly, in that we who are alive do not sacrifice to dead gods or worship them, but through him have come to know the Father of truth"; and then comes the question, "what is knowledge (γνῶσις) in reference to him, save refusing to deny him through whom we came to know the Father?" What follows clearly indicates that this gnosis is to be made manifest and concrete in deeds and actions. This same relationship between gnosis and action is found in 1 Clem. 48:5-49:1.

It is also important to observe that both 1 and 2 Clement are opposing those who deny God's eschatological promises, a position which the pneumatics held.[2] There are a number of interesting similarities

---

[1] Note also the references in 36:2 and 40:1.

[2] Because of this hesitation to believe God's promises concerning the future, both the authors of 1 and 2 Clement put a great stress on ἐπαγγελία: 1 Clem. 10:2; 26:1; 27:1; 34:7 and 2 Clem. 5:5; 10:3,4; 11:1,7; 15:4. Otherwise the word is not very frequent in the other Apostolic Fathers or in the later New Testament writings, with the exception of Hebrews. Since these persons do not believe in the future promises of God, their words and actions do not coincide (cf. 1 Clem. 15; 2 Clem. 4) and they get carried away with their own desires (1 Clem. 3:4; 28:1; 30:1; 2 Clem. 16:2; 17:3; 19:2). Thus, both 1 Clement (30:3; 35:2; 38:2; 62:2; 64:1) and 2 Clement (4:3; 15:1) find it necessary to exhort their congregation to self-control (ἐγκράτεια/ἐγκρατής).

between 2 Clement 9ff. and 1 Clement 23ff. While both 1 and 2 Clement contain elements of traditional paraenesis present in other early Christian writings, they contain a unique overlap of similar themes. The fact that both are dealing with a group opposed to the presbyters cannot simply be explained on the basis of a transmission of traditional paraenesis; rather, both are addressing a real and contemporary situation. In short, it appears most likely that both 1 and 2 Clement are directing their exhortations against a similar distortion of the Christian faith.

The third aspect we dealt with above was the suggestion that there might have been some controversy regarding the time and place of worship in Corinth. This is suggested not only by 1 Clement 40-41, but also by 2 Clem. 17:3: "Rather should we strive to come here more often and advance in the Lord's commands, so that 'with a common mind' we may all be gathered together to gain life."[1] All that we can ascertain from this passage is that there were some who did not worship regularly with the congregation. That there may have been some division on this point could be suggested by the exhortation that we should come together with "a common mind," but it is difficult to determine precisely from this limited information whether 1 and 2 Clement are responding to the same situation, although that is likely.

We must now proceed with our investigation of 1 Clement and raise the question concerning its central purpose—in other words, what goal it is trying to achieve. The obvious intention is to end the schism in Corinth and to restore the presbyters to their former position. But how is this to occur? The congregation in Corinth must repent. We agree fully with Beyschlag in his recent study on 1 Clement when he states: "In der Tat ist auch der I Clem im Kern nichts anderes als eine Schrift zur 2. Busse."[2] Just a few quick glances at 1 Clement are sufficient to show the accuracy of this statement. Chapters 51-57 have exactly one goal: to bring the Corinthians to repentance. In 51:1 the readers are exhorted to ask for pardon and in 51:3 we hear that it "is better for a man to confess his sins ...." In chapter 57 we learn that the spiritual superiority of the pneumatics makes it impossible for them to repent and because of this attitude they revolted against the presbyters. In

---

[1] See 1 Clem. 34:7. In 2 Clem. 17:3 the Greek, πυκνότερον προσερχόμενοι, could mean "to the presence of God," but with the majority of commentators the meaning "to this place of meeting" is to be preferred in view of the context.

[2] Beyschlag, *Clemens Romanus*, p. 145.

57:1 we read: "And that is why you who are responsible for the revolt must submit to the presbyters. You must humble your hearts and be disciplined so that you repent. You must learn obedience, and be done with your proud boasting and curb your arrogant tongues." 1 Clement 39 is directed precisely against those pneumatics who are foolish enough to think that they can do without repentance. 1 Clement 13-16 is directed against their hardness of heart. Chapters 17-18, highlighted by the example of David, illustrate how the great Old Testament heroes themselves confessed their transgressions and repented of their wrong. One must concur with Lütgert when he concludes: "Festzustehen scheint mir aber, dass die Pneumatiker als solche grundsätzlich die Busse und die Unterordnung unter die Presbyter verweigert haben und dass darin ihr Hochmut bestand."[1] Therefore they must repent and do good works.

Our investigation of 2 Clement will reveal that it too had a similar purpose: a call to repentance. That 1 and 2 Clement are interrelated at this point is evident. What 1 Clement appeals for in general terms, 2 Clement is able to carry out more intimately and specifically. 2 Clement can do this because it is an exhortation spoken by one of the presbyters, on behalf of the others, in the presence of the actual congregation.[2] Thus 2 Clement is far better acquainted with the reality of the situation than 1 Clement.

---

[1] Lütgert, *Amt und Geist*, p. 74.

[2] This point can be further substantiated by an examination of the terminology shared by 1 and 2 Clement in this area. In 1 Clem. 7:1, the purpose of that letter is described as follows: "We are writing ... not only to admonish you. ..." The verb νουθετέω as used here is also found in 2 Clem. 17:2, 3 and 19:2. Otherwise it is not found in the Apostolic Fathers, with the exception of a few references in Hermas, and infrequently in the New Testament. The combination μετανοέω/μετάνοια hardly appears in the later books of the New Testament, but it does appear with frequency in 1 and 2 Clement: 1 Clem. 7:4; 5, 6, 7; 8:1, 2, 3, 5; 57:1; 62:2; 2 Clem. 8:1, 2, 3; 9:8; 13:1; 15:1; 16:1, 4; 17:1; 19:1. One should also note the word θέλημα, used in the sense of doing the will of God. It appears only in Ignatius among the Apostolic Fathers, and never with a great degree of frequency in any of the late New Testament writings, yet one notes the following frequent usage in 1 and 2 Clement: 1 Clem. 14:2; 20:4; 21:4; 32:3, 4; 33:8; 34:52; 36:6; 40:3; 42:2; 49:6; 56:1, 2; 61:1; 2 Clem. 5:1; 6:7; 8:4; 9:11; 10:1; 14:12. In both writings the term ἀγών is used to describe the nature of the Christian life, a term not used elsewhere in the Apostolic Fathers and infrequently in the New Testament: 1 Clem. 2:4; 7:1; 2 Clem. 7:1, 2, 3, 4, 5. One should also observe the common stress on δικαιοσύνη: 1 Clem. 3:4; 5:7; 10:6; 13:1; 18:15; 31:2; 33:8; 35:2; 42:5; 48:2, 4; 60:2; 62:2; 2 Clem. 4:2; 6:9; 11:7; 12:1; 13:1; 18:2; 19:2, 3.

Finally, we must ask whether these remarks in any way help clarify the meaning of 2 Clem. 19:1: "Ὥστε, ἀδελφοὶ καὶ ἀδελφαί, μετὰ τὸν θεὸν τῆς ἀληθείας ἀναγινώσκω ὑμῖν ἔντευξιν εἰς τὸ προσέχειν τοῖς γεγραμμένοις, ἵνα καὶ ἑαυτοὺς σώσητε καὶ τὸν ἀναγινώσκοντα ἐν ὑμῖν.[1] We shall give our understanding of this verse straightaway and then attempt to support it. The expression "after the God of truth" does not refer to a scripture lesson which preceded the preaching of 2 Clement.[2] The expression, "I am reading you an exhortation" refers to 2 Clement which was composed and written prior to the worship service and which had just been read to the congregation. The remainder of this expression "to heed what was there written" refers not to a scripture lesson, but to 1 Clement.

Almost all scholars who have dealt with 2 Clem. 19:1 have insisted that γεγραμμένοις must refer to an Old Testament text which was read prior to 2 Clement. While γράφειν in the perfect can often refer to the Jewish scriptures, this is by no means always the case or must it be the case. In 1 Clem. 63:2 it is used to describe 1 Clement itself. In fact, we suggest that the presbyter had 1 Clem. 63:2 very clearly in mind as he was writing his summary in 2 Clement 19. In 1 Clem. 63:2 we find the same key words, γράφειν in the perfect and ἔντευξις, both of which occur in 2 Clem. 19:1. The actual text of 1 Clem. 63:2 is: χαρὰν γὰρ καὶ ἀγαλλίασιν ἡμῖν παρέξετε, ἐὰν ὑπήκοοι γενόμενοι τοῖς ὑφ' ἡμῶν γεγραμμένοις διὰ τοῦ ἁγίου πνεύματος ἐκκόψητε τὴν ἀθέμιτον τοῦ ζήλους ὑμῶν ὀργὴν κατὰ τὴν ἔντευξιν.[3] It is clear that the Roman church describes its own writing to the Corinthians as γεγραμμένοις; in the same way our author refers to 1 Clement as τοῖς γεγραμμένοις. What is the relation of ἔντευξις[4] in 1 Clem. 63:2

---

[1] Richardson's translation: "So my brothers and sisters, after God's truth I am reading you an exhortation to heed what was there written, so that you may save yourselves and your reader."

[2] Against R. Knopf, "Die Anagnose zum zweiten Clemensbrief," *ZNW* 3 (1902), pp. 266-79; see also the discussion on pp. 55-56 below.

[3] Richardson's translation: "Yes, you will make us exceedingly happy if you prove obedient to what we, prompted by the Holy Spirit, have written, and if, following the plea of our letter for peace and harmony, you rid yourselves of your wicked and passionate rivalry."

[4] In both 1 and 2 Clement, ἔντευξις may be translated as a "petition." This term in itself does not define a genre; for example, an ἔντευξις could take the form of a letter (1 Clement) or a hortatory address (2 Clement). See also Moulton-Milligan, *Vocabulary*, p. 218; J. S. White, *The Form and Structure of the Official Petition* (Missoula, 1972), and our discussion of ἔντευξις on pp. 34-36 below.

and 2 Clem. 19:1? How can both 1 and 2 Clement claim to be an
ἔντευξις? This can be explained easily: 2 Clement is an ἔντευξις from
the Corinthian presbyters to their congregation. That which enabled the
presbyters to make their ἔντευξις was the prior ἔντευξις from the
Roman congregation and, because of it, the presbyters were able to
urge their fellow believers "to heed what was there written," viz.,
in 1 Clement.[1]

We turn for a moment to the opening phrase μετὰ τὸν θεὸν κτλ.
Lightfoot cites Bryennios as giving the correct understanding: "After
you have heard the voice of God in the Scriptures."[2] But this is purely
conjectural and we find no basis for understanding this phrase as referring to the scriptures. A more accurate paraphrase in light of our
discussion might be, "After you have heard the voice of God in the
letter from the Romans (1 Clement)."[3] The Greek phrase μετὰ τὸν
θεὸν τῆς ἀληθείας should best be translated as "after God's truth."
That 1 Clement made a great impact and had a continuing authority
in the Corinthian congregation is beyond doubt, and that this truth
is to be found in 1 Clement is suggested by that letter itself. For example, in 1 Clem. 59:1 there is a consciousness that God himself is speaking
in and through this letter: "If, on the other hand, there be some who
fail to obey what God has told them through us, they must realize
that they will enmesh themselves in sin and in no insignificant danger."
One could point to a variety of similar texts,[4] such as 1 Clem. 63:2,
where it is stated that 1 Clement "was prompted by the Holy Spirit."
In view of such statements it is very natural for our author to
summarize 1 Clement with the statement "after God's truth."[5]

---

[1] See Beyschlag, *Clemens Romanus*, pp. 173-74.

[2] Lightfoot, *Apostolic Fathers*, p. 257.

[3] These observations, if correct, remove the basis for Schüssler's ("Ist der zweite
Klemensbrief ein einheitliches Ganzes," *ZKG* 28 [1907], pp. 1-13) argument that 2 Clement 19-20 are a later addition. We, of course, consider these chapters as part of the whole.
Many of Schüssler's arguments against this can be explained by the fact that chapters
19 and 20 serve as a summary.

[4] For example, 1 Clem. 35:5; 56:1.

[5] Adolf Ziegler, *Neue Studien zum ersten Klemensbrief* (München, 1958), supports our
understanding of 1 Clement. Speaking of Clement he says (p. 111): "Hier spricht er mahn-
end zu den Korinthern, zu einer anderen Gemeinde, um die A[utorität] der abgesetzten
Presbyter wieder herzustellen; es ist nicht eine einfache Mahnung zwischen Mensch
und Mensch, es steht hinter ihr der Wille und die A[utorität] Gottes, denn nach 56, 2 ist
die Mahnung, die wir einander geben, gut und überaus nützlich, denn sie verbindet uns
eng mit dem Willen Gottes." And on p. 117 we read: "Der Verfasser des Briefes trete

2. Previous Studies

In 1903 Di Pauli wrote: "Ein noch ungelöstes Problem der altchristlichen Literaturgeschichte bietet der 2. Korintherbrief des Clemens
Romanus."[1] Research since that time has not invalidated this statement. There has been little agreement among scholars as to the date,
place of origin, purpose or "Sitz im Leben" of 2 Clement. The actual
situation which may have produced this document and the kind of
problem to which it may have been addressed is hardly entertained,
except in such extreme forms as Schwegler's suggestion that it was
written against the Ebionites,[2] or R. Harris' suggestion that the
author was the encratite Julius Cassianus.[3] Even the most recent
studies of R. Grant and Holt Graham add little new. Both suggest
that 2 Clement was written in Rome during the time of Hyginus
(136-140), but Grant himself admits that this is "a wild hypothesis."[4]
Since there is such little clarity concerning the basic reason for
2 Clement's existence, it is not surprising that the literature reveals
a great diversity of opinion concerning both the date and place of its
origin. Pfleiderer, Bartlet, Streeter and C. Richardson all argue for
Alexandria.[5] Wocher, Funk, Zahn, Quasten, Lightfoot, Bardenhewer
and Krüger suggest a Corinthian origin.[6] But even within this second
group there is wide diversity of opinion. Lightfoot holds 2 Clement
to be a homily written about 120 *or earlier*, while Wocher holds it to

---

als Richter und Stellvertreter Gottes auf. ..." In light of what Ziegler concludes, we can
only reassert what was said before: μετὰ τὸν θεὸν τῆς ἀληθείας can be understood as
a perfectly natural reference to 1 Clement. It is God himself who wants an end to this
schism—and that is why 1 Clement was written.

  [1] Di Pauli, "Zum sogennanten," p. 321.

  [2] A. Schwegler, *Das nachapostolischen Zeitalter*, I (Tübingen, 1846), pp. 448-55.

  [3] R. Harris, "The Authorship of the So-called Second Epistle of Clement," *ZNW* 23
(1924), pp. 193-200. This position has been effectively refuted by H. Windisch, "Julius
Cassianus und die Clemenshomilie," *ZNW* 25 (1926), pp. 258-62.

  [4] Robert M. Grant and Holt Graham, *The Apostolic Fathers*, II (New York, 1965),
pp. 109-10; Robert M. Grant, *The Apostolic Fathers*, I (New York, 1964), p. 46.

  [5] Otto Pfleiderer, *Das Urchristentum, seine Schriften und Lehren* (Berlin, 1902),
p. 596; Vernon Bartlet, "The Origin and Date of 2 Clement," *ZNW* 7 (1906), pp. 123-35;
B. H. Streeter, *The Primitive Church* (London 1929), pp. 238ff.; C. Richardson, *Early
Christian Fathers*, pp. 186-87.

  [6] Wocher, *Der Brief des Clemens und des Polykarp* (Tübingen, 1830); Funk, "Der
sogennanten," p. 349; Johannes Quasten, *Patrology I* (Utrecht, 1962), p. 54; Lightfoot,
Apostolic Fathers, pp. 197ff.; Otto Bardenhewer, *Geschichte der altkirchlichen Literatur*,
I (Freiburg, 1913), p. 489; Krüger, "Bemerkungen," p. 423.

be an epistle from the hand of Bishop Dionysius (c. 170). A third group of scholars, including Harnack, Hilgenfeld, Hagemann, von Schubert, Knopf, Grant, Di Pauli, Graham and Goodspeed, postulate a Roman origin.[1] Some within this group, such as Knopf, would urge a date as early as 130 and others, such as Harnack and Di Pauli, a date closer to 170.

Of all the past attempts to explain the historical setting of 2 Clement the most ingenious is surely that of Harnack. Harnack argues that 2 Clement is a letter from Bishop Soter of Rome (c. 165/7-173/5) to the Corinthian congregation.[2] He attempts to support this argument in a number of ways. First, he draws our attention to the statement of Eusebius in *H.e.* 3.38.4: Ἰστέον δ' ὡς καὶ δευτέρα τις εἶναι λέγεται τοῦ Κλήμεντος ἐπιστολή. This whole section in translation reads: "It must be known that there is also a second letter ascribed to Clement, but we have not the same knowledge of its recognition as we have of the former, for we do not even know if the primitive writers used it." Secondly, he refers to the comments of Bishop Dionysius of Corinth (c. 170), as recorded by Eusebius. Eusebius states:

> There is, moreover, extant a letter of Dionysius to the Romans addressed to Soter who was then bishop, and there is nothing better than to quote the words in which he welcomes the custom of the Romans, which was observed down to the persecutions in our own times. 'This has been your custom from the beginning, to do good in manifold ways to all Christians, and to send contributions to the many churches in every city, in some places relieving the poverty of the needy, and ministering to the Christians in the mines, by the contribution which you have sent from the beginning, preserving the ancestral custom of the Romans, true Romans as you are. Your blessed bishop Soter has not only carried on this habit but has even increased it, by administering the bounty distributed to the saints and by exhorting with his blessed words the brethren who come to Rome, as a loving father would his children.'
>
> In this same letter he also quotes the letter of Clement to the Corinthians, showing that from the beginning it had been the custom to read it in the church. τὴν σήμερον

---

[1] Harnack, "Chronologie," p. 440; A. Hilgenfeld, *Die apostolische Väter* (Halle, 1853), p. 120; Hagemann, "Über den zweiten Brief des Clemens von Rom," *ThQ* 43 (1861), pp. 522ff.; H. von Schubert, "Der sog. zweite Clementsbrief, eine Gemeindepredigt" in *Neutestamentliche Apokryphen*, ed., E. Hennecke (Tübingen, 1924), p. 589; Knopf, *Zwei Clemensbriefe*, p. 152; Grant, *Apostolic Fathers*, p. 46; Di Pauli, "Zum sogenannten," pp. 324ff.; Graham, *Apostolic Fathers*, II, p. 109; Edgar Goodspeed, *The Apostolic Fathers* (New York, 1950), p. 83.

[2] Harnack, *Chronologie*, pp. 438-50. This position has been accepted by such prominent scholars as Kirsopp Lake in his translation of *Eusebius*, I (London, 1965), p. 383, and by Goodspeed, *Apostolic Fathers*, p. 83.

οὖν κυριακὴν ἁγίαν ἡμέραν διηγάγομεν, ἐν ᾗ ἀνέγνωμεν ὑμῶν τὴν ἐπιστολήν, ἣν ἕξομεν ἀεί
ποτε ἀναγινώσκοντες νουθετεῖσθαι, ὡς καὶ τὴν προτέραν ἡμῖν διὰ Κλήμεντος γραφεῖσαν."[1]

From Dionysius' letter, Harnack draws the following conclusions:
(1) that the Corinthians have just now, or in the recent past, received a
communication from the Roman church; (2) that the Corinthians read a
letter from Clement of Rome during their worship; (3) a. that they will
regard this current letter highly by continuing to read it, like the
first; b. and, further, that "... sie schicken sich bereits an, die beiden
römischen Schreiben an sie als erster und zweiter zu zählen ..."[2];
and (4) that this communication will serve them as a νουθεσία.

Except for assertion 3b, for which there is no evidence,[3] one can
agree with Harnack's line of reasoning. But there is difficulty in
following Harnack's logic in his identification of ὑμῶν τὴν ἐπιστολήν
with the present text of 2 Clement. "Lässt sich von hier aus nicht seine
Geschichte in der Kirche, das Aufkommen der Meinung, er sei auch ein
Clemensschreiben, und das Ansehen, welcher er gewonnen hat, auf das
beste erklären? Ja, 'erklären' ist hier nicht das richtige Wort: es ist
bereits alles gegeben."[4] But has Harnack really demonstrated this
adequately? We will return to this momentarily.

Harnack deals with three possible arguments against his supposition
that 2 Clement is really a letter of Bishop Soter of Rome to the church
of Corinth: 1) that 2 Clement comes from Corinth, not Rome; 2) that
2 Clement is not a letter, but a homily; and 3) that it was probably
written earlier than the reign of Bishop Soter. We have already suggested why Corinth is more probable than Rome[5] and we have proposed a considerably earlier date of composition.[6] Thus far, however,
we have not discussed the second possible argument against Harnack's
hypothesis, the question of genre. From the beginning of the nineteenth
century to the present there has been considerable ambiguity concerning
the basic nature of 2 Clement. In addition to Harnack, Lake, Goodspeed and others have strongly supported the view that 2 Clement is in

---

[1] *H.e.* 4.23.9-11.

[2] Harnack, *Chronologie*, p. 440.

[3] Lightfoot, *Apostolic Fathers*, p. 192, n. 1, refers to this passage in Eusebius: "The
passage however has been strongly misinterpreted, as though τὴν προτέραν meant *the
former of Clement's two epistles*—a meaning which the context does not at all favour and
which the grammar excludes, for then we should require τὴν προτέραν τῶν διὰ Κλήμεντος
γραφεισῶν."

[4] Harnack, *Chronologie*, p. 440.

[5] See pp. 1-7 above.

[6] See p. 1 above.

the form of a letter, and beyond that, that it was sent by Bishop Soter of Rome (c. 166-174) to Corinth.[1] Lightfoot, Knopf, Windisch, von Schubert and Grant have argued that it is either a sermon or a homily.[2] Since Harnack's thesis raises the fundamental question of literary genre, it will be best to deal with his arguments in that larger context.

3. GENRE LITTÉRAIRE

A variety of recent studies have sensitized us to the importance and the complexity of literary generic determination.[3] We would agree with Peterson that valid genre determination is "a pre-requisite to historical understanding and historical reconstruction.... Thus the genre question is for the historian methodologically unavoidable, and it is therefore imperative that the ambiguity of our categories be resolved."[4] It is precisely this ambiguity which is at issue with Harnack. For Harnack's hypothesis to be valid, 2 Clement must be both a letter and a homily. Commenting on Harnack, Richardson concludes that the difficulties of his "thesis are insuperable. A sermon is not a letter ...."[5] Let us examine Harnack's arguments in greater detail.

a) *2 Clement as letter*

"Allein sobald das Schriftstück für uns auftaucht — das Schriftstück, welches unzweifelhaft eine Homilie ist, — wird es als Brief bezeichnet

---

[1] In addition to Harnack, *Chronologie*, and Wocher, *Brief des Clemens*, see Harnack's article, "Zum Ursprung des sogennanten zweiten Klemensbriefes," *ZNW* 6 (1905), pp. 67-71; Albert Schwegler, *Das nachapostolischen Zeitalter*, I (Tübingen, 1846), pp. 448-55; Thomas M. Wehofer, *Untersuchungen zur altchristlichen Epistolographie* (Vienna, 1901), pp. 102-37; G. A. van der Bergh van Eysinga, *La littérature chrétienne primitive* (Paris, 1926). Hagemann, "Über den zweiten Brief," p. 516, summarizes this position: "Nirgends findet sich auch nur die leiseste Andeutung, dass der angebliche Brief eigentlich nicht Brief, sondern Homilie sei."

[2] Lightfoot, *Apostolic Fathers*, pp. 194ff.; Knopf, *Zwei Clemensbriefe*, p. 151; von Schubert, "Der sogennante," pp. 480ff.; Grant, *Apostolic Fathers*, p. 44; H. Windisch, "Das Christentum des zweiten Klemensbriefes" in *Harnack-Ehrung, Beiträge zur Kirchengeschichte* (Leipzig, 1921), pp. 119-34.

[3] Norman R. Petterson, Jr., "So-called Gnostic Type Gospels and the Question of the Genre 'Gospel,'" *Society of Biblical Literature annual meeting papers*, 1970; William G. Doty, "The Concept of Genre in Literary Analysis," in *Proceedings of the Society of Bilical Literature*, vol. 2, 1972, pp. 413-48.

[4] Peterson, "Gnostic Type Gospels," pp. 4-5.

[5] Richardson, *Early Christian Fathers*, p. 186.

(bei Eusebius und vielleicht schon bei Origenes), gewiss dann auch als Brief an die Korinther." Harnack continues, "Soll nun diese Predigt, die doch Brief genannt wird, etwas anderes sein als eben jener Brief (viz., from Bishop Soter) ?"[1]

Harnack's logic rests on two assumptions. The first is that in the tradition 2 Clement is referred to as an epistle. We have already noted that Eusebius was the first to do so. Yet one should not overlook the caution with which Eusebius refers to 2 Clement[2] — "$\tau\iota\varsigma$" and "$\lambda\acute{\epsilon}\gamma\epsilon\tau\alpha\iota$". In fact it appears unlikely from Eusebius' comments that he himself had ever seen 2 Clement.

What other references, in addition to Eusebius' possible one, are there to 2 Clement as an epistle? The earliest extant manuscript of 2 Clement is Codex A (5th cent. A.D.). In the table of contents added by a seventh or eighth century scribe,[3] 2 Clement is regarded equally with 1 Clement as an epistle of Clement of Rome. Toward the end of that table of contents we read:

ΑΠΟΚΑΛΥΨΙC[ΙѠΑ]ΝΝΟΥ

ΚΛΗΜΕΝΤΟCΕ[ΠΙCΤ]ΟΛΗ Ā

ΚΛΗΜΕΝΤΟCΕ[ΠΙCΤ]ΟΛΗ B̄

Moreover, in this manuscript directly above the text of 1 Clement we read ΠΡΟC ΚΟΡΙΝΘΙΟΥC Ā, but the corresponding ΠΡΟC ΚΟΡΙΝΘΙΟΥC B̄ which we would expect over 2 Clement is missing. This would be most important if we could be certain the omission was intentional. One would then have a reasonable argument for the anonymity of 2 Clement—the fact that is was not yet assigned to Clement of Rome. However, this cannot be made fully definite, since one has to take into account the possibility that the manuscript has been mutilated at this point.

The Syriac MS (12th cent. A.D.) also refers to 2 Clement as an epistle. However, the Constantinopolitan MS (11th cent. A.D.) lists 1 and 2 Clement in the following way:

---

[1] Harnack, *Chronologie*, pp. 443-44.

[2] Assuming, of course, that Eusebius is referring to our present document as 2 Clement.

[3] T. S. Pattie, The Assistant Keeper of the British Museum, London, makes the following comment in a letter addressed to me on May 19, 1967: "The table of contents appears to be in a 7th or 8th century hand, similar in style to the note at the foot of F. 76. of the CODEX SINAITICUS, Old Testament, illustrated in Milne and Skeat, *Scribes and Correctors of the Codex Sinaiticus*, 1938, figure 2, facing p. 2."

Κλήμεντος πρὸς Κορινθίους Α'
Κλήμεντος πρὸς Κορινθίους Β'

But since both stand in parallelism one cannot draw any conclusion from the absence of the word ἐπιστολή.

In short, the tradition does not speak with the kind of authority that Harnack would have us believe. Aside from Eusebius, the first specific reference that can present 2 Clement as an epistle stems from the table of contents of Codex A, which belongs to the seventh or eighth century. In other words, a large part of Harnack's case must rest on the accuracy of Eusebius' description.[1] Unfortunately, Harnack makes no attempt to distinguish between the genre intended by the original author and the generic designations secondarily or tertiarily added to the texts.

From this assumption about Eusebius, Harnack makes the ingenious connection between this reference to ἐπιστολή and that ἐπιστολή referred to by Dionysius as coming from Soter. The critical question is the one raised by Richardson, whether Harnack's second assumption, that a sermon and a letter can be equated, is justified.[2] The further question is whether Dionysius, who from the whole context of *H.e.* 4.23.1ff. wrote many letters, would himself have referred to 2 Clement as Soter's ἐπιστολή in view of the fact that 2 Clement itself does not give us the slightest reason to believe that it falls within the commonly recognized epistolographic patterns.

A number of recent studies have shown that despite the variety in the genre ἐπιστολή, all letters in the period demonstrate certain common characteristics.[3] The complete absence of these common features from 2 Clement make it very difficult to understand how 2 Clement would have been mistaken for an ἐπιστολή.

Koskenniemi's study of the Greek letter is divided into two major parts: 1) the letter as understood by the academicians and the theorists, such as Demetrius [c. 1st cent. B.C.], *Περὶ ἑρμηνείας*; Dionysius of Alexandria [1st cent. A.D.], *Περὶ το ὑὲν τῇ συνηθείᾳ χαίρειν τοῦ τε ἐν ταῖς ἐπιστολαῖς*; Apollonius Dyscolos [2nd cent. A.D.], *Περὶ*

---

[1] For a study challenging Eusebius' accuracy at a number of points, see Robert M. Grant, "Eusebius and His Church History," in *Understanding the Sacred Text*, ed. by John Reumann (Valley Forge, 1972), pp. 233-47.

[2] See p. 19, n. 5.

[3] Heikki Koskenniemi, *Studien zur Idee und Phraseologie des griechischen Briefes bis 400 n. Chr.* (Helsinki, 1956); Robert Funk, *Language, Hermeneutic and Word of God*

συντάξεως; Philostratus of Lemnos [3rd cent. A.D.], Letter to Aspasius; 2) and the more primary understanding of the letter that one receives from the Greek papyri. Although there are obvious differences between these two approaches, they do, on the whole, confirm each other. Both approaches vividly demonstrate that the Greek letter is firmly shaped by tradition in its phraseology, style and structure.

Beginning with the academicians, Koskenniemi finds in this literature three elements which are essential to the basic character of the letter. The first is φιλοφρόνησις, the basic element of friendship which exists between the writer and the recipient. Every letter presupposes the existence of this relationship.[1] The second characteristic is that of παρουσία. In fact, this is considered *the* most important function of the letter: "eine Form eben dieses Zusammenlebens während einer Zeit räumlicher Trennung darzustellen, d.h. die ἀπουσία zur παρουσία machen."[2] The third characteristic of the Greek letter is ὁμιλία, primarily in the sense of a conversation, but with the added thought that this ὁμιλία through a letter leads into communion and intercourse one with the other.

The second and more substantial part of Koskenniemi's work is a careful examination of the Greek papyri letters and their especially characteristic formulae of which not a single one is to be found in 2 Clement. Within the context of this study, we wish to single out only two of Koskenniemi's further observations. He examines the question of the separation between writer and addressee as being of decisive importance for the basic motivation of the letter, a point already observed as significant for the theorists. Most illuminating is the discussion of two letters from the hand of Basileius,[3] who expresses a sense of regret at being distant from the recipients, as well as a sense of power-

---

(New York, 1966), esp. pp. 250-74; *idem*, "The Form and Structure of II and III John," *JBL* 86 (1967), pp. 424-30; *idem*, "The Apostolic Parousia: Form and Significance," in *Christian History and Interpretation: Studies Presented to John Knox*, ed., by W. R. Farmer (Cambridge, 1967), pp. 249-68; Klaus Thraede, *Grundzüge griechisch-römischer Brieftopik* (München, 1970); Hildegard Cancik, *Untersuchungen zu Senecas epistulae morales* (Hildesheim, 1967).

[1] Koskenniemi, *Studien*, p. 36, writes: "freundschaftliche Gesinnung (ist) das innerste Wesen des Briefes."; Abraham J. Malherbe, "1 Thessalonians as a Paraenetic Letter," *Society of Biblical Literature annual meeting papers*, 1972; and Helmut Rahn, *Morphologie der antiken Literatur* (Darmstadt, 1969), pp. 157-59.

[2] *Ibid.*, p. 38.

[3] *Ibid.*, pp. 171ff.

lessness over against his condition of separation. In *Ep.* 47 it is expressed in this way: ὥστε με δυνηθῆναι διαβῆναι πρὸς τὴν ὑμετέραν ἀγάπην καὶ τόν τε πόθον ὃν ἔχω ἐφ᾽ ὑμῖν ἀναπαῦσαι; and in *Ep.* 140: καὶ πετασθήσομαι πρὸς ὑμᾶς καὶ καταπαύσω τὸν πόθον ὃν ἔχω ἐπὶ τῇ συντυχίᾳ τῆς ὑμετέρας ἀγάπης. Koskenniemi remarks: "Wenn wir jedoch berücksichtigen, dass der zweite an die Gemeinde von Antiochia geschrieben ist, also nicht an einen Einzelnen, so verstehen wir, dass der Anwendungsbereich dieser sehnsuchtsvollen Ausdrücke, was die Adressaten betrifft, weit war."[1] This characteristic, too, is absent from 2 Clement.

A second observation of Koskenniemi which is important for this present discussion is that the letter serves as a substitute for personal παρουσία or presence. Although not absent from the papyri prior to the second century A.D., this theme is consistently present thereafter. One example is a letter from a daughter to her mother (P. Oxy. VI 963 [II/III]): ἀσπάζομαί σε, μῆτερ, διὰ τῶν γράμματων τούτων ἐπιθυμοῦσα ἤδη θεάσασθαι. Such contrasts as τὰ γράμματα-θεάσασθαι are quite common in expressing this sense of παρουσία. "Es liegt in der Natur des Breifes," suggests Koskenniemi, "dass er nicht nur ein Benachrichtigungsmittel darstellt oder ein Mittel für all das, was man mit seiner Hilfe erledigen will, sondern zugleich ein vereinigendes Band, eine Form des Umgangs zwischen räumlich voneinander getrennten Menschen."[2] If this aspect, too, is missing from 2 Clement it may be because there was no need to express it. 2 Clem. 17:3 certainly suggests that the presbyter who was addressing this exhortation was actually present in the midst of his congregation. This further weakens Harnack's Soter hypothesis and the possibility that that hypothesis can adequately explain the original *Sitz im Leben* of 2 Clement.

After carefully investigating all the parts and phrases which comprise a letter, Koskenniemi draws two important conclusions from his investigation: 1) the letter shows itself to be tied to a tradition; 2) it demonstrates a certain formal character. It is precisely this latter element which determines not only the structure of the papyrus letter, but also its formulation (e.g., the recurrence of certain given phrases). From both these elements, Koskenniemi concludes: "Nicht nur die Grundstruktur des Briefes bleibt im grossen und ganzen unverändert, —auch in der Verteilung der einzelnen Elemente im Brief zeigt sich

---

[1] *Ibid.*, p. 172.
[2] *Ibid.*, p. 88.

die gleiche Tendenz."[1] Koskenniemi has convincingly shown that despite certain obvious differences between the literary letters and the papyrus letters, there is, so far as certain given phrases and formulae are concerned, a wide-reaching agreement; and, although the Greek papyrus letters found in Egypt had their unique local coloring, they can nevertheless be viewed as representative of a large proportion of letter writing in the Hellenistic culture.

From our discussion of the form of the Greek letter, it should have become sufficiently clear that 2 Clement is neither a letter[2] nor a homily put in the form of a letter.[3] 2 Clement contains no salutation. Every sign of a sender, addressee and greetings is absent. It contains no thanksgiving. It contains no closing greetings or benediction. In addition to this, both Funk and Koskenniemi have shown that an important element in the letter is that of anticipated παρουσία or in the case of Paul, apostolic parousia. Not only is this totally absent from 2 Clement, but 2 Clement speaks directly against it. There is no need for the expression of presbyterial parousia, that is, for the presbyters to desire their letter to be a substitute for their personal presence, because *they are in fact present.* They are present in the congregation as they preach. This is certainly the case in 17:3, "Not only at this moment (ἄρτι), while the presbyters are preaching to us, should we appear believing and attentive. But when we have gone home, we should bear in mind the Lord's commands ...," and from 15:2, ὁ λέγων καὶ ἀκούων. Clearly the substance of 2 Clement can in no way be understood as a letter, nor is there any evidence that 2 Clement was a homily sent as a letter from Rome to Corinth. When every characteristic unique to a letter is absent, it is difficult to insist that this writing is a homily in the form of a letter from the hand of Bishop Soter. When one recalls that Koskenniemi's investigation takes him into the fourth century A.D. and that he has clearly shown the tradition-bound nature of the letter, then it seems inconceivable that Bishop Soter's letter should have violated every formal characteristic of a letter. Our conclusion at this point is that it is impossible to place 2 Clement into the "letter" genre, or even to hold that it is a homily put into the form of a letter. Those traits associated with and typical of the letter genre, are totally absent from 2 Clement.

---

[1] *Ibid.*, p. 202.
[2] Against Hagemann, Wehofer.
[3] Against Harnack, Goodspeed.

It may be objected that Koskenniemi's heavy concentration on the Greek papyrus letters, as opposed to other letters known to us by way of literary transmission, may bias our conclusions concerning 2 Clement, since 2 Clement may have a closer proximity to the philosophical and paraenetic aims of Latin epistolography. However, Thraede's recent study has amply demonstrated that the themes of φιλοφρόνησις, παρουσία, and ὁμιλία are present and basic to the structure of pre-Christian Latin letters (Cicero, Ovid; cf. also Seneca, Pliny),[1] New Testament letters[2] and early Christian letters.[3] Thraede clearly demonstrates: 1) that in early Christianity the letter was consistently understood as a "*sermo absentium*,"[4] which is not the case in 2 Clement (cf. 17:3); 2) the letter can be filled with paraenetic, biblical, theological and philosophical discussions, but these are present "ohne dass die formgeschichtlichen Bedingungen in Stil und Topik auch nur im geringsten verändert wurden ...."[5] One of Thraede's final conclusions, which is directly relevant to our discussion, is this: "So konnten exegetische und dogmatische Texte, Themen und Inhalte in den spätantik-christlichen Brief einfliessen, ohne die Richtung der Tradition wesentlich zu verändern."[6]

This investigation would lead us to conclude that Harnack's ingenious hypothesis that 2 Clement was a letter from Bishop Soter of Rome to the Corinthians is not probable for the very reasons to which Harnack was sensitive: 1) 2 Clement is not a letter; 2) it is more likely to be dated in the first half of the second century, or earlier, than in the second half of that century; 3) it is more likely that the city of origin was Corinth, not Rome.

b) *2 Clement as homily*

Most recent works dealing with 2 Clement assume that it is either a "sermon"[7] or a "homily,"[8] with the majority favoring the term

---

[1] Thraede, *Grundzüge*, pp. 17-94; see also Cancik, *Untersuchungen*, pp. 46-88.

[2] Thraede, *Grundzüge*, pp. 95-108, and the important work of Robert Funk.

[3] Thraede, *Grundzüge*, pp. 109ff.

[4] *Ibid.*, pp. 162ff.

[5] *Ibid.*, p. 188.

[6] *Ibid.*, p. 187.

[7] Grant, *Apostolic Fathers*, p. 44.

[8] Helmut Köster, *Synoptische Überlieferung bei den apostolischen Vätern* (Berlin, 1957), p. 62.

"homily." To define 2 Clement as a "sermon" is not helpful since we know virtually nothing about the contours of such a genre in the first century A.D. Is "homily" a more adequate term?

The basic thrust of this section will be that the term "homily" is so vague and ambiguous that it should be withdrawn until its literarily generic legitimacy has been demonstrated. The crux of the problem lies in the definition of the term "homily." It has been employed to describe various types of Greek literature, Jewish midrash, the New Testament book of Hebrews, parts of the pseudo-Clementine literature and Melito's tract on the Pascha. Perhaps the greatest ambiguity in the current usage is when it is used to describe both a certain class of Hellenistic Jewish literature influenced by the Greek diatribe form,[1] on the one hand, and when it is used to define certain typically Jewish midrashic patterns, on the other hand.[2] These are not necessarily exclusive definitions,[3] but they are sufficiently different to warrant greater precision.

It was Norden who in his systematic categorization of the "Gattungen der Predigt" used the term ὁμιλία to describe that type of preaching in which "das lehrhafte Moment im Mittelpunkt stand."[4] As the earliest extant example of this type of preaching, Norden referred to 2 Clement. It is not unimportant to ask why he selected the term ὁμιλία for this type of paraenetic and didactic preaching. ὁμιλέω and ὁμιλία have a wide range of meaning in the Classical and Hellenistic period

---

[1] Hartwig Thyen, *Der Stil der Jüdisch-Hellenistischen Homilie* (Göttingen, 1955).

[2] Peder Borgen, *Bread from Heaven* (Leiden, 1965); Wilhelm Wuellner, "Haggadic Homily Genre in 1 Corinthians 1-3," *JBL* 89 (1970), pp. 199-204.

[3] We should note here the important work of David Daube and Henry Fischel in attempting to relate Hellenistic rhetoric and the study of midrash: David Daube, "Rabbinic Methods of Interpretation and Hellenistic Rhetoric," *HUCA* 22 (1949), pp. 239-64; Henry A. Fischel, "Story and History: Observations on Greco-Roman Rhetoric and Pharisaism" in *American Oriental Society, Middle West Branch, Semi-Centennial Volume*, edited by Denis Sinor, (Bloomington, 1969); Henry A. Fischel, "Greco-Roman Rhetoric and the Study of Midrash" (unpublished).

[4] Norden describes this type of preaching with precision: "Da in dieser Art der Predigt das lehrhafte Moment im Mittelpunkt stand, so nannte man sie ὁμιλία (*sermo*), ein Wort, in dem die Anschauung ausgesprochen liegt, dass der Prediger zu seiner Gemeinde in rein persönliche Beziehung trat, wenn er sie fast im Tone gewöhnlichen Gesprächs belehrte: mit demselben Wort wurde seit alter Zeit von den Griechen die persönliche Belehrung bezeichnet, welche die Philosophen ihren Schülern (τοῖς ὁμιληταῖς) zuteil worden liessen...." Eduard Norden, *Die Antike Kunstprosa*, II (Darmstadt, 1958), p. 541.

and only one, not very frequent meaning, relates to this description. In Xenophon's *Memorabilia* I.2.15,39, ὁμιλέω frequently means a teacher's lectures and in *Mem.* I.2.6 and 15, ὁμιλία refers to instruction. In Aelianus' (2/3 cent. A.D.) *Varia Historia* 3.19, ὁμιλία refers to a lecture. Thus the terms are not used frequently in the Classical and Hellenistic periods and only tangentially describe this particular classification of Norden.

Norden's selection of this term is based primarily on Acts 20:11 and Ign. Polyc. 5:1. If Acts 20:11 were less ambiguous, it would be a good illustration of the use of ὁμιλέω to refer to preaching before persons who were already Christian. Unfortunately, Acts 20:11 could refer to the continuation of Paul's previous discourse, or it could simply mean "conversation." Luke's use of this verb elsewhere (Lk. 24:14,15; Acts 24:26) in the sense of "conversation" adds to the uncertainty of this particular reference in Acts 20. At best, the use of ὁμιλέω in Acts 20 might possibly refer to preaching before a Christian audience. The reference in Ignatius is more secure, and most commentators understand the use of ὁμιλία there as referring to some type of paraenetic preaching. This employment of the term in Ignatius, together with its use in Justin (not mentioned by Norden), *Dial.* 85, τὸν ἀπὸ τῶν γραφῶν τῶν προφητικῶν ὁμιλίας ποιούμενον and *Dial.* 28, ἀπό τε τῶν γραφῶν καὶ τῶν πραγμάτων τάς τε ἀποδείξεις καὶ τὰς ὁμιλίας ποιοῦμαι, may justify Norden's use of the term as a description of didactic and paraenetic preaching.

We are inclined to hold that Norden's general impulse was sound and that one might possibly use his work as a starting point to further define a genre which might include 2 Clement. The problem is that the term "homily" has been employed so broadly and ambiguously in recent literature that its continued use may bring about even greater confusion. For this reason we are hesitant to use this designation in the present study. The following review of selected literature which employs the term "homily" as a generic definition reveals how divergently it is used.

Hartwig Thyen's, *Der Stil der Jüdisch-Hellenistischen Homilie*, attempts to demonstrate how both the style and rhetoric of the diatribe influenced a large variety of Jewish-Hellenistic and early Christian texts. There are two basic weaknesses in Thyen's work: 1) He never defines a homily in terms of literary form despite his introductory assertion that his method will be "eine streng formgeschichtliche

Betrachtung."[1] How can a method be "streng formgeschichtlich" when the criterion for the definition of a homily is "Abschnitte der jüdisch-hellenistischen Literatur, deren homiletischer Charakter am Tage liegt."[2] When one tries to determine which writings are composed "mit deutlich homiletischem Charakter" one is referred to Bultmann's work on the diatribe. Thyen's method is both arbitrary and circular: he selects writings which he thinks are of a homiletic character, proceeds to analyse them, and then says, he has carefully analyzed the form of the homily! One could justifiably ask why the Pauline epistles were not included—they certainly would have to be designated as homilies according to Thyen's methodological criterion. 2) The second weakness of Thyen's study is his uncritical dependence upon Bultmann's 1910 doctoral dissertation, *Der Stil der paulinischen Predigt und die kynisch-stoische Diatribe*.[3] Bultmann tried to demonstrate the dependence of Pauline preaching upon the Cynic-Stoic "Gattung der Diatribe."[4] It is likely that Bultmann described this relationship as much closer than it really was and that his description of the diatribe as a "Gattung" is inaccurate.[5] Thyen's study follows Bultmann's pattern, and therefore also has its shortcomings. He fails to consider seriously that the diatribe style may have influenced not only the "homily" but also a wider variety of literature, as well as the fact that the Jewish-Hellenistic texts he singles out could have been influenced by rhetorical patterns of the period and not exclusively or necessarily by the diatribe style. Thyen's work on the Jewish-Hellenistic homily does not, unfortunately, contribute to a precise form-critical analysis of the homily genre.

Another group of eminent scholars[6] are using the term "homily"

---

[1] Thyen, *Stil*, p. 7.

[2] *Ibid*, p. 7.

[3] Rudolf Bultmann, *Der Stil der paulinischen Predigt und die kynisch-stoische Diatribe* (Göttingen, 1910).

[4] Bultmann, *Diatribe*, pp. 107-109.

[5] See the criticism of Bultmann by Adolf Bonhöffer, *Epiktet und das Neue Testament* (Giessen, 1911), p. 179, n. 1. See also the helpful discussion of diatribe by the classicist Cancik, *Untersuchungen*, p. 47, n. 79, and the summary remark found there ("Die Frage nach der Diatribe ist noch nicht geklärt..."), as well as the discussion in Rahn, *Morphologie*, pp. 153-56.

[6] J. W. Bowker, "Speeches in Acts: A Study in Proem and Yellammedenu Form," *NTS* 14 (1967), pp. 96-111; *idem, The Targums and Rabbinic Literature* (Cambridge, 1969), pp. 72ff.; W. O. E. Oesterley and G. H. Box, *The Religion and Worship of the Syna-*

and derivations thereof, such as "homiletic midrash,"[1] in a quite different way and it is imperative for our purposes that this development be reviewed as well. Peder Borgen, in his pioneering work, *Bread from Heaven*, uses the term "homily" with reference to certain portions of the New Testament, especially John 6. While at many points Borgen brings keen insight to his interpretation of John 6, his contributions with regard to the use of the term "homily" are questionable, especially since he never defines how he is using the term.[2]

Before Borgen's homiletic pattern is examined, is it possible to ascertain what he means by the adjective "homiletic"? Borgen appears to have a teaching function in mind: "The environment for Philo's writing was the synagogue, whereas John's environment seems to have been a 'school' of a church after the break with the synagogue had become a definite fact."[3] Discussing the *Sitz im Leben* of this homiletic pattern, Borgen suggests that it "was originally used for lecturing (preaching) in the synagogue."[4] While this school situation

---

gogue (London, 1911), pp. 89ff.; Borgen, *Bread from Heaven*; Wuellner, "Haggadic Homily"; Jacob Mann, *The Bible as Read and Preached in the Old Synagogue*, I (New York, 1971); W. Bacher, *Die Pröoemien der alten jüdischen Homilie* (Leipzig, 1913); L. Zunz, *Die gottesdienstlichen Vorträge der Juden historisch entwickelt* (Hildesheim, 1966); S. Maybaum, *Die ältesten Phasen in der Entwicklung der jüdischen Predigt* (Berlin, 1901); *idem, Jüdische Homiletik* (Berlin, 1890); A. G. Wright, *The Literary Genre Midrash* (New York, 1967), pp. 57ff.; Renée Bloch, "Midrash," *SDB*, 5, cols. 1263-81; Roger Le Déaut, "Apropos a Definition of Midrash," *Int* 25 (1971), pp. 259-82; E. E. Ellis, "Midrash, Targum and New Testament Quotations," in *Neotestamentica et Semitica*, ed. by E. E. Ellis and Max Wilcox (Edinburgh, 1969), pp. 61-69; G. W. Buchanan, *To the Hebrews* (New York, 1972), pp. xix-xxii and p. 246.

[1] The exact meaning of this term is ambiguous. This is largely due to the fact that the form criticism of rabbinic texts is still in its infancy. What the term appears to mean is haggadic exposition of scriptural texts. Such midrash involves a complex interpretation of the scriptural text by a series, sometimes a large series, of other texts.

[2] It is this failure to be precise which makes it difficult to accept Borgen's (*Bread from Heaven*, p. 54-55) criticism of Thyen: "In his analysis of the Jewish Hellenistic homily H. Thyen abstains from making a comparison with the Palestinian homily. Against Thyen it must now be said that such a comparison is of great importance, and it will lead to the conclusion that there are homiletic patterns which both have in common. Thus the distinction between the terms 'Jewish Hellenistic' and 'Palestinian' homilies is artificial and misleading as far as homiletic patterns are concerned."

[3] Borgen, *Bread from Heaven*, p. 3. This stress on the "school" situation is quite correct and is now supported by the work of J. Louis Martyn, *History and Theology in the Fourth Gospel* (New York, 1968).

[4] Borgen, *Bread from Heaven*, p. 55.

is likely to be correct, one must be very careful not to confuse lecturing or teaching with preaching: they are overlapping, but not synonymous functions. That this homiletic pattern is not to be simply identified with *actual* preaching is recognized by Borgen: "So, although authentic sermons are not preserved here, the homiletic pattern has been the collecting basin for material of different kinds from the tradition."[1] Since this homiletic pattern does not represent an actual sermon, but rather a "collecting basin," perhaps it would be best to call this phenomenon an exegetical or midrashic pattern, a pattern that in fact could serve a wide variety of purposes. Such an exegetical pattern might illuminate the way in which scripture was interpreted in certain synagogues and Christian beth-midrashim. Yet it is crucial to remember that while certain forms or exegetical patterns are similar, they may be used in a wide variety of genres; exegetical patterns do not necessarily assist in defining the genre in which they are used.

---

[1] *Ibid.*, p. 57. Very important in this context is the work of Lou H. Silberman, "A Midrash on Midrash" (unpublished paper distributed to members of seminar on Jewish Exegesis, 1971 annual meeting of *Studiorum Novi Testamenti Societas*) in which he distinguishes between "actual" and "literary" sermons (p. 5). After reviewing a variety of midrashim, Silbermann cites Joseph Heinemann's observations: "Although these homilies were preached for many centuries in the Palestinian communities and although we possess a considerable collection whose redactors made use basically of materials from the tannaitic and amoraic periods, we do not have precise knowledge of their structures and forms. For in most instances the sermons themselves as they were preached to congregations have not been transmitted to us but only their adaptations. Sometimes they are fragments only, sometimes collections of scraps not emanating from one but from several sermons on the same subject. Further, before they were put into writing, they passed through a period of oral transmission during which some were shortened, others mutilated, others combined, so that in general they suffered a multitude of vicissitudes. Thus there are but few of which we can say with certainty that they exist today in their original form and not in summary" (p. 3). Silbermann carries this a step further and concludes that "a major task confronting the student of midrash is the development of form-critical studies that will enable us to move back through the literary structures of the texts to or near to the original forms as is possible. Without such studies, carried out with rigor and reflecting what has happened in other areas, particularly O.T. and N.T., the midrashim will remain no more than partially opened books and their use as aids in other fields, for example, N.T. studies will be subject to the greatest suspicion so that studies thus based will fall into the realm of doubtful value" (p. 3). Important advances in the form-critical study of rabbinic literature may be found in the work of Jacob Neusner; most recently see his "Types and Forms in Ancient Jewish Literature: Some Comparisons," *HR* 11 (1972), pp. 354-90. *Idem, Rabbinic Traditions about the Pharisees before 70*, 3 vols., (Leiden, 1971).

Borgen regards the following elements as central to his homiletic pattern: (1) the opening and closing of the homily correspond to one another; (2) there is always a main quotation from the Old Testament, as well as some subordinate Old Testament quotations; and (3) there is a repetition, expansion or paraphrase of words from the text in the homily. It is suggested that such a pattern can be found in independent units, when isolated from their present contexts. Borgen suggests that examples can be found in Philo, Leg All III 162-168; Mut 253-263; and in the New Testament, Gal. 3:6-29 and Rom. 4:1-22.[1] Borgen has shown that a similar exegetical pattern does exist in some of these texts. But whether this pattern can be lifted out of its present context quite so easily is open to question.[2] In his attempt to show similarities between John 6 and the Palestinian midrashim, he may have oversimplified some very complex, and sometimes, patternless material.[3]

One of the most problematic of Borgen's theses is that Jn. 6:31-58 was originally an independent homily which the author of John inserted into the present context.[4] Here it might be asked what the relationship of a literary pattern to a historical situation is ? More comprehensive than Borgen's is Martyn's understanding of the gospel of John as an ongoing apologetic dialogue with Judaism.[5] It was in such a context that John 6 developed, rather than as an independent homily which was taken up and inserted into its present context. As the author

---

[1] Borgen, *Bread from Heaven*, pp. 47ff.

[2] Can Leg All III 162-68 be separated from what precedes ? Can Jn. 6:31-58 ? This pericope seems to begin with Jn. 6:27. Should not the relationship of Jn. 6:27 to Deut. 8:3 have been discussed ? One should also not overlook that to obtain this correspondence of beginning to end, Borgen views all of Jn. 6:31-58 as a unit, a view not held by most New Testament scholars. Most recently Borgen's understanding of John 6 has been challenged by Georg Richter, "Zur Formgeschichte und literarischen Einheit von John 6,31-58," *ZNW* 60 (1969), pp. 21-55 and Günther Bornkamm, "Vorjohanneische Tradition oder nachjohanneische Bearbeitung in der eucharistischen Rede Johannes 6 ?" in *Geschichte und Glaube*, 2 (München, 1971), pp. 51-64.

[3] Borgen has stressed the similarities; what about the vast differences ? Further, what distinguishes Borgen's homiletic pattern from a broader rhetorical one. How does John 6 differ from Epictetus II.1,14ff., where we have a discussion of death which begins with a text from an unknown tragic poet, a subordinate citation from Socrates and a play on the word death throughout ? (I owe this reference to Prof. Harvey K. McArthur). Also, how does Jn. 6:27-51b differ from John 10, where we have the words of Jesus replacing the Old Testament texts ?

[4] Borgen, *Bread from Heaven*, pp. 59ff.; 96ff.

[5] Martyn, *History and Theology*, pp. 45ff.

of the gospel was writing in this situation, he took up certain exegetical
principles common to those of Jewish background and applied them to
situations of the actual dialogue.

Before this section is concluded, brief attention must be given to
the article by J. W. Bowker, "Speeches in Acts: A Study in Proem and
Yelammedenu Form."[1] His basic concern is whether the speech attributed to Paul in Acts 13 "may in fact have originated as a genuine
synagogue sermon, and the second is to ask whether any of the other
speeches in Acts may have been in origin homilies or parts of homilies,
preached in synagogues, which were then adapted to fit their present
context in Acts."[2] Although Bowker is aware of the problem of "what
constitutes a sermon" and that even though Tannaitic literature
contains many examples of "sustained biblical exegesis ... it would
be rash to conclude that they must have originated as sermons," he
seems not to have made any attempt at solving the problem and goes
on to use the terms "homily" and "sermon" interchangeably and impre-
cisely.[3]

It is Bowker's cautious suggestion that there is a close relationship
between the speeches in Acts and the proem and yelammedenu homilies
of the synagogue. Yet a number of questions need to be raised. Bowker
indicates that "the meaning of scripture ... was brought home to the
people present ... by a homily."[4] But was it the primary purpose
of Luke and other early Christians to bring home "the meaning of
scripture" or the meaning of Jesus, that is, the kergyma to which scripture testified ? If there are similar exegetical patterns, do they serve
the same ends ? It is more likely that for primitive Christianity,
midrash is always at the service of the kerygma. Thus, Bowker is fully
right when he recognizes that "at the same time the sermon as a whole
is unlike a proem homily in so far as it has an introductory section ..."
and when he realizes that "the problem is to know whether it is a
case of the material demanding the pattern or of the pattern being

---

[1] *NTS* 14 (1967), pp. 96-111.

[2] *Ibid.*, p. 96.

[3] *Ibid.*, pp. 102ff. W. D. Davies' criticism of Morton Smith's *Tannaitic Parallels to
the Gospels* (Philadelphia, 1968) in his *The Setting of the Sermon on the Mount* (Cambridge
1964), pp. 8ff., seems equally applicable to Bowker: "Morton Smith himself recognizes
that even in most of the Tannaitic sermons that he cites there is no sustained sequence
of thought, and the propriety of applying the term 'sermon' to the Tannaitic material
he adduces is open to question."

[4] Bowker, "Speeches in Acts," p. 103.

imposed on the material." [1] Also important in this respect is Bowker's observation about yelammedenu homilies: "However, since yelam-medenu homilies evolved from requests for instruction, some of them are not so closely related to the lectionary.... The problem in that case is to know whether the exposition can be accepted as a formal homily."[2] We would suggest that the overlap between Christian and Jewish materials is due to a similar exegetical method and not to the use of the same genre.[3]

Bowker also reviews the relationship of the yelammedenu homily to Acts 15. Since both proem and yelammedenu are late texts, it is unfortunate that he provides no methodological discussion con-cerning the validity of relating fourth and fifth century texts to first century ones. Bowker does acknowledge, however, that Acts 15 only partially reflects a yelammedenu homily pattern and that there are a number of differences between them. Therefore, it is well to keep in mind the tentativeness of his suggestion, "that what has survived in Acts is a fragment of a longer discourse, which may well have been an actual homily; but obviously it is impossible to be sure."[4] Despite the ambiguity of the terminology involved, Bowker has demonstrated that Luke and the synagogue interpret scripture by the use of similar methodologies, even if their ultimate purposes may have been different.

A final word must be added about the use of comparative Jewish midrash for the illumination of early Christian literature.[5] Its signifi-cance must not be underestimated, but neither must the difficulty of this comparative work. This latter point is well stated by Roger Le Déaut in his discussion concerning the characterization of midrash as a literary *genre*: "It is ... an explicitly *modern* literary category in

---

[1] *Ibid.*, p. 106.

[2] *Ibid.*, p. 101.

[3] Concerning the speeches in Acts, one should consult the important works of Wilckens, Schweizer and Plümacher: Ulrich Wilckens, *Die Missionsreden der Apostelge-schichte* (Neukirchen, 1962); Eduard Schweizer, "Concerning the Speeches in Acts" in *Studies in Luke-Acts*, ed. by L. E. Keck and J. L. Martyn (Nashville, 1966), pp. 208-16; Eckhard Plümacher, *Lukas als hellenistischer Schriftsteller* (Göttingen, 1972).

[4] Bowker, "Speeches in Acts," p. 109.

[5] See Matthew Black, "The Christological Use of the Old Testament in the New Testament," *NTS* 18 (1971), pp. 1-14; Barnabas Lindars, *New Testament Apologetic* (London, 1961); E. Earle Ellis, *Paul's Use of the Old Testament* (Edinburgh, 1957); Krister Stendahl, *The School of St. Matthew* (Philadelphia, 1968); Merrill P. Miller, "Targum, Midrash and the Use of the Old Testament in the New Testament," *JSJ* 2 (1971), pp. 29-82.

question, established on the basis of rabbinic writings, which are for the most part late and whose structure is known to be artificial."[1] Until such time that form criticism of rabbinic texts moves to a more advanced stage, one must be extraordinarily cautious and precise so as to avoid misleading comparisons with genres that are possibly non-existent or highly artificial.[2]

c) *2 Clement as μικράν συμβουλίαν περὶ ἐγκρατείας*

In view of the fact that the generic legitimacy of the concept "homily" has not yet been demonstrated and its continued use is more likely to confuse than to illuminate, it will be a wise methodological procedure to define 2 Clement in light of its own self-description. This involves basically three assertions:[3]

15:1 Οὐκ οἴομαι δέ, ὅτι μικρὰν συμβουλίαν ἐποιησάμην περὶ ἐγκρατείας, ἣν ποιήσας τις οὐ μετανοήσει, ἀλλὰ καὶ ἑαυτὸν σώσει κἀμὲ τὸν συμβουλεύσαντα.

Now I do not think that I have given you any small counsel about self-control, and anyone who takes it will have no cause to regret it, but shall save both himself and me his counsellor.

17:3 καὶ μὴ μόνον ἄρτι δοκῶμεν πιστεύειν καὶ προσέχειν ἐν τῷ νουθετεῖσθαι[4] ἡμᾶς ὑπὸ τῶν πρεσβυτέρων, ἀλλὰ καὶ ὅταν εἰς οἶκον ἀπαλλαγῶμεν, μνημονεύωμεν τῶν τοῦ κυρίου ἐνταλμάτων ...

Not only at this moment, while the presbyters are admonishing us, should we appear believing and attentive; but likewise when we have gone home we should remember the Lord's commands ...

19:1 Ὥστε, ἀδελφοὶ καὶ ἀδελφαί, μετὰ τὸν θεὸν τῆς ἀληθείας ἀναγινώσκω ὑμῖν ἔντευξιν εἰς τὸ προσέχειν τοῖς γεγραμμένοις, ἵνα καὶ ἑαυτοὺς σώσητε καὶ τὸν ἀναγινώσκοντα ἐν ὑμῖν·

---

[1] Le Déaut, "Definition of Midrash," pp. 264-65.

[2] See Silberman, "Midrash" and W. Sibley Towner, "Form Criticism of Rabbinic Literature," *Society of Biblical Literature annual meeting papers*, 1971.

[3] The translations which follow are our own and are not taken from Richardson, *Early Christian Fathers*, as elsewhere.

[4] See also 2 Clem. 19:2.

So, my brothers and sisters, after the God of truth, I am reading to you an address, to heed what was there written, in that you may save yourselves and him who does the reading before you.

This description of the intention of 2 Clement given by its author, together with the fact that each of the key terms in the verses cited reflects the Greek rhetorical tradition, lead us to suggest that 2 Clement is a hortatory address. Let us examine the background of 2 Clement's terminology as it is used in the classical tradition.

It is significant to note that all three terms under primary discussion, συμβουλία (or its related συμβουλευτικός and συμβουλέυω), νουθετέω and ἔντευξις, are found in Aristotle's *Rhetoric*. In *Rhet* I.3.1ff., we read: "The kinds of Rhetoric are three in number, corresponding to the three kinds of hearers. For every speech is composed of three parts: the speaker, the subject of which he treats, and the person to whom it is addressed, I mean the hearer, to whom the end or object of the speech refers." In 2 Clement the speaker is one of the presbyters speaking on behalf of all of them, the subject is ἐγκράτεια set over against a gnosticizing libertinism, and the hearers are the congregation in Corinth. Aristotle continues: "Therefore there are necessarily three kinds of rhetorical speeches, deliberative (συμβουλευτικόν), forensic and epideictic. The deliberative kind (συμβουλῆς) is either hortatory or dissuasive; for both those who give advice in private (οἱ ἰδίᾳ συμβουλεύοντες) and those who speak in the assembly invariably exhort or dissuade .... Further, to each of these a special time is appropriate: to the deliberative the future (τῷ συμβουλεύοντι ὁ μέλλων)."[1] This is very much what we have in 2 Clement: a hortatory address in which advice is given in the present with reference to the future.

In *Rhet* II. 18, where Aristotle is discussing the topics common to all three kinds of rhetoric, we find not only the use of the term οἱ νουθετοῦντες (those who give advice), but also περὶ ὧν βουλεύονται and the use of συμβουλεύοντες as a synonym for the deliberative speech. In *Rhet*. I.1.12 Aristotle suggests that "our proofs and arguments must rest on generally accepted principles ... when speaking of converse with the multitude (περὶ τῆς πρὸς τοὺς πολλοὺς ἐντεύξεως)." Commenting on this use of ἔντευξις in Aristotle, Cope defines it as "a meeting which leads to a 'conversation'; or as arising casually out of that,

---

[1] In *Rhet* I.6.1 and 8.7 Aristotle also mentions the present as a time appropriate to deliberative rhetoric.

a dialectical 'encounter.' "[1] It is not far from this to the ἐντεύξεις
ὀχλιναί (speeches to the mob) of Dionysius Halicarnassus, *On Thucy-
dides* 50.

Is 2 Clement unique in the fact that this hortatory address was read
to the congregation? Certainly not. The very fact that Plato[2] and
Alcidamas (*On those writing written speeches or on the sophists*) defend
extemporaneity vividly indicates that there was literary composition
of oratory. An important discussion of the written speech can be found
in Aristotle, *Rhet* III.12.1-3. Clearly the written composition is one
kind of rhetoric.[3]

One could easily become involved in a lengthy discussion concerning
different ways by which some of these terms could have been and were
used in both the pre-Chirstian and Christian period,[4] as well as a
lengthy list of complementary references to the ones already noted.[5]
However, all that we are attempting to suggest is that use of the terms
συμβουλία, νουθετέω and ἔντευξις in close relationship with one another
reveals a usage quite similar to that of the Greek rhetorical traditions,
and permits us to understand 2 Clement as a hortatory address influenced by Hellenistic rhetoric. It is obviously difficult to specify the exact
source of this influence other than to say that it was through a particular rhetorical trajectory prevailing in Graeco-Roman Hellenism which
was accessible and meaningful to the author of 2 Clement.

---

[1] Edward M. Cope, *The Rhetoric of Aristotle with a Commentary*, I (Cambridge,
1877), p. 24.

[2] *Phaedrus* 257d.5ff.

[3] For a further discussion see George Kennedy, *The Art of Persuasion in Greece*
(Princeton, 1963), pp. 203-205 and pp. 112-13; also, Cope, *Rhetoric*, III, p. 144.

[4] For example, the development of deliberative oratory into the *suasoria* in Rome.
On this point see Stephen Usher, "Oratory" in *Greek and Latin Literature*, ed. by John
Higginbotham (London, 1969), esp. pp. 386ff. See also Donald L. Clark, *Rhetoric in
Greco-Roman Education* (New York 1957), pp. 220, 224, 226-67, 255-57; Antonio Quac-
quarelli, *Retorica E Liturgia Antenicena* (Rome, 1960); and W. C. van Unnik, "Studies
over de zogenaamde eerste Brief van Clemens. I. Het litteraire genre", *Mededelingen der
Koninklijke Nederlandse Akademie van Wetenschappen, Afd. Letterkunde*. Nieuwe Reeks
33 (1970), pp. 151-204.

[5] In addition to the approriate references in Liddell-Scott and those already referred
to above, one may find the following especially instructive. συμβουλία - συμβουλευτικός:
Quintilian, *Inst. Orat.* III. 3.14 and 8.6. βουλένω: Dio Chrysostom, *Orat* 26 and 13.22; Ps.
Isocrates, *Ad Demonicus* 34ff.; Philodemus, *Rhet.* 2.2145; *Stoicorum Veterum Fragmenta*
2.96; Pseudo-Cicero, *Rhetorica ad Herennium*. ἔντευξις: Ps. Isocrates, *Ad Demonicus* 20;
Cicero, *de Oratore* I. 46 and 202; Moulton-Milligan, p. 218. νουθετέω: Xenophon, *Mem.*
I. 2.21; Dio Chrysostom, *Orat* 78.42; Justin, *Apol.* 67:4.

(i) Style

Aristotle suggested that the end or object of any speech is the hearer. It may be helpful for our total analysis of 2 Clement to ascertain by what rhetorical means its author tried to communicate effectively to the congregation at Corinth his central theological and ethical concerns. A few examples must suffice.

Even a brief examination of 2 Clement suggests that its author was interested in producing a strong rhetorical effect upon his listeners. Found not infrequently are parallellism, antithesis, play on words with the same root, and the hortatory subjunctive.

At the outset in chapter 1, one discovers a positive thesis (a) and a negative thesis (b) in parallelism.

<table>
<tr><td align="center">a</td><td align="center">b</td></tr>
<tr><td>Ἀδελφοί, οὕτως δεῖ ἡμᾶς φρονεῖν περὶ Ἰησοῦ Χριστοῦ, ὡς περὶ θεοῦ, ὡς περὶ κριτοῦ ζώντων καὶ νεκρῶν·</td><td>καὶ οὐ δεῖ ἡμᾶς μικρὰ φρονεῖν περὶ τῆς σωτηρίας ἡμῶν.</td></tr>
</table>

Standing in distinct relationship to one another are the following elements:

$$\delta\epsilon\hat{\iota}\ \phi\rho o\nu\epsilon\hat{\iota}\nu\ =\ o\dot{\upsilon}\ \delta\epsilon\hat{\iota}\ \phi\rho o\nu\epsilon\hat{\iota}\nu$$
$$\dot{\eta}\mu\hat{a}s\ =\ \dot{\eta}\mu\hat{a}s$$
$$\pi\epsilon\rho\dot{\iota}\ \mathrm{I}\eta\sigma o\hat{\upsilon}\ X\rho\iota\sigma\tauο\hat{\upsilon}\ =\ \pi\epsilon\rho\dot{\iota}\ \tau\hat{\eta}s\ \sigma\omega\tau\eta\rho\dot{\iota}as\ \dot{\eta}\mu\hat{\omega}\nu$$
$$\dot{\omega}s\ \pi\epsilon\rho\dot{\iota}\ \theta\epsilon o\hat{\upsilon}\ =\ o\dot{\upsilon}\ ...\ \mu\iota\kappa\rho\dot{a}$$

In 2 Clem. 1:2a another parallelism occurs with a continued play on the words μικρά and φρονεῖν:

ἐν τῷ γὰρ φρονεῖν ἡμᾶς μικρὰ   μικρὰ καὶ ἐλπίζομεν λαβεῖν·
περὶ αὐτοῦ

2 Clem. 1:2b is a good example of parataxis as well as a chiasmic structure:[1]

---

[1] On chiasmus see the older work by T. Wehofer, *Altchristlichen Epistolographie*, especially pp. 102-37. Often Wehofer's analysis is extreme and unconvincing, but at several points he has amplified our investigation with helpful insights. In addition, one should consult the work of Joachim Jeremias, "Chiasmus in den Paulusbriefen,"

καὶ οἱ ἀκούοντες ὡς περὶ μικρῶν]   [καὶ ἡμεῖς ἁμαρτάνομεν

ἁμαρτάνουσιν,]   [οὐκ εἰδότες, πόθεν ἐκλήθημεν ...

        [καὶ ὅσα ὑπέμεινεν Ἰησοῦς Χριστὸς

        ...

The remainder of chapter 1 contains confessional elements. These will be discussed in detail below.[1] For the moment, let us note the parallelism in the structure of 2 Clem. 1:3-6. We have here a two-fold question followed by a two-fold answer:[2]

Question 1a   *Question 1b*

τίνα οὖν ἡμεῖς αὐτῷ δώσομεν ἀντιμισθίαν,   ποῖον οὖν αἶνον αὐτῷ δώσομεν

ἢ τίνα καρπὸν ἄξιον οὗ ἡμῖν αὐτὸς ἔδωκεν; (1:3)   ἢ μισθὸν ἀντιμισθίας ὧν ἐλάβομεν; (1:5)

Confession 2a   *Confession 2b*

πόσα δὲ αὐτῷ ὀφείλομεν ὅσια; τὸ φῶς γὰρ ἡμῖν ἐχαρίσατο, ὡς πατὴρ υἱοὺς ἡμᾶς προσηγόρευσεν, ἀπολλυμένους ἡμᾶς ἔσωσεν. (1:4)   πηροὶ ὄντες τῇ διανοίᾳ ... ἀμαύρωσιν οὖν περικείμενοι καὶ τοιαύτης ἀχλύος γέμοντες ἐν τῇ ὁράσει, ἀνεβλέψαμεν ἀποθέμενοι ἐκεῖνο ὃ περικείμεθα νέφος τῇ αὐτοῦ θελήσει. (1:6)

Chapter 2 is also very carefully and artfully constructed. First, one should not overlook the parallelism in the quotation from Isaiah:

Εὐφράνθητι, στεῖρα ἡ οὐ τίκτουσα,
ῥῆξον καὶ βόησον ἡ οὐκ ὠδίνουσα

The explanation of this verse is structured as follows:

ZNW 49 (1958), pp. 145-56; N. W. Lund, *Chiasmus in the New Testament: A Study in Formgeschichte* (Chapel Hill, 1942); John C. Hurd, "Concerning the Structure of 1 Thessalonians," *Society of Biblical Literature annual meeting papers*, 1972.

[1] See pp. 103-107 below.

[2] In all likelihood the hymnic confession was originally a whole and only subsequently interspersed with questions by the author; he did this to heighten the rhetorical impact.

(1) ὅ εἶπεν· Εὐφράνθητι, στεῖρα... στεῖρα γὰρ ἦν ἡ ἐκκλησία ἡμῶν
πρὸ τοῦ δοθῆναι αὐτῇ τέκνα. (2:1)

(2) ὅ δὲ εἶπεν· Βόησον ... τοῦτο λέγει· τὰς προσευχὰς ἡμῶν
ἁπλῶς ἀναφέρειν πρὸς τὸν θεόν, μὴ
ὡς αἱ ὠδίνουσαι ἐγκακῶμεν. (2:2)

(3) ὅ δὲ εἶπεν· "Ότι πολλὰ τὰ ἐπεὶ ἔρημος ἐδόκει εἶναι ἀπὸ τοῦ
τέκνα τῆς ἐρήμου μᾶλλον ἢ θεοῦ ὁ λαὸς ἡμῶν, νυνὶ δὲ πιστεύ-
τῆς ἐχούσης τὸν ἄνδρα· σαντες πλείονες ἐγενόμεθα τῶν
δοκούντων ἔχειν θεόν. (2:3)

We have proceeded far enough to observe the repetition of certain
themes in both chapters, as well as a play on certain words:

1:7 — ἔσωσεν ... μηδεμίαν ἐλπίδα ἔχοντας σωτηρίας
2:5 — δεῖ τοὺς ἀπολλυμένους σώζειν
1:8 — ἠθέλησεν ἐκ μὴ ὄντος εἶναι ἡμᾶς
2:7 — ἠθέλησεν σῶσαι τὰ ἀπολλύμενα
1:8 — ἐκάλεσεν γὰρ ἡμᾶς οὐκ ὄντας
2:7 — καλέσας ἡμᾶς ἤδη ἀπολλυμένους.

There is a curious parallelism here as well as an interesting repetition
of the verb ἀπόλλυμι (1:4; 2:5,7) which suggests that our author is
interpreting the hymnic confession of chapter 1 in chapter 2. This
play on words occurs at other points in 2 Clement as well. Another
clear example can be found in 3:1: ἀλλὰ ἔγνωμεν δι' αὐτοῦ τὸν
πατέρα τῆς ἀληθείας· τίς ἡ γνῶσις ἡ πρὸς αὐτόν, ἢ τὸ μὴ ἀρνεῖσθαι
δι' οὗ ἔγνωμεν αὐτόν; In 2 Clement 7, too, the play on words
gives it a strongly rhetorical character. Variations of ἀγών or ἀγωνίζομαι are employed ten times (ἀγωνισώμεθα, ἀγών, ἀγῶνας, ἀγωνισάμενοι, ἀγωνισώμεθα, ἀγῶνα, ἀγωνισώμεθα, ἀγῶνα, ἀγωνιζόμενος,
ἀγῶνα). Variations of στέφανος or στεφανόω appear five times (στεφανοῦνται, στεφανωθῶμεν, στεφανωθῶμεν, στεφανωθῆναι, στεφάνου).
And all this within five verses!

Noteworthy, too, in this regard are chapters 9 and 10. The key-word
of chapter 9 is σάρξ and it echoes throughout the chapter: ἡ σάρξ οὐ
κρίνεται, ἐν τῇ σαρκὶ ταύτῃ ὄντες, φυλάσσειν τὴν σάρκα, ἐν τῇ
σαρκὶ ἐκλήθητε, καὶ ἐν τῇ σαρκὶ ἐλεύσεσθε, Χριστὸς ... ὢν μὲν
τὸ πρῶτον πνεῦμα ἐγένετο σάρξ, καὶ ἡμεῖς ἐν ταύτῃ τῇ σαρκί.

Returning to the use of parallelism, we note how in chapter 8 the
exegesis carefully parallels the illustration.[1]

---

[1] Wehofer, _Altchristlichen Epistolographie_, p. 131.

A

1. ὃν τρόπον γὰρ ὁ κεραμεύς, ἐὰν ποιῇ σκεῦος

2. καὶ ἐν ταῖς χερσὶν αὐτοῦ διαστραφῇ ἢ συντριβῇ,

3. πάλιν αὐτὸ ἀναπλάσσει,

6. οὕτως καὶ ἡμεῖς,

7. ἕως ἐσμὲν ἐν τούτῳ τῷ κόσμῳ, ἐν τῇ σαρκὶ ἃ ἐπράξαμεν πονηρὰ μετανοήσωμεν ἐξ ὅλης τῆς καρδίας, ἵνα σωθῶμεν ὑπὸ τοῦ κυρίου, ἕως ἔχομεν καιρὸν μετανοίας.

B

4. ἐὰν δὲ προφθάσῃ εἰς τὴν κάμινον τοῦ πυρὸς αὐτὸ βαλεῖν,

5. οὐκέτι βοηθήσει αὐτῷ·

8. μεὰ γὰρ τὸ ἐξελθεῖν ἡμᾶς ἐκ τοτ κόσμου

9. οὐκέτι δυνάμεθα ἐκεῖ ἐξομολογήσασθαι ἢ μετανοεῖν ἔτι.

10. ὥστε, ἀδελφοί,
ποιήσαντες τὸ θέλημα τοῦ πατρὸς
καὶ τὴν σάρκα ἁγνὴν τηρήσαντες
καὶ τὰς ἐντολὰς τοῦ κυρίου φυλάξαντες
ληψόμεθα ζωὴν αἰώνιον.

Chapters 15, 16, 17 and 18 form a self-contained unit, the basic theme being expressed in the words of the author, σπουδάζω τὴν δικαιοσύνην διώκειν. A certain parallelism can also be detected in this section:

I - (15:1-16:4)

a: Responsibility to heed the instructions and to act on them (15:1,2)

b: The Lord's promise for the obedient (15:3-5); paraenesis

c: Threat of punishment for the disobedient at the Last Judgment; paraenesis (16:1-4)

II - (17:1-18:2)

a: Responsibility to heed the instructions and to act on them (17:1-3)

b: Punishment of the disobedient at the Last Judgment (17:4-6)

c: Promise and reward for the obedient; paraenesis (17:7-18:2)

A careful examination of these verses reveals the following structure:[1]

Ia = IIa
Ib — chiastic — IIb
Ic — — IIc

One should also note the interweaving and variations on the themes μετανοέω (15:1; 16:1; 17:1) and κρίσις (16:3; 17:6; 18:2).

Chapters 19 and 20 are a concluding summary taking up themes already discussed earlier in the writing and putting them in the framework of a comparison of the suffering of this present life to the joys of the life to come. The basic theme is expressed in 20:2: "We are engaged in the contest of the living God and are being trained by the present life in order to win laurels in the life to come."

One can note a further example of parallelism in 19:3 and 4:

κἂν ὀλίγον χρόνον κακοπαθήσωσιν ἐν τῷ κόσμῳ τούτῳ,
τὸν ἀθάνατον τῆς ἀναστάσεως καρπὸν τρυγήσουσιν.

μὴ οὖν λυπείσθω ὁ εὐσεβής, ἐὰν ἐπὶ τοῖς νῦν χρόνοις ταλαιπωρῇ·
μακάριος αὐτὸν ἀναμένει χρόνος·

The discourse concludes with this doxology:

I
a. Τῷ μόνῳ θεῷ ἀοράτῳ, πατρὶ τῆς ἀληθείας,
b. τῷ ἐξαποστείλαντι ἡμῖν τὸν σωτῆρα καὶ ἀρχηγὸν τῆς ἀφθαρσίας,
c. δι' οὗ καὶ ἐφανέρωσεν ἡμῖν τὴν ἀλήθειαν καὶ τὴν ἐπουράνιον ζωήν,

II [αὐτῷ ἡ δόξα εἰς τοὺς αἰῶνας τῶν αἰώνων. ἀμήν.

Finally, a word must be said about two other features of the rhetorical style of 2 Clement. First, the use of illustrations and examples. One need only recall the illustrations of the athletic contest (2 Clement 7). Secondly, the use of the hortatory subjunctive (ποιήσωμεν, 5:1; ἀγωνισώμεθα, 7:1; μετανοήσωμεν, 8:1) and prohibition as expressed by the subjunctive with μή (μὴ ... ἐγκακῶμεν, 2:2; μὴ ... καλῶμεν, 4:1).

(ii) The form and structure of 2 Clement

It was Klaus Baltzer who made a first step toward a form-critical analysis of 2 Clement as well as other Jewish-Hellenistic and early

---

[1] *Ibid*, p. 131.

Christian texts.[1] Although his central concern is that of the book's title, *The Covenant Formulary*, he also attempted to trace the continued influence of this covenant formulary into the intertestamental and early Christian period. His investigation revealed, albeit in a fragmentary way, a recurring pattern in this literature: a theological section, a section filled with ethical exhortations and a final section including eschatological sanctions. Even though some of Baltzer's applications are strained and sometimes only partially correct, for example, with reference to 2 Clement,[2] one must appreciate this effort which attempted to determine whether a form-critical pattern could be discovered in certain Jewish-Hellenistic and early Christian texts. Further, his conjecture as to the historical setting of such a pattern is probably correct, namely, that "the common *Sitz im Leben* we are after is the use of the form in Jewish and Christian worship."[3]

Our own analysis also leads to the conclusion that 2 Clement follows a very definite three-fold pattern, comprised of the following elements: 1) a theological section (1:1-2:7), which serves as the basic foundation for the address. Here God's saving action in Jesus Christ is described; 2) an ethical section (3:1-14:5) which develops the ethical consequences of the theological assertions made in the first section. The transitional character of 2 Clement 3 is evident: *because* God has saved us in Jesus Christ, *therefore* we must obey him. This ethical section is filled with paraenetic material and contains the central emphasis of the whole; (3) an eschatological section (15:1-18:2), in which the major theme of blessing and curses is summarized in this way: "For these sayings hold as much pleasure in store for those who act on them, as they do condemnation for those who disregard them" (15:5).

At certain points these results are parallel to those of Baltzer;[4] at other points they are quite different. We would agree with him that 2 Clement makes use of a pattern, but we would differ as to its application. Our investigation will show that this three-fold pattern governs most of 2 Clement and does not end with 7:6, as Baltzer suggests. Further, Baltzer's main concern in discussing 2 Clement is to demonstrate that the covenant formulary of the Old Testament had a continuing influence in early Christianity. There is indeed a pattern in

---

[1] Klaus Baltzer, *The Covenant Formulary* (Philadelphia, 1971).

[2] *Ibid.*, pp. 132-36.

[3] *Ibid.*, p. 167.

[4] *Ibid.*, pp. 132-36.

some early Christian texts, but the evidence appears to be too meager and too diversified to hold categorically to a definite influence of the Old Testament covenant formulary.[1]

In what other literature might one find this three-fold pattern which is common to 2 Clement ? Baltzer finds this pattern in Qumran's Manual of Discipline: the dogmatic part in 3:15-4:1, the ethical in 4:2-6 and 9-11 and the eschatological sanctions in 4:6b-8 and 12-14.[2] A similar three-fold analysis is given for the Damascus Document of Qumran: Part I, 1-6:11; Part II, 6:11-7:4; Part III, 7:4ff. Less convincing are some other texts collected by Baltzer, specifically, Barnabas and Didache. That both of these writings have a clearly defined ethical section (Barn. 18:1-20:2; Did. 1:1-15:4) and eschatological section (Barn. 21:1-9; Did. 16:1-8) is evident. However, there is no theological section in the Didache, and to claim that Barnabas 2-17 is a theological section is to stretch that term to the point of imprecision. A careful analysis of Barnabas 1-17 prohibits such a lumping together into one theological section.[3] Barnabas and the Didache do not represent this three-fold pattern in its purity; the use of parts two and three of this pattern might well be a reflection of the influence of the worship service where this pattern had its "Sitz im Leben."

Most illuminating and convincing is Baltzer's reference to the Acts of John 106-107 where one finds a brief paraenetic sermon (perhaps a summary) with the same three-fold pattern as in 2 Clement.[4] Because this section of the Acts of John parallels so closely the structure of 2 Clement, we will quote the whole of it.

I—*Theological Part*

My brethren and fellow-servants, joint-heirs and partners with me in the kingdom of God, you know the Lord, how many great works he has granted you through me, how many wonders, how many healings, how many signs, what gifts of grace, (what) teachings, directions. refreshments, services, enlightenments, glories, graces, gifts, and acts of faith and fellowship, which you have seen with your eyes are given you by him, (though) they are not seen with these eyes nor heard with these ears.

---

[1] On this point note some of the critical reviews of Baltzer's work. These reviews are conveniently cited at the end of the German second edition of Baltzer, *Das Bundesformular* (Neukirchen, 1964).

[2] Baltzer, *Covenant*, pp. 123ff.

[3] See Robert Kraft, *The Didache and Barnabas* (New York, 1965), pp. 78ff.

[4] See Hans Lietzmann, *Messe und Herrenmahl* (Berlin, 1955), pp. 240ff.

II—*Ethical Exhortation*

Therefore be firmly settled in him, remembering him in all you do, understanding the mystery of (God's) providence that has been accomplished for men, why the Lord has performed it. He entreats you through me, my brethren, and makes request, desiring to continue free from distress, free from insult, and from disloyalty, and from injury; for he knows the insult that comes from you, he knows that dishonour, he knows that disloyalty, he knows even injury from those who do not listen to his commandments.

So let not our gracious God be grieved, the compassionate, the merciful, the holy, the pure, the undefiled, the immaterial, the only, the one, the unchanging, the simple, the guileless, the patient, the one that is higher and loftier than every name we can utter or conceive, our God Jesus Christ. Let him rejoice with us because we behave honourably, let him be glad because we live purely, let him be refreshed because our ways are sober, let him be easy because we live strictly, let him be pleased at our felloswhip, let him smile because we are chaste, let him be merry because we love him. I give you this charge, my brethren, because I am not hastening toward the task that is prepared for me, which is already being perfected by the Lord. For what else could I have to say to you? You have the pledges of our God, you have the securities of his goodness, you have his presence that is inescapable.

III—*Eschatological Sanction*

If, then, you sin no longer, he forgives you what you did in ignorance; but if when you have known him and found mercy with him you resort again to such (deeds), then both your former (sins) will be laid to your charge, and you shall have no part nor mercy is his presence.[1]

Baltzer made no attempt to ascertain whether such a three-fold pattern might be found in the New Testament. We will suggest that this pattern may possibly be reflected in at least four New Testament writings: 1 John, 1 and 2 Peter and Hebrews. Much of the current discussion with regard to each of these documents testifies to the difficulty of defining their genre with precision. However, the fact that they have a three-fold pattern similar to the hortatory address known as 2 Clement suggests that we may be dealing with hortatory addresses put in letter form, or letters heavily influenced by such hortatory addresses.[2]

Marxsen describes well the frustration involved in attempting to define 1 John:

We certainly cannot describe 1 Jn. as a 'letter,' as it lacks all the concrete details which would justify such a description. On the other hand, it is quite plain that

---

[1] English translation from Hennecke, Schneemelcher and Wilson, *New Testament Apocrypha*, II (London, 1965), pp. 254-55.

[2] See Cancik, *Epistulae Morales*, pp. 46-61.

the author frequently has in mind a circle of readers to whom he addresses himself directly (2:1, 7f., 12ff., 18, 21, 26, etc.). The document has been spoken of as a 'homily,' an 'admonitory letter', a 'tract' or a 'manifesto', but none of these is a really adequate description. It is a document the form of which has no parallel elsewhere.[1]

Bultmann's commentary on the Johannine epistles contains the suggestion that 1 John originally ended with 2:27, since after that point nothing specifically new in terms of content is found.[2] This may be. If this suggestion is accepted, then a clear three-fold pattern can be detected: theological section, 1 Jn. 1:1-4; ethical exhortations, 1:5-2:17; eschatological warnings, 2:18-24. Perhaps a hortatory discourse addressed to this congregation was edited, expanded and sent on to other congregations forming the Johannine circle, or a hortatory discourse preached by this writer was influential in determining the pattern of this paraenetic letter. The latter option is the more likely, since the first option involves a fairly complex theory of composition. If this should be the case, the form of 1 John would not be without parallel as Marxsen suggested. In terms of form there would be a parallel to the three-fold pattern of 2 Clement, and in terms of paraenetic intention the letters from the hand of Seneca, Cicero and Pliny offer interesting analogies.

A number of scholars have suggested that 1 Peter is a baptismal sermon, while others hold that it is an epistle.[3] 1 Peter reveals a three-fold pattern similar to 2 Clement: I) theological section, 1 Pet. 1:3-12; II) ethical exhortations, 1:13-4:6. Within this section one finds the not uncommon alternation between theme and paraenesis; [4] III) eschatological section, 4:7-11. Perhaps a hortatory discourse was taken over and made to serve as an encyclical letter to the churches of Asia Minor by the addition of 1:1-3 and 4:12-5:14.[5] However, one has also to reckon with the possibility that this document was originally intended to be a pseudonymous letter to the churches

---

[1] Willi Marxsen, *Introduction to the New Testament* (Philadelphia, 1968), p. 261.

[2] Rudolf Bultmann, *Die drei Johannesbriefe* (Göttingen, 1967), p. 47.

[3] Among them Perdelwitz, Streeter, Windisch, Beare, Schneider and Nauck. See summary in W. G. Kümmel, *Introduction to the New Testament* (Nashville, 1966), pp. 295ff., although Kümmel himself disagrees with this position. See also the excellent discussion in Marxsen, *Introduction*, pp. 199ff.

[4] See pp. 110ff. below.

[5] The arguments for this position are well summarized by Reginald H. Fuller, *A Critical Introduction to the New Testament* (London, 1966), p. 158.

named and that its form and content were significantly influenced by the preaching situation in the church of its origin. One should not overlook the fact that those who wrote letters to the churches also preached regularly, and thus the oral communication undoubtedly influenced the written.

To determine the formation of 2 Peter is also not simple. Lying behind the present form of 2 Peter we can still discern remnants of a three-fold pattern: theological section, 2 Pet. 1:3-4; ethical exhortations, which have been abbreviated, 1:5-19; eschatological section, 3:3-13. Into this basic pattern Jude was taken up in the second chapter. That 2 Pet. 1:20-3:2 does not belong to the original document is suggested by three factors: 1) the dependence, at points *verbatim*, on Jude; 2) the repetition of τοῦτο πρῶτον γινώσκοντες in 1:20 and 3:3. We would suggest that 1:19 originally continued with 3:3; 3) the seemingly new introduction to the false teachers and scoffers in 3:3ff. This would hardly seem necessary if 2 Peter 2 belonged to the original. To make use of a hortatory discourse for a more general church situation a later redactor may also have added 1:1-2; 3:1-2, and possibly 3:14-18, although the latter might simply be a concluding summary of the original address, much as in the case of 2 Clement 19-20. The definite and awkward insertion of a section as long as 1:20-3:2 into a previous document, suggests that we may be dealing with a hortatory address put into letter form, rather than the form of a hortatory address having influenced the formation of the letter.

In this section of the discussion, which is intended to be more suggestive than final, it is important to include the book of Hebrews, despite its complexity. It refers to itself as "a word of exhortation" (τοῦ λογοῦ τῆς παρακλήσεως) and we find a number of texts which refer to the author's speaking, rather than writing (2:5; 5:11; 6:9; 8:1; 9:5). An increasing number of scholars now refer to Hebrews as having been originally a sermon.[1] But there is still little agreement with regard to the literary structure of Hebrews. Thyen, Héring and Coppens suggest a two-fold division and Vaganay and Vanhoye argue for at least a five-fold division.[2] After carefully reviewing the manifold solution to these questions, Grässer writes: "Strittig war und ist dagegen noch immer die Abgrenzung der einzelnen Gedankenkreise

---

[1] For a thorough discussion of the contemporary literature on Hebrews, see the survey by Erich Grässer, "Der Hebräerbrief 1938-1963," *ThRu* 30 (1964), pp. 138-236.

[2] For a precise summary of these positions see Grässer, "Hebräerbrief," pp. 159-67.

innerhalb des Gesamtaufrisses wie das die kunstvolle Komposition bestimmende Motiv überhaupt."[1]

If Hebrews is "pastoral preaching to an established community,"[2] does it make use of a three-fold pattern similar to that of 2 Clement? Tentatively and cautiously we suggest that it may: I) theological section, Heb. 1:1-14. Verses 1-4 are a clear example of a hymnic confession which, incidentally, have no other parallel in Hebrews.[3] This confession is then amplified by the use of the Old Testament, exactly as in 2 Clement; II) ethical exhortations, 2:1-10:18. In this section we also find a pattern present in 2 Clement: the alternation of theme and paraenesis. For example, in 5:1-10 we have the theme of Jesus as high priest, followed by paraenesis in 5:11-6:12. Where Hebrews differs from 2 Clement is that its thematic section, which has its goal in the paraenesis, is developed to a much further degree than in 2 Clement; III) eschatological section, 10:19-12:19. We are not suggesting that the theme of eschatology is absent elsewhere in Hebrews, but that it is present in a more concentrated form in this section and that it is the predominant concern. This is evident from such references as 10:25, "as you see the Day drawing near;" 10:35, the "great reward"; 10:36ff., "that you may do the will of God and receive what is promised"; all of chapter 11—especially verses 10, 13-16, 26, 35, 40; also 12:2, 15, 17, 22-29. Hebrews 13 would be a final paraenetic summary, similar to 2 Clement 19-20. Once again it is likely that we may have a hortatory discourse which was subsequently put into letter form and circulated, rather than having been originally composed as a letter. [4]

These observations suggest that the three-fold pattern found in 2 Clement is not unique, and, in fact, may have been used with some

---

[1] *Ibid.*, p. 160.

[2] Fuller, *Introduction*, p. 147.

[3] See Günther Bornkamm, "Das Bekenntnis im Hebräerbrief," *Studien zu Antike und Urchristentum*, II (München, 1959), pp. 188-203; Reinhard Deichgräber, *Gotteshymnus und Christushymnus in der frühen Christenheit* (Göttingen, 1967), pp. 137-40; and Jack T. Sanders, *The New Testament Christological Hymns* (Cambridge, 1971), pp. 19-20.

[4] These observations have important implications for the common distinction made between "letter" and "epistle." This differentiation, which goes back to the work of Adolf Deissmann (*Light from the Ancient East*, Grand Rapids, 1965, pp. 228ff.), is neither helpful nor clarifying. For Deissmann, a letter is essentially "non-literary" in form and was meant only for the person or persons to whom it is addressed. In this sense it is private and not meant for the wider public. It is thus spontaneous in its

degree of frequency in early Christianity. The probable sociological setting was the oral exhortation to an assembled Christian congregation. This oral setting of the three-fold pattern, which may well have its roots in Judaism, undoubtedly exercised influence upon the written correspondence of early Christianity. Thus, certain early Christian letters may have been shaped by this pattern, and some hortatory addresses may have been put in letter form and circulated among a wider audience.

---

motivation. The epistle, however, "has nothing in common with the letter except its form" (p. 229). It is an artistic literary form which is intended primarily for the wider public. Whereas the letter relates genuine experience, the literary epistle presents mere manufactured experiences. "The father of the epistle was no great pioneer spirit, but a mere paragraphist, a mere mechanic. ... If the true letter might be compared to a prayer, the epistle which mimicked it was only a babbling; if there beamed forth in the letter the wondrous face of a child, the epistle grinned stiffly... like a puppet" ([*Bible Studies*, Edinburgh, 1928], p. 10). Certainly one must appreciate Deissmann's acute perception of the necessity for classifying those writings in the New Testament and elsewhere which he designates as "epistles"; he touches on the whole problem of genre in the New Testament. Yet one cannot help but feel that Deissmann's distinction between letter and epistle is both too sharply and too rigidly drawn. Further, one must ask whether his category "epistle" has not become a catchall for writings which are difficult to classify, such as the ones just discussed. Deissmann's "epistle" genre is simply too restrictive and artificial to be of much value. From both a style and form critical approach, Koskenniemi (*Studien*, pp. 90ff.) has pointed out some of the weaknesses inherent in Deissmann's position. His fundamental criticism is that Deissmann's classification avoids the complexity of the problem. To distinguish between a letter and an epistle primarily using the criteria "non-literary"—"literary" is inadequate, since the style of a letter is largely dependent upon the background and training of the author. Another of Deissmann's points, namely, that the letter is marked by intimacy and personal reflections and the epistle by artificiality, is disputed. In fact, argues Koskenniemi, one could establish the reverse. Not only is it important to ascertain what type of person might have written a certain letter, but also one should ask, what kind of relationship exists between the writer and the recipient. This, too, could play a large role as to whether the letter is "personal" or "artificial."

CHAPTER TWO

QUOTATIONS FROM AUTHORITATIVE SOURCES

Since 2 Clement specifically cites a large number of quotations from the Jewish scriptures and the gospel tradition and introduces them with specific formulas, it will be helpful to examine these in a separate chapter. Such an examination should assist us in more precisely determining the setting of 2 Clement in early Christianity. The attempt will be made to determine which sources the writer of 2 Clement utilized, as well as in what manner and for what purpose he used them. In the first two sections dealing with "conscious quotations," only those quotations specifically introduced by an introductory formula will be examined.

INTRODUCTORY FORMULAS

Jewish Scriptures	*Gospel Tradition*
2 Clem.	2 Clem.
3:5 λέγει δὲ καὶ ἐν τῷ Ἡσαΐᾳ	2:4 καὶ ἑτέρα δὲ γραφὴ λέγει
6:8 λέγει δὲ καὶ ἡ γραφὴ ἐν τῷ Ἰεζεκιήλ	3:2 λέγει δὲ καὶ αὐτός (Χριστός)
7:6 φησίν	4:2 λέγει γάρ (ὁ κύριος)
11:2 λέγει γὰρ καὶ ὁ προφητικὸς λόγος	4:5 εἶπεν ὁ κύριος
	5:2 λέγει γὰρ ὁ κύριος
13:2 λέγει γὰρ ὁ κύριος	6:1 λέγει δὲ ὁ κύριος
14:1 ... ἐκ τῆς γραφῆς τῆς λεγούσης	8:5 λέγει γὰρ ὁ κύριος ἐν τῷ εὐαγγελίῳ
14:2 λέγει γὰρ ἡ γραφή	9:11 καὶ γὰρ εἶπεν ὁ κύριος
15:3 ... τὸν θεὸν τὸν λέγοντα	12:2 ὁ κύριος ... εἶπεν
17:4 εἶπεν γὰρ ὁ κύριος	13:4 λέγει ὁ θεός

Those quotations not so introduced but bearing some relationship to a known source will be discussed in the third section, "literary affinities and allusions." Aspects of the introductory formulas calling for special comment will be treated in the context of the actual quotation they introduce as well as at other points throughout the chapter.

1. Conscious Quotations from the Jewish Scriptures

2 Clem. 3:5

(λέγει δὲ καὶ ἐν τῷ 'Ησαΐᾳ) 'Ο λαὸς οὗτος τοῖς χείλεσίν με τιμᾷ, ἡ δὲ καρδία αὐτῶν πόρρω ἄπεστιν ἀπ' ἐμοῦ.

The old Greek of Is. 29:13 reads:

'Εγγίζει μοι ὁ λαὸς οὗτος τοῖς χείλεσιν αὐτῶν τιμῶσίν με, ἡ δὲ καρδία αὐτῶν πόρρω ἀπέχει ἀπ' ἐμοῦ....

In Mt. 15:8 // Mk. 7:6 we read:

οὗτος ὁ λαὸς τοῖς χείλεσίν με τιμᾷ, ἡ δὲ καρδία αὐτῶν πόρρω ἀπέχει ἀπ' ἐμοῦ·

In 1 Clem. 15:2 we read:

Οὗτος ὁ λαὸς τοῖς χείλεσίν με τιμᾷ, ἡ δὲ καρδία αὐτῶν πόρρω ἄπεστιν ἀπ' ἐμοῦ.

The above comparison indicates that the quotation in 2 Clement stands closer to the synoptic tradition than to the old Greek; however, it is identical with that found in 1 Clem. 15:2, except for the insignificant change of position of οὗτος. Especially noteworthy is the use of the verb ἄπεστιν in both 1 and 2 Clement against the use of ἀπέχει in the old Greek and the synoptic tradition. It is, of course, possible that 2 Clement is dependent upon 1 Clement.[1] Another solution is that both 1 and 2 Clement are drawing upon the same source, which may have been a different recension of the old Greek, or possibly, a collection of proof-texts.[2]

---

[1] Helmut Köster, *Synoptische Überlieferung bei den apostolischen Vätern* (Berlin, 1957), p. 22, denies the dependence of 2 Clement on 1 Clement because 2 Clement cited this specifically as an Isaiah text while 1 Clement does not. While this point is worthy of consideration it cannot bear the full burden of proof. It is imaginable that 2 Clement cites the text from 1 Clement knowing full well that this is an Isaiah text and consequently states this. In the last analysis, though, we agree with Köster that no final certainty can be attained as to precisely where 2 Clement has derived this text.

[2] For a review of the variety of hypotheses concerning the existence of proof-texts and testimony books, see the survey of the literature by M. P. Miller, "Targum, Midrash and the Use of the Old Testament in the New Testament," *JSJ* 2 (1971), pp. 28-82.

This quotation appears in the paraenetic section of chapter 3. It is to be placed in that category of quotations which Thyen characterizes as follows: "Hier dient das Zitat nicht so sehr dem Beweis, als vielmehr der Bestätigung oder Erläuterung des Gesagten, ja oft erscheint es auch nur rein rhetorisch als Schmuck der Rede verwandt."[1] The purpose of our quotation is both supportive and illustrative.

2 Clem. 6:8

(λέγει δὲ καὶ ἡ γραφὴ ἐν τῷ Ἰεζεκιήλ) ἐὰν ἀναστῇ Νῶε καὶ Ἰὼβ καὶ Δανιήλ, οὐ ῥύσονται τὰ τέκνα αὐτῶν ἐν τῇ αἰχμαλωσίᾳ.

This material resembles Ezek. 14:14-20 which refers to *Νωε καὶ Δανιηλ καὶ Ιωβ ... οἱ τρεῖς ἄνδρες οὗτοι ... οὐ μὴ ῥύσωνται υἱοὺς οὐδὲ θυγατέρας, αὐτοὶ μόνοι σωθήσονται ... καὶ Νωε καὶ Δανιηλ καὶ Ιωβ ... ἐὰν υἱοὶ ἢ θυγατέρες ὑπολειφθῶσιν, αὐτοὶ ... ῥύσονται τὰς ψυχὰς αὐτῶν.* The bulk of the material found in this section of Ezekiel is absent from 2 Clement. Further, the order of the names in 2 Clement is different, as well as the fact that 2 Clement uses three terms not found in any of the old Greek texts to Ezekiel: *ἀναστῇ, τὰ τέκνα* and *τῇ αἰχμαλωσίᾳ*. It is difficult to argue for an exact quotation from Ezekiel, even if one leaves open the possibility of differing old Greek translations. On balance, it appears as if our author is summarizing a well known account from Ezekiel for the purpose of illustrating and supporting his point that only by doing the will of Christ will his listeners be saved.

2 Clem. 7:6 [17:5b; cf. p. 92 below]

(τῶν γὰρ μὴ τηρησάντων, φησίν, τὴν σφραγῖδα) ὁ σκώληξ αὐτῶν οὐ τελευτήσει καὶ τὸ πῦρ αὐτῶν οὐ σβεσθήσεται, καὶ ἔσονται εἰς ὅρασιν πάσῃ σαρκί.

Save for the insignificant omission of *γάρ*, this quotation is taken directly from the old Greek of Is. 66:24. An abridged version of Is. 66:24 is also found in Mk. 9:48: *ὁ σκώληξ αὐτῶν οὐ τελευτᾷ καὶ τὸ πῦρ οὐ σβέννυται*. It is impossible, however, that 2 Clement is dependent on Mark at this point. The quotation serves as an illustration of what happens to those who do not guard the seal.

---

[1] Hartwig Thyen, *Der Stil der Jüdisch-Hellenistischen Homilie* (Göttingen, 1955), p. 72.

2 Clem. 11:2

1 Clem. 23:3-4	2 Clem. 11:2
(πόρρω γενέσθω ἀφ' ἡμῶν ἡ γραφὴ αὕτη, ὅπου λέγει)	(λέγει γὰρ καὶ ὁ προφητικὸς λόγος)
Ταλαίπωροί εἰσιν οἱ δίψυχοι, οἱ διστάζοντες τῇ ψυχῇ, οἱ λέγοντες ·	Ταλαίπωροί εἰσιν οἱ δίψυχοι, οἱ διστάζοντες τῇ καρδίᾳ, οἱ λέγοντες·
Ταῦτα ἠκούσαμεν καὶ ἐπὶ τῶν πατέρων ἡμῶν, καὶ ἰδού, γεγηράκαμεν, καὶ οὐδὲν ἡμῖν τούτων συνβέβηκεν.	Ταῦτα πάλαι ἠκούσαμεν καὶ ἐπὶ τῶν πατέρων ἡμῶν, ἡμεῖς δὲ ἡμέραν ἐξ ἡμέρας προσδεχόμενοι οὐδὲν τούτων ἑωράκαμεν.
ὦ ἀνόητοι, συμβάλετε ἑαυτοὺς ξύλῳ· λάβετε ἄμπελον· πρῶτον μὲν φυλλοροεῖ, εἶτα βλαστὸς γίνεται, εἶτα φύλλον, εἶτα ἄνθος, καὶ μετὰ ταῦτα ὄμφαξ, εἶτα σταφυλὴ παρεστηκυῖα.	ἀνόητοι, συμβάλετε ἑαυτοὺς ξύλῳ· λάβετε ἄμπελον· πρῶτον μὲν φυλλοροεῖ, εἶτα βλαστὸς γίνεται, μετὰ ταῦτα ὄμφαξ, εἶτα σταφυλὴ παρεστηκυῖα· οὕτως καὶ ὁ λαός μου ἀκαταστασίας καὶ θλίψεις ἔσχεν· ἔπειτα ἀπολήψεται τὰ ἀγαθά.

The introductory formula ὁ προφητικὸς λόγος is unique in 2 Clement and only appears at one other point in all of the New Testament and the Apostolic Fathers, 2 Pet. 1:19, where it refers to the Jewish Scriptures in general. In Philo, Plant 117 it refers to Gen. 1:14, in Leg All III 43 to Moses and Ex. 9:24, and in Sobr 68 to Gen. 49:22. Finally, there is one other reference to the term ὁ προφητικὸς λόγος: in Justin, *Dial.* 56:6 where it refers to Gen. 18:10. In light of this usage elsewhere it is likely that 2 Clement also has the Jewish Scriptures in mind when he uses this term.[1]

The matter is complicated by the fact that this quotation is not found in the Old Testament or any other Jewish writing known to us. It appears in only one other place, 1 Clem. 23:3-4. While it is conceivable that 2 Clement is dependent upon 1 Clement and incorporates minor alterations, this possibility is weakened by the fact that 2 Clement adds a final sentence. Thus Grant's conclusion that both 1 and 2 Clement, independently of one another, are directly based on

---

[1] See the further discussion on pp. 151-52 below.

a Jewish apocryphal writing is the most likely.[1] At the time the authors of 1 and 2 Clement were writing, this unknown source must have enjoyed an authoritative status. Lightfoot's[2] suggestion that the lost book may be that of Eldad and Modad, referred to in a similar context in Hermas, Vis. 2:4, is worth considering. Eldad and Modad is mentioned in a list of 'apocrypha of the Old Testament' in *The Stichometry of Nicephorus*; it is also listed under the heading of "apocrypha" in the so-called "List of the Sixty (Canonical) Books" attached to certain manuscripts of the *Quaestiones et Responsiones of Anastasius of Sinae*.[3]

In 2 Clement 11, this quotation is the central one, serving as an illustration and support for the theme of the chapter that one must believe in the promises of God.

2 Clem. 13:2

(λέγει γὰρ ὁ κύριος) Διὰ παντὸς τὸ ὄνομά μου βλασφημεῖται ἐν πᾶσιν τοῖς ἔθνεσιν.

In the old Greek of Is. 52:5, the verse is introduced very similarly: τάδε λέγει κύριος. 2 Clement is close to the old Greek, but lacks δι' ὑμᾶς at the beginning and includes πᾶσιν before τοῖς ἔθνεσιν. Is. 52:5 is also reflected in Rom. 2:24, but since the divergence is so great, it is hardly possible that 2 Clement is dependent on Romans.

(καὶ πάλιν) Οὐαὶ δι' ὃν βλασφημεῖται τὸ ὄνομά μου.

The source of this half of the quotation is unknown.[4] Since Ignatius, Trall. 8:2 has a similar quotation, Οὐαὶ γάρ, δι' οὗ ἐπὶ ματαιότητι τὸ ὄνομά μου ἐπί τινων βλασφημεῖται, they both might be reflecting the same apocryphal source. Both parts of this quotation serve as a support for the major theme of chapter 13. The quotation is followed by a brief paraenetic interpretation.

2 Clem. 14:1

(ἐὰν δὲ μὴ ποιήσωμεν τὸ θέλημα κυρίου, ἐσόμεθα ἐκ τῆς γραφῆς τῆς λεγούσης) Ἐγενήθη ὁ οἶκός μου σπήλαιον λῃστῶν.

---

[1] Robert M. Grant, *The Apostolic Fathers* I (New York, 1965), pp. 48-50.

[2] J. B. Lightfoot, *The Apostolic Fathers* I, 2 (London, 1890), p. 80.

[3] D. S. Russell, *The Method and Message of Jewish Apocalyptic* (Philadelphia, 1964), pp. 391-94.

[4] See also pp. 86-88 and 154-59 below.

This quotation derives ultimately from the old Greek of Jer. 7:11 where ὁ οἶκός μου follows after σπήλαιον λῃστῶν. It is sufficiently different from the synoptics (Mk. 11:17 //) so as not to be dependent on them. This quotation serves an essentially illustrative purpose.

2 Clem. 14:2

(λέγει γὰρ ἡ γραφή) Ἐποίησεν ὁ θεὸς τὸν ἄνθρωπον ἄρσεν καὶ θῆλυ.

This more closely resembles the old Greek of Gen. 1:27 than Mk. 10:6 // Mt. 19:4, except that it lacks κατ᾽ εἰκόνα θεοῦ ἐποίησεν αὐτον after ἄνθρωπον. This verse is then interpreted: τὸ ἄρσεν ἐστὶν ὁ Χριστός, τὸ θῆλυ ἡ ἐκκλησία. Since an exegesis of this verse would get us deeply involved in the complex problem of chapter 14, we will reserve our discussion until chapter three.[1]

2 Clem. 15:3

(ἵνα μετὰ παρρησίας αἰτῶμεν τὸν θεὸν τὸν λέγοντα) Ἔτι λαλοῦντός σου ἐρῶ· ἰδοὺ πάρειμι.

Our text comes from the old Greek of Is. 58:9. The only change is that 2 Clement has ἐρῶ instead of ἐρεῖ. This might be explained by the introduction to the quotation, or possibly by a different version of the old Greek. It serves as a proof-text for the "blessings" part of the "blessings and curses" section.

2 Clem. 17:4

(εἶπεν γὰρ ὁ κύριος) Ἔρχομαι συναγαγεῖν πάντα τὰ ἔθνη, φυλὰς καὶ γλώσσας.

This quotation is similar to the old Greek of Is. 66:18, except that φυλάς is lacking in Isaiah. The trio τὰ ἔθνη, φυλὰς καὶ γλώσσας is found in the Greek of Dan. 3:2, as well as in Rev. 11:9 and 14:6. This quotation, along with its interpretation, is used as a proof for the final day of judgment, which then leads over to the blessings and curses motif.

Summary

Before we proceed to the section which follows dealing with conscious quotations from the gospel tradition, the following observations are

---

[1] See pp. 160-66 below.

important. Twice the source of 2 Clement's quotation is specifically stated — 3:5 and 6:8; yet in neither case do we find an exact quotation from the old Greek versions as we know them. All exact or almost exact quotations are taken from the old Greek of Isaiah (52:5; 58:9; 66:18; 66:24) and one from the Greek of Gen. 1:27.

The fact that a number of quotations are taken from Isaiah has led Knopf to suggest that the scripture lesson read immediately prior to 2 Clement was Isaiah 54-66.[1] Knopf's basic starting point is 2 Clem. 19:1: "Ὥστε, ἀδελφοὶ καὶ ἀδελφαί, μετὰ τὸν θεὸν τῆς ἀληθείας ἀναγινώσκω ὑμῖν ἔντευξιν εἰς τὸ προσέχειν τοῖς γεγραμμένοις, ἵνα καὶ ἑαυτοὺς σώσητε καὶ τὸν ἀναγινώσκοντα ἐν ὑμῖν. According to his interpretation τοῖς γεγραμμένοις refers to the scripture lesson read prior to 2 Clement and upon which it is based. This practice would then parallel Justin's description of the life of his congregation in mid-second century Rome: "And on the day called Sunday, all who live in cities or in the country gather together to one place, and the memoirs of the apostles or the writings of the prophets are read, as long as time permits; then, when the reader has ceased, the president verbally instructs, and exhorts to the imitation of these good things."[2]

However, in view of our previous remarks concerning τοῖς γεγραμμένοις[3] we are not inclined to agree with Knopf that this phrase refers to a scripture lesson read prior to the delivery of 2 Clement. Even if for the moment we were to accept the accuracy of Knopf's position it is still difficult to hold to the view that the text preceding 2 Clement included chapters 54 through 66 of Isaiah. First, we know of no precise parallel in early Christianity or Judaism[4] which suggests anything like a thirteen chapter text. Usually such texts from the prophets included a few verses.[5] Secondly, Knopf's evidence is not sufficient to support his case. He cites only four verses out of thirteen chapters, and only one of them plays an important role. Then, too, he is forced to omit 2 Clement's quotation of Is. 52:5 since it

---

[1] R. Knopf, "Die Anagnose zum zweiten Clemensbrief," *ZNW* 3 (1902), pp. 266-79.

[2] Justin, *Apol.* 67.

[3] See pp. 14-15 above.

[4] See Paul Glaue, *Die Vorlesung heiliger Schriften im Gottesdienste* (Berlin, 1907), pp. 62-78; Leopold Zunz, *Die gottesdienstlichen Vorträge der Juden historisch entwickelt* (Hildesheim, 1966).

[5] S. Maybaum, *Die ältesten Phasen in der Entwicklung der jüdischen Predigt* (Berlin, 1901); J. W. Doeve, *Jewish Hermeneutics in the Synoptic Gospels and Acts* (Assen, 1954).

precedes Isaiah 54. The argument that the general context of Isaiah 54-66 influenced 2 Clement is too vague to be of any real significance.

In light of C. H. Dodd's[1] work concerning the use of the Old Testament in the early church, it is much more probable that 2 Clement is dependent upon those blocks of Jewish scriptures which the early church selected as most appropriate for its didactic, homiletic and apologetic task, than that it is dependent upon a thirteen chapter text which preceded it. This suggestion is supported by our previous analysis in which it has become evident that 2 Clement cites some of the classic Christian references to the Jewish Scriptures—Genesis, Jeremiah and Isaiah.[2] For the most part the writer is not unique in his selection of texts, but uses those texts which are widely employed in other parts of the early church. Whereas primitive Christianity used these texts in its apologetic, we observe in 2 Clement a shift in application from an apologetic to a paraenetic use.[3]

2. CONSCIOUS QUOTATIONS FROM THE GOSPEL TRADITION

This section proposes to examine and evaluate those quotations in 2 Clement which suggest, or which have been thought to suggest, acquaintance with the gospel tradition.[4] Important questions to be considered are whether 2 Clement is dependent upon our synoptic gospels or independent traditions, or both; and if independent traditions, what the nature of these traditions is. Do they have parallels elsewhere? Also to be considered is what significance we should attribute to the fact that 2 Clement cites a Jesus logion as $\gamma\rho\alpha\phi\acute{\eta}$. Obviously these and related questions are extraordinarily important not only for our understanding of 2 Clement, but also for our understanding of the development of early Christianity. The complexity of the problems makes any suggestion or anything approaching a conclusion, at best, tentative. Such caution is advisable since at practically every turn one is forced to select one hypothesis over another. Very seldom does one tread on firm ground. This is illustrated by the fact that the two most thoroughgoing studies of the matter at hand, *The New Testament in the Apostolic Fathers* by the Oxford Committee of the

---

[1] C. H. Dodd, *According to the Scriptures* (London, 1961); see also Miller, "Targum."

[2] See pp. 50-55.

[3] See especially Barnabas Lindars, *New Testament Apologetic* (London, 1961).

[4] Possible synoptic allusions, as well as possible allusions to other New Testament texts, will be examined in the following section of this chapter, pp. 82-93.

Society of Historical Theology[1] and *Synoptische Überlieferung bei den Apostolischen Vätern* by Helmut Köster, come to completely different conclusions on most issues. With these preliminary remarks in mind, we proceed to our first text, 2 Clem. 2:4.

2 Clem. 2:4

2 Clem. 2:4	Mk. 2:17	Mt. 9:13
οὐκ ἦλθον καλέσαι δικαίους, ἀλλὰ ἁμαρτωλούς	οὐκ ἦλθον καλέσαι δικαίους ἀλλὰ ἁμαρτωλούς	οὐ γὰρ ἦλθον καλέσαι δικαίους ἀλλὰ ἁμαρτωλούς

Lk. 5:32	Justin, Apol. 15:8
οὐκ ἐλήλυθα καλέσαι δικαίους ἀλλὰ ἁμαρτωλοὺς εἰς μετάνοιαν	οὐκ ἦλθον καλέσαι δικαίους, ἀλλὰ ἁμαρτωλοὺς εἰς μετάνοιαν

Barn. 5:9	1 Tim. 1:15
οὐκ ἦλθεν καλέσαι δικαίους, ἀλλὰ ἁμαρτωλούς	Χριστὸς Ἰησοῦς ἦλθεν εἰς τὸν κόσμον ἁμαρτωλοὺς σῶσαι

In 2 Clement this material is introduced as follows: καὶ ἑτέρα δὲ γραφὴ λέγει. A comparison of the texts shows that 2 Clement's quotation is identical with that of Mk. 2:17. It is also possible that 2 Clement is dependent upon Mt. 9:13, for Matthew's οὐ γάρ is indeed a minor alteration. In Matthew, γάρ serves as a connective; when this is removed it is necessary that οὐ be changed to οὐκ.

Both Dibelius[2] and Bultmann[3] suggest that we are dealing here with a saying of Jesus in free circulation which was only secondarily combined with Mk. 2:15-16. They correctly observe that our logion does not fit into the context very smoothly. As Haenchen pointedly remarks: "Es passt hier auch nicht allzugut: die Teilnahme an einem

---

[1] *The New Testament in the Apostolic Fathers* (Oxford, 1905) by A Committee of the Oxford Society of Historical Theology.

[2] Martin Dibelius, *From Tradition to Gospel* (New York, n.d.), p. 46.

[3] Rudolf Bultmann, *The History of the Synoptic Tradition* (New York, 1963), p. 18.

grossen Gastmahl mit Zöllnern und Sündern ist etwas anderes als das,
was Jesus meint, wenn er sich um solche Menschen bemüht. Ein
solches Fest ist keine Seelsorge."[1] In this sense the author of 2
Clement has preserved the original context more correctly, although
with a somewhat greater soteriological emphasis. He interprets this
quotation in verse 5, τοῦτο λέγει, ὅτι δεῖ τοὺς ἀπολλυμένους
σώζειν, and verse 7, οὕτως καὶ ὁ Χριστὸς ἠθέλησεν σῶσαι τὰ ἀπολλύμενα, καὶ ἔσωσεν πολλούς, ἐλθὼν καὶ καλέσας ἡμᾶς ἤδη ἀπολλυμένους.

In view of this observation, the question must be raised whether
we can with certainty claim that 2 Clement is really dependent upon
Mark. Could our author not have received this saying via an independent tradition? When one notes the context of Barn. 5:9 and 1 Tim.
1:15 this becomes more probable. None of the the three (2 Clement,
Barnabas and 1 Timothy) share the motif of misunderstanding which is
present in Mark, Matthew and Luke. All three are concerned with sin
and forgiveness. In fact, all three stress the "einst-jetzt" pattern
which is characteristic of the theological section of 2 Clement.[2]
The point of 1 Timothy 1 is to tell of God's great mercy in calling
Paul from his former life to be "an example to those who were to
believe in him for eternal life" (v. 16). The theme of Barn. 5:5-10
is that Jesus came in the flesh so that sinful man could see him and
be saved. In a very similar manner 2 Clement stresses the fact that
Jesus came to save those who were perishing.

Barnabas and 2 Clement preserve the logion in a more original
form than does Timothy. The verse in 1 Timothy beginning with
πιστὸς ὁ λόγος is probably a free variation of this logion. It is unlikely that any of these three go back to the synoptic tradition since
they do not share a single common theme with that context. Köster
rightly concludes "es (ist) auch so gut wie unmöglich, dass das Barn.
5,9 angeführte Logion aus einem Evangelium stammt. Es ist Barn.
(evtl. in Verbindung mit dem Sündermotiv) aus der freien Gemeindetradition zugeflossen."[3] While Köster is tempted to make this same
conclusion concerning 2 Clement, he does not because the logion is
introduced by γραφὴ λέγει.[4] Yet one must keep in mind that 2

---

[1] Ernst Haenchen, *Der Weg Jesu* (Berlin, 1966), p. 110.

[2] See pp. 107-109.

[3] Köster, *Synoptische Überliefering*, p. 145.

[4] "Doch wird 2. Clem. dies Logion nicht aus der mündlichen Überlieferung über-

Clement does not use ἡ γραφή with the kind of precision which one would expect from later church fathers.[1] For example, in 2 Clem. 6:8 we read: λέγει δὲ καὶ ἡ γραφὴ ἐν τῷ Ἰεζεκιήλ. In our previous discussion of this text we have noticed only a vague reflection of Ezekiel in this quotation from "scripture."[2] The author of 2 Clement uses the phrase γραφή in a rather general way, intending only to lend some authority to his citations. It is probable, but by no means certain, that in his use of γραφή our preacher is referring to words of Jesus transmitted orally, and not to the canonical books of a later New Testament.[3] Therefore, we suggest that the author of 2 Clement is

---

kommen haben; denn gerade hier, an der einzigen Stelle, an der er der Form des Zitates nach von der freien Überlieferung abhängig sein könnte, zitiert er mit γέγραπται." *Ibid.*, p. 71.

[1] For a concise review of the term γραφή as used in the first two Christian centuries, see Edwin D. Freed, *Old Testament Quotations in the Gospel of John* (Leiden, 1965), pp. 51-59. Our understanding of 2 Clement's use of γραφή has many points of contact with the central thrust of Freed's study in which he shows that in several places (Jn. 7:42; 17:12 and 20:9), γραφή refers to synoptic or intra-Johannine sayings of Jesus.

[2] Hans von Campenhausen, *Die Entstehung der christlichen Bibel* (Tübingen, 1968), p. 82, in referring to 2 Clement's use of the Old Testament as an authoritative source, suggests that "auch dies geschieht weniger auf Grund einer durchdachten Konzeption von der Bedeutung des Alten Testaments, als naiv, mehr oder weniger willkürlich und ad hoc auf Grund eines anerkannten Verfahrens, das sich nach Belieben anwenden, fortführen und veriieren lässt."

[3] von Campenhausen's study of the development of a New Testament canon supports this general understanding, against Köster. Referring specifically to Barn. 4:14 and 2 Clem. 2:4, von Campenhausen, *Entstehung*, pp. 142ff., states: "Oft rücken die 'im Evangelium' erteilten Befehle des Herrn in die nächste Nachbarschaft der alttestamentlichen Gebote, soweit diese übernommen werden. Das erscheint ganz unproblematisch; Jesus hat ja schon im alten Bunde geredet, und gelegentlich werden seine Worte umgekehrt auch wie ein Schriftwort zitiert." Turning precisely to the discussion at hand, von Campenhausen continues (in n. 63): "II. Clem. 2,4 bietet im Anschluss an Jes. 54,1 den Text von Mt. 9,13 ausdrücklich als eine ἑτέρα γραφή. Gerade in Zitatenkombinationen kann eine solche durch die alttestamentlichen Worte nahegelegte Bezeichnung leicht auftreten." In conclusion, von Campenhausen makes this significant observation in reference to the use of γραφή in Barnabas and 2 Clement: "Aber das bleibt die Ausnahme und bedeutet nicht, dass diese Worte darum gälten, weil sie in heiligen Büchern verzeichnet wären. Die Autorität, die hinter ihnen steht, ist immer noch—wie bei Paulus—die Autorität des Herrn selbst, nicht die Autorität eines bestimmten, als 'kanonisch' angesehenen Schriftwerks, in dem seine Worte bewahrt und zu finden wären" (pp. 143-44). Finally, if 2 Clem. 2:4 is not taken from Mark, we have here an example of where oral and written tradition are identical. To this point von Campenhausen adds: "Schriftliche und mündliche Überlieferungen laufen ununterscheidbar und ununterschieden nebeneinander her, kreuzen, bereichern und verwirren einander" (p. 144).

not dependent on Matthew or Mark, but rather that he has received this logion from the "Gemeindetradition."[1]

2 Clem. 3:2

2 Clem. 3:2	Mt. 10:32	Lk. 12:8	Rev. 3:5
Τὸν ὁμολογήσαντά με ἐνώπιον τῶν ἀνθρώπων,	πᾶς οὖν ὅστις ὁμολογήσει ἐν ἐμοὶ ἔμπροσθεν τῶν ἀνθρώπων,	πᾶς ὃς ἂν ὁμολογήσῃ ἐν ἐμοὶ ἔμπροσθεν τῶν ἀνθρώπων, καὶ ὁ υἱὸς τοῦ ἀνθρώπου	
ὁμολογήσω	ὁμολογήσω κἀγὼ	ὁμολογήσει	ὁμολογήσω τὸ ὄνομα
αὐτὸν ἐνώπιον τοῦ πατρός μου.	ἐν αὐτῷ ἔμπροσθεν τοῦ πατρός μου τοῦ ἐν τοῖς οὐρανοῖς.	ἐν αὐτῷ ἔμπροσθεν τῶν ἀγγέλων τοῦ θεοῦ.	αὐτοῦ ἐνώπιον τοῦ πατρός μου καὶ ἐνώπιον τῶν ἀγγέλων αὐτοῦ.

The author of 2 Clement appears to be following an independent tradition which is far less semitic than either Matthew or Luke.[2] This can be seen in his use of τὸν ὁμολογήσαντα,[3] and his failure to express the object of the verb by means of the preposition ἐν; both Matthew and Luke use ἐν ἐμοί and ἐν αὐτῷ. Neither 2 Clement nor Revelation uses this Aramaism.[4]

Perrin is probably right in suggesting that the original form of this logion read: "Everyone who acknowledges me before men, will be

---

[1] It is interesting to observe that Justin's text (*Apol.* 15.8) shows evidence of harmonization of this synoptic text. Similar harmonization can be observed, for example, in Pseudo-Justin, *On the Resurrection*, 7.23; Epiphanius, *Haereses* 51. 5. 1. etc., as well as in the manuscript tradition.

[2] By using the term "less semitic" we are not expressing a negative judgment concerning "antiquity" of the tradition. We are not at all convinced that Semitisms prove the historical authenticity of given traditions. See the excellent summary of the problem in E. P. Sanders, *The Tendencies of the Synoptic Tradition* (Cambridge, 1969), pp. 190-225.

[3] Sanders, *Tendencies*, p. 227.

[4] See the perceptive discussion in Norman Perrin, *Rediscovering the Treaching of Jesus* (New York, 1967), pp. 188ff.

acknowledged before the angels of God."[1] In this form, he suggests, it could go back to the historical Jesus. The tradition then altered this in an apocalyptic and christological direction, adding a second half to the saying (Mt. 10:33 // Lk. 12:9). In its final form, then, we are dealing with a logion created by the church in a situation of persecution. The setting is that of a heavenly law court in which decisions will be made concerning the disciples. Apocalyptically determined, it stresses the necessity for perseverance in suffering and this is motivated by appeal to the last judgment and its reward. The criterion for this judgment is one's attitude toward Jesus. Man's decision about Jesus determines the future decisions of the last judgment.

The emphasis in 2 Clement is not that of Q and it may be possible that 2 Clement had access to this logion at an earlier point in its trajectory. The stress is not on remaining loyal to Jesus before a human court, but on obedience to his commands — μὴ παρακούειν αὐτοῦ τῶν ἐντολῶν. Doing this will also influence a future heavenly decision, but the context in which this obedience takes place is totally different from that of Q.

We have noted substantial differences between 2 Clem. 3:2 and the synoptic versions. These differences make it difficult to accept Köster's[2] conclusion that 2 Clement is dependent upon Matthew.[3] In view of this evidence, there are really only two probable views: 1) that the author of 2 Clement has freely reworked Matthew's text so as to fit his context and theological purpose; or, 2) one could hold with the Oxford Committee that "Clement's wording is sufficiently different to suggest the direct use of another source altogether, whether oral or written."[4] In light of the tenuous relationship between 2 Clement and Matthew, the conclusion of the Oxford Committee is the more probable. The hypothesis which suggests the use of an independent source is further strengthened by the close similarities to Rev. 3:5. It is rather difficult to argue that Revelation and 2 Clement have altered Matthew in an almost identical manner.

---

[1] *Ibid.*, p. 189.

[2] Köster, *Synoptische Überlieferung*, pp. 72ff.

[3] Köster's reference (p. 72) to the similarity between 2 Clement and Matthew in their use of τοῦ πατρός μου is not persuasive in demonstrating dependence. This phrase might well be pre-Matthean; so Perrin, *Rediscovering*, p. 189. It is also congenial to Clement's choice of vocabulary; πατήρ is used eleven times, as well as the phrase τοῦ πατρός μου (12:6).

[4] The Oxford Committee, p. 130.

2 Clem. 4:2 and 5

(See table on pp. 64-65)

The relationship of these verses both to the synoptics and the apocryphal traditions is an extraordinarily difficult and complex one. We shall attempt to show that the most likely explanation which takes into account all the data is that 2 Clement is here dependent upon an early sayings source which has close similarities to Q.[1] Basic to the discussion which follows is the understanding that 2 Clem. 4:2 and 5 followed directly upon one another in the source. This is highly probable since verses 3 and 4 are merely an exegesis of verse 2, as well as the fact that the parallel in Matthew forms a cohesive whole. In this case it is Matthew, not Luke, who has preserved the original order of Q.[2]

---

[1] At this point it is well to keep in mind one of Köster's (*Synoptische Überlieferung*, p. 258) conclusions: "... die 'Apostolischen Väter' [dürften] noch mitten in der lebendigen Geschichte der Tradition stehen. Sie entnehmen für ihre Bedürfnisse den synoptischen Stoff z.T. den gleichen Quellen, aus denen auch die synoptischen Evangelien schöpften. Sie sind also nicht von den Evangelien abhängig, sondern stehen neben ihnen." One example of a specific application of this conclusion by Köster (p. 18) is in reference to the Jesus word cited in 1 Clem. 46:8: "Es bleibt nur die Annahme, dass 1. Clem. 46,8 mit einer Vorstufe der Synoptiker, und zwar wäre an Q zu denken, verwandt ist. In der Tat können alle Wörter, in denen sich 1. Clem. 46,8 mit den Synoptikern berührt, bereits in Q gestanden haben." Also important in this context is the article by James M. Robinson, "*ΛΟΓΟΙ ΣΟΦΩΝ* Zur Gattung der Spruchquelle Q" in *Zeit und Geschichte* (Tübingen, 1964), ed. Erich Dinkler, pp. 77-96. One of Robinson's (p. 91) preliminary conclusions is this: "Damit können wir in der Mitte des 2. Jahrhunderts die letzten Spuren einer frühchristlichen Gattung der Sammlung von Sprüchen = λόγοι feststellen, die dann durch λόγοι als Reden, in Dialogen und Traktaten in der Grosskirche wie in der Gnosis ersetzt wurde, die aber in Verbindung mit den Zitationsformeln der Herrenworte als λόγοι verständlich geworden war und die lebendig war, solange Herrenworte mündlich überliefert wurden." See also Dieter Lührmann, *Die Redaktion der Logienquelle* (Neukirchen, 1969), p. 91.

[2] J. M. Creed, *The Gospel according to St. Luke* (London, 1960), p. 184. This observation is contrary to the maxim, "Prefer Luke for the order of Q, prefer Matthew for its wording." However, F. Grant's (*The Gospels: their origin and growth* [New York, 1957], p. 58) remarks in reference to this phrase are supported by our exegetical observation: "But the conviction has steadily grown stronger, as we have studied the use which Matthew and Luke made of Mark, that Luke as a rule (to which there are, of course, certain obvious exceptions) exercises far greater care in following the exact wording of his source in relating *the words of our Lord*. This is not true of their settings, which he often enough rewrites. But the sayings of Jesus he alters far less, to say the least,

It is likely that 2 Clem. 4:2, rather than Mt. 7:21 or Lk. 6:46, stands closest to an original sayings source which may have been shared by the synoptics. A comparison of 2 Clem. 4:2 with Matthew indicates that 2 Clement is the earlier. Such phraseology as εἰσελεύσεται εἰς τὴν βασιλείαν τῶν οὐρανῶν and τὸ θέλημα τοῦ πατρός μου τοῦ ἐν τοῖς οὐρανοῖς clearly belongs in the realm of Matthean redaction. It would be more difficult to explain why the author of 2 Clement would have reduced Matthew to its present form, since he himself uses this "Matthean" terminology elsewhere.[1] Bultmann[2] has suggested the priority of Lk. 6:46, but this is unlikely since Luke reworked these words into a question which serves as an introduction to the section dealing with the hearers and doers of the word beginning in verse 47.[3]

Following this verse dealing with "Lord, Lord," 2 Clement continues with the words Ἐὰν ἦτε μετ' ἐμοῦ συνηγμένοι κτλ. These words do not appear to be a later insertion into 2 Clement's source and may well be original. One could well ask, *if* they were known to Matthew and Luke, why were they not included? Luke has already so drastically reshuffled these verses for his own editorial needs that it is little wonder that they are not included. *If* Matthew had these words in his Q source, one can understand why for theological reasons he might have eliminated these words and instead substituted his own formulation in 7:22. As Bultmann suggests, in Matthew "it is the false Christian teacher who is rejected; and this is of course secondary. But in any case this rests on a secondary community formulation, one that looks back to Jesus' completed ministry and depicts him as proclaiming himself judge of the world."[4]

---

than he does the narrative.... Matthew, on the other hand, does not scruple to introduce later exegesis into the very formulation of Jesus' words. I prefer, therefore, to follow Luke's wording of Q wherever possible."

[1] 5:5; 9:6; 11:7; 12:1,2,6.

[2] Bultmann, *Synoptic Tradition*, pp. 116ff.

[3] In commenting on Lk. 6:46, Heinz Schürmann, *Das Lukasevangelium*, I (Freiburg, 1969), p. 379, footnote 1, states: "Derartige 'Vorbauten' sind für Lk charakteristisch, mögen sie nun ursprünglich sein (so vielleicht Lk 12,57 diff Mt) oder redaktionell (wie 7,29f; 17,20f)." He comments further, p. 380: "VV 47f geht es - s.u. - ursprünglich um den Gegensatz: Hören-Tun, V 46 um den verwandten: Lippenbekenntnis-Tatbekenntnis, ein Unterschied, der es immerhin zweifelhaft lässt, ob V 46 in der vorliegenden Gestalt das Gleichnis VV 47ff ursprünglich einleitete."

[4] Bultmann, *Synoptic Tradition*, p. 117.

2 Clem. 4:2,5	*Mt. 7:21ff; 13:42ff*	*Lk. 6:46; 13:26ff*
2) Οὐ πᾶς ὁ λέγων μοι· Κύριε κύριε, σωθήσεται,	7:21) Οὐ πᾶς ὁ λέγων μοι κύριε κύριε, εἰσελεύσεται εἰς τὴν βασιλείαν τῶν οὐρανῶν,	6:46) τί δέ με καλεῖτε· κύριε κύριε,
ἀλλ' ὁ ποιῶν τὴν δικαιοσύνην.	ἀλλ' ὁ ποιῶν τὸ θέλημα τοῦ πατρός μου τοῦ ἐν τοῖς οὐρανοῖς.	
		καὶ οὐ ποιεῖτε ἃ λέγω;
5) Ἐὰν ἦτε μετ' ἐμοῦ συνηγμένοι ἐν τῷ κόλπῳ μου καὶ μὴ ποιῆτε τὰς ἐντολάς μου, ἀποβαλῶ ὑμας	7:22) πολλοὶ ἐροῦσίν μοι ἐν ἐκείνῃ τῇ ἡμέρᾳ· κύριε κύριε, οὐ τῷ σῷ ὀνόματι	13:26) τότε ἄρξεσθε λέγειν· ἐφάγομεν ἐνώπιόν
	ἐπροφητεύσαμεν, καὶ τῷ σῷ ὀνόματι δαιμόνια ἐξεβάλομεν, καὶ τῷ σῷ ὀνόματι δυνάμεις πολλὰς ἐποιήσαμεν,	σου καὶ ἐπίομεν, καὶ ἐν ταῖς πλατείαις ἡμῶν ἐδίδαξας·
καὶ ἐρῶ ὑμῖν· Ὑπάγετε ἀπ' ἐμοῦ, οὐκ οἶδα ὑμᾶς, πόθεν ἐστέ,	7:23) καὶ τότε ὁμολογήσω αὐτοῖς ὅτι οὐδέποτε ἔγνων ὑμᾶς, ἀποχωρεῖτε ἀπ' ἐμοῦ οἱ	13:27) καὶ ἐρεῖ λέγων ὑμῖν· οὐκ οἶδα (ὑμᾶς) πόθεν ἐστέ· ἀπόστητε ἀπ' ἐμοῦ
ἐργάται ἀνομίας.	ἐργαζόμενοι τὴν ἀνομίαν 13:42b) ἐκεῖ ἔσται ὁ κλαυθμὸς καὶ ὁ βρυγμὸς τῶν ὀδόντων. 43) τότε οἱ δίκαιοι ἐκλάμψουσιν ὡς ὁ ἥλιος. 42a) καὶ βαλοῦσιν αὐτοὺς εἰς τὴν κάμινον τοῦ πυρός.	πάντες ἐργάται ἀδικίας. 13:28) ἐκεῖ ἔσται ὁ κλαυθμὸς καὶ ὁ βρυγμὸς τῶν ὀδόντων, ὅταν ὄψησθε Ἀβραὰμ κτλ.

Gospel of the Nazarenes	Justin. Apol. 16:9-12.	Justin. Dial. 76:5
	9) Οὐχὶ πᾶς ὁ λέγων μοι Κύριε κύριε εἰσελεύσεται εἰς τὴν βασιλείαν τῶν οὐρανῶν, ἀλλ' ὁ ποιῶν τὸ θέλημα τοῦ πατρός μου τοῦ ἐν τοῖς οὐρανοῖς. 10) ῝Ος γὰρ ἀκούει μου καὶ ποιεῖ ἃ λέγω, ἀκούει τοῦ ἀποστείλαν-	
ἐὰν ἦτε ἐν τῷ κόλπῳ μου καὶ τὸ θέλημα τοῦ πατρός μου τοῦ ἐν οὐρανοῖς μὴ ποιῆτε ἐκ τοῦ κόλπου μου ἀπορρίψω ὑμᾶς.	τός με. 11) Πολλοὶ δὲ ἐροῦσί μοι· Κύριε, οὐ τῷ σῷ ὀνόματι ἐφάγομεν	Πολλοὶ ἐροῦσί μοι τῇ ἡμέρᾳ ἐκείνῃ· Κύριε, κύριε, οὐ τῷ σῷ ὀνόματι ἐφάγομεν
	καὶ ἐπίομεν	καὶ ἐπίομεν καὶ προεφητεύσαμεν καὶ
	καὶ δυνάμεις ἐποιήσαμεν; καὶ τότε ἐρῶ αὐτοῖς·	δαιμόνια ἐξεβάλομεν; Καὶ ἐρῶ αὐτοῖς·
	'Αποχωρεῖτε ἀπ' ἐμοῦ, ἐργάται τῆς ἀνομίας. 12) Τότε κλαυθμὸς ἔσται καὶ βρυγμὸς τῶν ὀδόντων, ὅταν οἱ μὲν δίκαιοι λάμψωσιν ὡς ὁ ἥλιος, οἱ δὲ ἄδικοι πέμψωνται εἰς τὸ αἰώνιον πῦρ.	'Αναχωρεῖτε ἀπ' ἐμοῦ.

What is striking is that this otherwise unknown logion in 2 Clem. 4:5a is found in "τὸ 'Ιουδαϊκόν" to Mt. 7:5,[1] and what we find there is a conflation of the saying in 2 Clem. 4:5a with Mt. 7:21! Do we have here in this "Judaic" Gospel, which Vielhauer identifies as the Gospel of the Nazarenes, another indication of a document which preserved part of the original source? Vielhauer in his discussion of the Gospel of the Nazarenes suggests that at "all events we can see here, as already in Q (Mt. 11:24ff. and parallels) an infiltration of 'Johannine' motifs."[2] That is certainly the case in reference to the verse under discussion (cf. Jn. 1:18; 13:23).[3] Could it be that Q was originally more "Johannine" than we now know from its preservation in Matthew and Luke?[4] At any rate, 2 Clement is not quoting from the Gospel of the Nazarenes directly, since it is impossible to conceive of 2 Clement separating and expanding what was conflated in the Gospel of the Nazarenes.

We come now to 2 Clem. 4:5b. A striking similarity between 2 Clement and Luke is the joint use of οὐκ οἶδα ὑμᾶς, πόθεν ἐστέ as opposed to Matthew's ὅτι οὐδέποτε ἔγνων ὑμᾶς. Does this indicate a dependence on Luke? Köster[5] has argued this on the basis that Matthew represents the original of Q. But is there not another possibility? From a close examination of Mt. 25:12 // Lk. 13:25 it appears that the original behind the two read οὐκ οἶδα ὑμᾶς, and perhaps also with the addition πόθεν ἐστέ. When one moves from this observation to Mt. 7:23 // Lk. 13:27, is it not likely that Luke has preserved the more

---

[1] See Vielhauer's discussion of this gospel in *New Testament Apocrypha*, I (Philadelphia, 1963), ed. Hennecke, Schneemelcher, Wilson, p. 136. Text found in Erich Klostermann, *Apocrypha* II (Berlin, 1929), p. 7.

[2] *Ibid.*, p. 145.

[3] Rudolf Meyer in his discussion of κόλπος, *TWNT*, III, p. 824, sees "das gleiche Motiv" present in Jn. 13:23 as in 2 Clem. 4:5. "Am κόλπος eines Menschen befindet sich das Wesen, mit dem er die innigste Gemeinschaft pflegt ..." suggests W. Bauer, *Johannes* (Tübingen, 1912), p. 19. Also note list of Old Testament and other parallel passages cited there.

[4] J. Robinson's article, *ΛΟΓΟΙ ΣΟΦΩΝ*, certainly moves in this direction. One definite text which supports our conjecture is Mt. 11:25ff.//Lk. 10:21ff. Commenting upon these verses in Matthew, K. Stendahl ("Matthew" in *Peake's Commentary on the Bible* [London, 1962], ed. M. Black and H. H. Rowley, p. 784) summarizes: "Consequently we are inclined to consider the passage as having originated from an interplay between actual words of Jesus and the formative activity of a church similar to that behind the Fourth Gospel."

[5] Köster, *Synoptische Überlieferung*, pp. 83ff.

original reading of Q ? W. D. Davies[1] has shown that we can understand the Sermon on the Mount only over against a formative and threatening Judaism. Could it not be, therefore, that Matthew is purposely giving a literal translation — οὐδέποτε ἔγνων ὑμᾶς — of a Jewish "Bannformel"[2] אֵינִי מַכִּירְךָ מֵעוֹלָם ? This would fit the polemical context of Mt. 7:21ff. very well, as well as continuing Matthew's tendency to alter Q (eg. Mt. 7:21//Lk. 6:46) to fit his own theological purposes. We are convinced that it is Luke who preserves Q accurately and that once again 2 Clement is dependent on Q, or a source very similar to it, and not on Luke. This dependence on Q seems to be further confirmed by 2 Clement's use of the term ἐργάται ἀνομίας. As Bultmann observes, it "is much more likely that Luke has changed a original ἀνομίας into ἀδικίας, since he always avoids the use of ἀνομία."[3]

Finally, we must consider the suggestions made by Köster and his student, Bellinzoni, that there is a relationship between the harmonization found in Justin and in 2 Clement. Bellinzoni, for example, asserts that a "comparison of this harmonization of Matthew and Luke [Mt. 7:22,23//Lk. 13:26,27] in the patristic quotations with the analysis of *Apol.* 16:11 and *Dial.* 76:5 leaves little doubt that Justin used a harmony of Mt. 7:22f. and Lk. 13:26f. and that this harmony was known to other fathers in substantially the same form as that used by Justin. Further, the witness of *2 Clement* here proves the existence of this harmonization of Matthew and Luke previous to Justin."[4] It is difficult to see any significant relationship between 2 Clement and Justin. To draw upon 2 Clement in support of Justin's use of a harmonized text at this point is unjustified and 2 Clement cannot carry the burden of proof.

---

[1] W. D. Davies, *The Setting of the Sermon on the Mount* (Cambridge, 1964), esp. pp. 191ff; cf. also R. Hummel, *Die Auseinandersetzung zwischen Kirche und Judentum im Matthäusevangelium* (München, 1963).

[2] Strack-Billerbeck, I, p. 469.

[3] Bultmann, *Synoptic Tradition*, p. 116, n. 3.

[4] A. J. Bellinzoni, *The Sayings of Jesus in the Writings of Justin Martyr* (Leiden, 1967), p. 25. Köster, *Synoptische Tradition*, p. 92, proceeds in the same fashion, although somewhat more cautiously than Bellinzoni. "Irgendwelche Beziehungen zwischen dem harmonisierten Zitat 2. Clem. 4 ... zu der Harmonie Justins sind sicher vorhanden; nur muss eben fraglich bleiben, ob es sich dabei um gemeinsame Benutzung derselben Evangelienharmonie handelt oder um Beeinflussung dieser Harmonie Justins durch 'eingebürgerte' harmonistische Zitate, die auch 2. Clem. geläufig waren."

Our investigation of 2 Clem. 4:2-5 reaches a conclusion similar to that of Schneemelcher after his discussion of 2 Clem. 4:5. "Reminiscences of Lk. 13:27 and Mt. 7:23 can in any case be found only in single words, the altered form of these passages in Justin, *Apol.* 16:11 and *Dial.* 76:5 cannot be drawn upon in explanation. Here extra-canonical tradition must indeed be assumed, but the source must have been very similar to the Synoptic tradition."[1] We have gone a step further by suggesting that this source was not only similar to the synoptic tradition, but possibly the same source from which Matthew and Luke drew their material.

2 Clem. 5:2-4

(See table on p. 69)

A comparison of this text with that of the synoptics leads to two possibilities: 1) that 2 Clement is dependent upon the synoptics and that he inserted verse three from another source, or; 2) that 2 Clement draws upon a source which is similar to the synoptic source, but independent of it. The second alternative is to be preferred. The dialogue between Peter and Jesus does not appear to be an afterthought which the author of 2 Clement himself inserted or created; rather it appears to fit into the context smoothly and, in all likelihood, was already in that form prior to 2 Clement. Also in favor of this latter alternative is the fact that 2 Clement reads ὡς ἀρνία and Luke ὡς ἄρνας. 2 Clement is hardly dependent on Luke at this point since Luke's ἄρνας is the accusative plural of ἀρήν, ἀρνός, ὁ, while 2 Clement's ἀρνία is the accusative plural of ἀρνίον, ου, τό, which is the diminutive of ἀρήν. This points to a tradition other than that of Luke, and of course, different from Matthew who reads πρόβατα.

Verse 3 is without parallel. Could it be that we are dealing with a source prior to the synoptics (such as Q) which has preserved an authentic Jesus logion ? Such a position would be difficult to maintain and Jeremias[2] is probably correct in seeing this logion as a later creation of the tradition.[3] Is verse 4 dependent on Matthew or Luke ? Both 2 Clement and Matthew read μὴ φοβεῖσθε against Luke's

---

[1] *New Testament Apocrypha* I, pp. 171-72.

[2] J. Jeremias, *Unbekannte Jesusworte* (Gütersloh, 1963), p. 42.

[3] See E. P. Sanders, *Tendencies*, pp. 259ff.; H. Köster, *Synoptische Überlieferung*, p. 98.

	Mt. 10:28	**Lk. 12:4-5**		
Ἰδοὺ ἐγὼ ἀποστέλλω ὑμᾶς ὡς πρόβατα ἐν μέσῳ λύκων·	ὑπάγετε· ἰδοὺ ἀποστέλλω ὑμᾶς ὡς ἄρνας ἐν μέσῳ λύκων.	Ἔσεσθε ὡς ἀρνία ἐν μέσῳ λύκων. 3) ἀποκριθεὶς δὲ ὁ Πέτρος αὐτῷ λέγει· Ἐὰν οὖν διασπαράξωσιν οἱ λύκοι τὰ ἀρνία; 4) εἶπεν ὁ Ἰησοῦς τῷ Πέτρῳ· Μὴ φοβείσθωσαν τὰ ἀρνία τοὺς λύκους μετὰ τὸ ἀποθανεῖν αὐτά·		
καὶ μὴ φοβεῖσθε ἀπὸ τῶν ἀποκτεννόντων τὸ σῶμα,	4) μὴ φοβηθῆτε ἀπὸ τῶν ἀποκτεννόντων τὸ σῶμα καὶ μετὰ ταῦτα	καὶ ὑμεῖς μὴ φοβεῖσθε τοὺς ἀποκτέννοντας ὑμᾶς καὶ μηδὲν ὑμῖν δυναμένους	Μὴ φοβεῖσθε τοὺς ἀναιροῦντας ὑμᾶς καὶ μετὰ ταῦτα μὴ δυναμένους τι	
τὴν δὲ ψυχὴν μὴ δυναμένων ἀποκτεῖναι·	μὴ ἐχόντων περισσότερόν τι ποιῆσαι. 5) ὑποδείξω δὲ ὑμῖν τίνα φοβηθῆτε·	ποιεῖν, ἀλλὰ	ποιῆσαι (εἶπε),	
φοβεῖσθε δὲ μᾶλλον τὸν δυνάμενον καὶ ψυχὴν καὶ σῶμα ἀπολέσαι ἐν γεέννῃ.	φοβήθητε τὸν μετὰ τὸ ἀποκτεῖναι ἔχοντα ἐξουσίαν ἐμβαλεῖν εἰς τὴν γέενναν.	φοβεῖσθε τὸν μετὰ τὸ ἀποθανεῖν ὑμᾶς ἔχοντα ἐξουσίαν ψυχῆς καὶ σώματος τοῦ βαλεῖν εἰς γέενναν πυρός.	φοβήθητε δὲ τὸν μετὰ τὸ ἀποθανεῖν δυνάμενον καὶ ψυχὴν καὶ σῶμα εἰς γέενναν ἐμβαλεῖν.	

μὴ φοβηθῆτε. Does this indicate dependence on Matthew? Probably
not. In view of the fact that just prior to this in the same verse, 2
Clement has used the present imperative middle (Μὴ φοβείσθωσαν),
it is rather logical that in the second half of the verse he would continue
with the present imperative middle (μὴ φοβεῖσθε). Although 2 Clement
uses δυναμένους (Mt. δυναμένων) and ποιεῖν (Lk. ποιῆσαι) it is really
difficult to speak of harmonization on the basis of such limited evidence.
Does τὸ ἀποθανεῖν ὑμᾶς ἔχοντα ἐξουσίαν indicate a dependence
on Luke's τὸ ἀποκτεῖναι ἔχοντα ἐξουσίαν? It is possible, but not
probable, insofar as both use different verbs. ψυχῆς καὶ σώματος
might be influenced by Matthew — ψυχὴν καὶ σῶμα — although one
should keep in mind that 2 Clement uses ψυχή and σῶμα together
in other contexts (12:3,4 — τὴν ψυχὴν λέγει τὸ ἔσω, τὸ δὲ ἔξω τὸ
σῶμα λέγει). It appears that this analysis, together with the expansion
in verse 3 so typical of the apocryphal gospels, lead to the conclusion
that this quotation, in the form of a "Schulgespräch," is here dependent
upon a non-canonical source which is perhaps closer to Luke than to
Matthew.

Referring to our passage, Bellinzoni makes the following statement:
"It is, therefore, quite possible that Justin and *2 Clement* are here
based on the same harmony of Matthew and Luke."[1] It is difficult
to agree with this conclusion. First, as we have tried to show, it is
very doubtful that our quotation shows any significant harmonization
of Matthew and Luke. Secondly, a similar comparison between Justin
and 2 Clement shows the unlikeliness of their dependence on the
same harmony of Matthew and Luke. Some of the differences between 2 Clement and Justin, *Apol.* 19.7 are :

2 Clement	*Justin*
ἀποκτέννοντας	ἀναιροῦντας
φοβεῖσθε	φοβήθητε δὲ
ἔχοντα ἐξουσίαν	δυνάμενον
εἰς γέενναν πυρός	εἰς γέενναν

While no one will deny certain resemblances between the text of 2
Clement and Justin, the obvious differences, as well as the places
where Justin and Luke agree *against* 2 Clement, make it unlikely

---

[1] Bellinzoni, *Sayings of Jesus*, p. 111.

that Justin and 2 Clement are drawing from the same harmonized text. The possibility that Justin may have used a harmonized text does not permit us to take this one step back to 2 Clement, as Bellinzoni does when he writes that "the parallel material in *2 Clement*...indicates rather that this harmony was not composed by Justin but that it was in use before Justin composed his *Apology*."[1] That 2 Clement and other early second century texts show possible signs of harmonization here and there is clear. But that they develop this to the extent and degree to which Justin does is not supported by the evidence, at least insofar as 2 Clement is concerned.

2 Clem. 6:1

(Λέγει δὲ ὁ κύριος) Οὐδεὶς οἰκέτης δύναται δυσὶ κυρίοις δουλεύειν.

This quotation is found in identical form in Lk. 16:3 and in the Gospel of Thomas 1:47: ⲘⲚ ϬⲞⲘ` ⲚⲦⲈⲞⲨⲨⲘⲨⲀ̅ⲗ ϢⲘϢⲈ ⲗⲞⲈⲓⲤ ⲤⲚⲀⲨ. Mt. 6:24 lacks *οἰκέτης*.

Whether 2 Clement is here dependent upon Luke or a source which is related to the Gospel of Thomas is difficult to judge, especially since there is a distinct difference of opinion concerning which sources the latter employed.[2]

The context in 2 Clement is clearly "gnosticizing" as is evident from verse 3: *ἔστιν δὲ οὗτος ὁ αἰὼν καὶ ὁ μέλλων δύο ἐχθροί.* These same tendencies are apparent in the Gospel of Thomas and in the Valentinian use of Luke. It is impossible to know which of these traditions 2 Clement used.

---

[1] *Ibid*, p. 110. We agree with Köster, *Synoptische Überlieferung*, p. 97, when he says in reference to our quotation: "... so dürfte sich das Gewicht doch zuungunsten einer von 2. Clem. und Just. gemeinsam benutzten Evangelienharmonie verlagern."

[2] The question as to the dependence of the Gospel of Thomas on the synoptics is at present still a disputed point. Puech (in Hennecke-Schnêemelcher-Wilson, I, p. 294), commenting on the work of C. H. Hunziger (in *Judentum, Urchristentum, Kirche* [Berlin, 1964], ed. W. Eltester, pp. 209ff.) states the case for independence in a fair manner: "C. H. Hunziger however justly observes that the fact that our present document is a Gnostic work does not preclude the possibility that the author may have made use of genuine early tradition; the structure of the gospel, the variation in the order of the sayings compared with the Synoptics, and the fact that sayings separate in our Gospels are here re-grouped, all suggest an independent tradition. Moreover some sayings are apparently more primitive, and elements recognized as secondary by Synoptic criticism are here missing."

2 Clem. 8:5

Lk. 16:10	2 Clem. 8:5	Irenaeus, Adv. Haer. 2.34.3	Hilary, Epist. seu libellus 1
	λέγει γὰρ ὁ κύριος ἐν τῷ εὐαγγελίῳ·	Et ideo dominus dicebat ingratis existen- tibus in eum:	
	Εἰ τὸ μικρὸν οὐκ ἐτηρήσατε, τὸ μέγα τίς ὑμῖν δώσει;	Si in modico fideles non fuistis, quod magnum est, quis dabit vobis?	Si in modico fideles non fuistis, quod maius est, quis dabit vobis?
ὁ πιστὸς ἐν ἐλαχίστῳ καὶ ἐν πολλῷ πιστός ἐστιν, καὶ ὁ ἐν ἐλαχίστῳ ἄδικος καὶ ἐν πολ- λῷ ἄδικός ἐστιν.	... ὁ πιστὸς ἐν ἐλαχίστῳ καὶ ἐν πολλῷ πιστός ἐστιν.		

This quotation in 2 Clement is introduced with ἐν τῷ εὐαγγελίῳ. This is noteworthy since the first half of this verse has no parallel in the synoptic gospels. 2 Clement is here using the term εὐαγγέλιον to mean the oral message of salvation, rather than as a designation for a written book.[1]

A part of the quotation coincides with Luke. Is there here a depen- dence on Luke or did our author receive this from the "freie Über- lieferung?" The latter is the more probable. Supporting this would be the fact that the parable of the dishonest steward in Luke ends in verse 9, and verses 11-12 are an interpretation of it.[2] If Jülicher is correct in his suggestion that in verse 10 we are dealing with a common maxim, then it is quite likely that 2 Clement could have received this independently of Luke.

The first part of our quotation has parallels in Irenaeus and Hilary. The fact that Irenaeus and Hilary read *fideles non fuistis* for 2 Clement's

---

[1] Schneemelcher, *New Testament Apocrypha*, I, p. 172, adds to our verse: "... the expression 'gospel' is used as a comprehensive term for the whole Christian message of salvation: there is only one gospel, although different gospels are used."

[2] So Bultmann, *Synoptic Tradition*, p. 90, and Jülicher, *Die Gleichnisreden Jesu*, II (Darmstadt, 1963), p. 508.

οὐκ ἐτηρήσατε can be easily explained. τηρεῖν is a common term in 2 Clement (6:9; 7:6; 8:4; 8:6; 14:3). It appears directly before (8:4) the verse under consideration and directly after (8:6). Therefore the author of 2 Clement most likely altered his source for theological reasons and Irenaeus and Hilary preserved the original. That we are here dealing with a non-canonical source is substantiated by the important suggestion of Bartlett that Irenaeus does not usually use *dicebat* for the citation of a definite gospel text, but that this usage generally points to "some *logion* handed down."[1] From this discussion, the most likely conclusion that can be reached is that 2 Clem. 8:5 is dependent on a non-synoptic source. What this source is cannot be determined, but it does seem to have certain points of contact with Luke.

2 Clem. 9:11

(See table on p. 74)

It appears that we are here dealing with a combination from Matthew and Luke. In agreement with Luke are ἀδελφοί μου οὗτοί εἰσιν οἱ ποιοῦντες (in a somewhat different order); with Matthew τὸ θέλημα τοῦ πατρός. It is unlikely that the author of 2 Clement was himself responsible for this conflation in view of the fact that both the Gospel of the Ebionites as cited in Epiph. *Haer.* 30.14.5, and the Gospel of Thomas (both early second century) have almost the identical quotations. Most likely, all three were dependent upon a non-canonical source, which had possibly already conflated these sayings of Matthew and Luke.[2]

2 Clem. 12:2,6

2 Clem. 12:2,6	Gospel of the Egyptians
2) ἐπερωτηθεὶς γὰρ αὐτὸς	πυνθανομένης
ὁ κύριος ὑπό τινος,	τῆς Σαλώμης,
πότε ἥξει	πότε γνωσθήσεται

(continued on p. 75)

---

[1] *The New Testament in the Apostolic Fathers*, p. 133.

[2] We would agree with Köster, *Synoptische Überlieferung*, p. 79, when he states in reference to our verse: "Es wird noch zu erwägen sein, ob nicht auch eine auf Mt. und Luk. basierende Herrenwortsammlung von 2. Clem. benutzt sein kann, deren Formulierungen auch auf das NE von Einfluss gewesen sind." Also, W. Schrage, *Das Verhältnis des Thomas-Evangeliums zur Synoptischen Tradition* (Berlin, 1964), p. 187.

2 Clem. 9:11	Mt. 12:49-50	Mk. 3:34-35	Lk. 8:21	Gospel of the Ebionites
Ἀδελφοί μου οὗτοί εἰσιν	ἰδοὺ ἡ μήτηρ μου καὶ οἱ ἀδελφοί μου·	ἴδε ἡ μήτηρ μου καὶ οἱ ἀδελφοί μου.	μήτηρ μου καὶ ἀδελφοί μου οὗτοί εἰσιν	οὗτοί εἰσιν οἱ ἀδελφοί μου καὶ ἡ μήτηρ καὶ ἀδελφοί,
οἱ	ὅστις γὰρ	ὃς	οἱ τὸν λόγον τοῦ θεοῦ ἀκούοντες καὶ ποιοῦντες.	
ποιοῦντες τὸ θέλημα τοῦ πατρός μου.	ἂν ποιήσῃ τὸ θέλημα τοῦ πατρός μου τοῦ ἐν οὐρανοῖς, αὐτός μου ἀδελφὸς ... ἐστίν.	ἂν ποιήσῃ τὸ θέλημα τοῦ θεοῦ, οὗτος ἀδελφός μου ... ἐστίν.		οἱ ποιοῦντες τὰ θελήματα τοῦ πατρός μου.

Gospel of Thomas 96

ΝΑΥ ΔΕ ΝΕΤΝΝΕΕΙΜΑ ΕΤΡΕ ΜΠΟΥΩϢ ΜΠΑΕΙΩΤ· ΝΑΕΙ ΝΕ ΝΑΣΝΗΥ ΜΝ ΤΑΜΑΑΥ

"Those here who do the will of my Father are my brothers (and my mother)."

αὐτοῦ ἡ βασιλεία,   τὰ περὶ ὧν ἤρετο,
εἶπεν·   ἔφη ὁ κύριος·
                 "Οταν τὸ τῆς αἰσχύνης
                 ἔνδυμα πατήσητε
"Οταν ἔσται   καὶ ὅταν γένηται
τὰ δύο ἕν,   τὰ δύο ἕν
καὶ τὸ ἔξω ὡς τὸ ἔσω,
καὶ τὸ ἄρσεν   καὶ τὸ ἄρσεν
μετὰ τῆς θηλείας,   μετὰ τῆς θηλείας
οτŭε ἄρσεν οὔτε θῆλυ. οὔτε ἄρσεν οὔτε θῆλυ.
6) ταῦτα ὑμῶν ποιούντων,
φησίν, ἐλεύσεται
ἡ βασιλεία τοῦ πατρός μου.

Gospel of Thomas 23

ϩΟΤΑΝ ΕΤΕΤΝ͞ϢΑР͞ ΠϹΝΑΥ ΟΥΑ ΑΥѠ Ε
ΤΕΤΝ͞ϢΑР͞ ΠϹΑ ΝϨΟΥΝ ͞ΝΟΕ ͞ΜΠϹΑ ΝΒΟΛ
ΑΥѠ ΠϹΑ ΝΒΟΛ ͞ΝΘΕ ͞ΜΠϹΑ ΝϨΟΥΝ ΑΥѠ ΠϹ͞Α
ΤΠΕ ͞ΝΘΕ ͞ΜΠϹΑ ΜΠΙΤ͞Ν ΑΥѠ ϢΙΝΑ ΕΤΕ
ΤΝΑΕΙΡΕ ͞ΜϕΟ·ΟΥΤ· Μ͞Ν ΤϹϨΙΜΕ ͞ΜΠΙΟΥΑ
ΟΥѠΤ ΑΕΚΑΑϹ ΝΕϕΟΟΥΤ· Р͞ ϨΟΟΥΤ· ͞ΝΤΕ
ΤϹϨΙΜΕ Р͞ ϹϨΙΜΕ

Translation:

(They said to him: If we are little ones, will we enter into the kingdom? Jesus said to them:) When you make the two one, and make the inside like the outside, and the outside like the inside, and the upper side like the under side and (in such a way) that you make the man (with) the woman a single one, in order that the man is not the man and the woman is not the woman...

We can observe here how close 2 Clement parallels the Gospel of Thomas and, to a lesser extent, the Gospel of the Egyptians as cited in Clem. Alex. *Strom.* 3.13.92. In fact, the whole context of the Gospel of Thomas 23 is a discussion concerning the kingdom which is precisely the point of 2 Clement's discussion. In the Gospel of Thomas the disciples ask Jesus: "If we are little ones, will we enter into the kingdom?

Jesus said to them...." Then follows our quotation. The context in
the Gospel of the Egyptians is different. It is essentially concerned
with the institution of the different sexes — not the kingdom — and
the introductory question is also different: "When Salome asked when
what she had inquired about would be known, the Lord said...."

Everything which the quotation in 2 Clement includes can be found
in the Gospel of Thomas, although the Gospel of Thomas version is
more extensive. Where 2 Clement has "the outside like the inside,"
the Gospel of Thomas reads "the inside like the outside, and the outside
like the inside, and the upper side like the under side...." After our
quotation ends, the Gospel of Thomas continues: "When you make
eyes in place of an eye, and a hand in place of a hand, and a foot in
place of a foot, an image in place of an image...." Then 2 Clement and
the Gospel of Thomas conclude in a similar fashion: "Then you will
go into (the kingdom)."

Is our quotation dependent on the Gospel of Thomas? This is certainly possible in view of the close parallels we have already observed.
However, it is more likely that the Gospel of Thomas represents a
somewhat later and more developed form of a common source. This
appears the more probable especially since we must seriously reckon
with the possibility that the Gospel of Thomas preserves a tradition
independent of the Gospels,[1] and as Cullmann[2] and R. McL. Wilson[3]
have shown, the tradition behind the Gospel of Thomas went through
a complex process of development. It is likely that 2 Clement had
access to this source at a stage prior to that of the presently known
(Coptic) Gospel of Thomas.

We must now consider the parallel with the Gospel of the Egyptians.
A comparison of all three sources (2 Clement, Gospel of Thomas and
Gospel of Egyptians) indicates that the Gospel of the Egyptians represents the latest stage in the development and that 2 Clement is
not dependent on it. The following considerations are important for
this observation:

(1) As we have already pointed out, the context of 2 Clement and the
Gospel of the Egyptians is quite different. That the Gospel of the
Egyptians is not concerned with "the kingdom" is apparent from its

---

[1] See footnote 2 on p. 71.
[2] *ThLZ* 85 (1960) cols. 321ff.
[3] *Studies in the Gospel of Thomas* (London, 1960).

omission of ἡ βασιλεία at the beginning and the phrase ἐλεύσεται ἡ βασιλεία which both 2 Clement and the Gospel of Thomas have.

(2) In 2 Clement we read: ἐπερωτηθεὶς γὰρ αὐτὸς ὁ κύριος ὑπό τινος. In the Gospel of the Egyptians it is Salome who raises the question. It seems easiest to assume that 2 Clement is earlier since it is difficult to see why the name would have been omitted, in addition to the fact that traditions generally tend to add specific names, not to omit them.[1]

(3) Ὅταν τὸ τῆς αἰσχύνης ἔνδυμα....[2] More likely than 2 Clement's omission of this from his source is the suggestion that this phrase was added by the Gospel of the Egyptians at a more encratitic stage in the development of the saying.

(4) Where did 2 Clement obtain the phrase τὸ ἔξω ὡς τὸ ἔσω, if the Gospel of the Egyptians was his source? That 2 Clement added this to his source is difficult to hold in view of his somewhat forced exegesis of this in 12:4. Had this phrase contributed to the making of an important and central point, one could understand 2 Clement adding this to his source; but this is not the case. It is easier to assume that the Gospel of the Egyptians omitted this phrase since it did not substantially contribute to its encratitic tendency, i.e., it was not radical enough for its purposes.

There is little reason, therefore, to believe that 2 Clement is dependent on the Gospel of the Egyptians. With this conclusion must end speculation that the remainder of 2 Clement's quotations are derived from the Gospel of the Egyptians, a deduction often made on the basis of this verse. This conclusion also considerably weakens the hypothesis that 2 Clement was written in Alexandria, a view largely based on 2 Clement's alleged use of the Gospel of the Egyptians. As we have seen, the verse quoted by 2 Clement stands close to the Gospel of Thomas, although the dependence is probably not on the Gospel of Thomas itself, but rather on their common source.

---

[1] E. P. Sanders, *Tendencies*, pp. 144ff.

[2] Bauer, Arndt, Gingrich, *A Greek-English Lexicon of the New Testament* (Chicago, 1963), p. 263, translate this as a "garment worn for modesty's sake."

2 Clem. 13:4

2 Clem. 13:4	Lk. 6:32,27	Mt. 5:46,44
Οὐ χάρις ὑμῖν, εἰ ἀγαπᾶτε τοὺς ἀγαπῶντας ὑμᾶς, ἀλλὰ χάρις ὑμῖν,	32) καὶ εἰ ἀγαπᾶτε τοὺς ἀγαπῶντας ὑμᾶς, ποία ὑμῖν χάρις ἐστίν; καὶ γὰρ κτλ.	46) ἐὰν γὰρ ἀγαπήσητε τοὺς ἀγαπῶντας ὑμᾶς, τίνα μισθὸν ἔχετε; οὐχὶ καὶ ...
εἰ ἀγαπᾶτε τοὺς ἐχθροὺς καὶ	27) ἀγαπᾶτε τοὺς ἐχθροὺς ὑμῶν, καλῶς ποιεῖτε	44) ἀγαπᾶτε τοὺς ἐχθροὺς ὑμῶν
τοὺς μισοῦντας ὑμᾶς·	τοῖς μισοῦσιν ὑμᾶς,	καὶ προσεύχεσθε ὑπὲρ τῶν διωκόντων ὑμᾶς·

We find here a certain resemblance to Luke. That 2 Clement is dependent on Luke appears unlikely for a number of reasons. Those sections of Luke which correspond to 2 Clement are separated by four verses and then in reverse order. We find in 2 Clement both a variation in the order and a regrouping — characteristics which, for example, mark the sayings source behind the Gospel of Thomas. Furthermore, there are differences in the text between Luke and 2 Clement. 2 Clement's οὐ χάρις ὑμῖν is missing in Lk 6:32a. For 2 Clement's ἀλλὰ χάρις ὑμῖν, Lk 6:32 has ποία ὑμῖν χάρις ἐστίν. We also note that this verse in Luke (and Mt. 5:46) is in the form of a question; in 2 Clement it is not. Furthermore, the καλῶς ποιεῖτε of Lk. 6:27 has no equivalent in Clement. Certainly it is possible that 2 Clement made some alterations for theological reasons. But surely one cannot convincingly explain all the differences on this basis.[1] Most likely 2 Clement had access to a non-canonical source and is quoting from this;[2] again one observes a certain similarity between this non-canonical source and Luke.[3]

---

[1] Against Köster, *Synoptische Überlieferung*, pp. 76ff.

[2] The conclusion of the Oxford Committee, p. 132, is very probable: "No sure argument for the use of Luke can be based on this passage.... Possibly, however, 2 Clement quotes the whole saying as known to him in an apocryphal Gospel."

[3] One should consult the suggestive chapter "Lukan Material in the Gospel of Thomas" in *The Theology of the Gospel of Thomas* (London, 1961) by Bertil Gärtner. Gärtner makes this interesting observation on p. 67: "Several other sayings show this

Summary

1. With reasonable certainty it can be asserted that in seven out of nine quotations from the gospel tradition, 2 Clement is dependent on a source other than the synoptic gospels. This might also be the case with the other two quotations (2:4; 6:1), but one must leave open the possibility that they are dependent on Mark and Luke, respectively.

In five of the quotations which are based upon independent tradition, we note that this non-canonical, probably oral, source is very close to either the Gospel of Thomas (2 Clem. 12:2) or the Gospel of Luke (2 Clem. 5:2-4; 8:5; 13:4). In another quotation (6:1) we are uncertain as to whether the affinity is with Luke or Thomas. This affinity of 2 Clement with Luke and Thomas, or sources standing behind them, is significant if one keeps in mind Thomas' "marked preference for Luke in certain details."[1] A further explanation of these similarities must await further investigation.

2. On the basis of our discussion of 2 Clem. 2:4, it is unlikely that ἡ γραφή introduces a quotation from a synoptic gospel. In addition to our previous comments, it may be added that the large majority, if not all, of 2 Clement's citations of early Christian tradition are taken from pre- or non-canonical materials. This would seem to strengthen our earlier suggestion. It should also not be overlooked that 2 Clement uses γραφή in a very loose, non-exact sense. At a number of points, γραφή, when referring to Old Testament texts, does not refer to an exact written text as we now find it in our Greek manuscripts. This last point is substantiated in 2 Clem. 6:8 where we read: λέγει δὲ καὶ ἡ γραφὴ ἐν τῷ Ἰεζεκιήλ. However, what follows is not, in large part, from the canonical Ezekiel. From 2 Clement's usage of introductory formulas for the Old Testament, we see that there are three essential terms by which he tries to stress the authority of the Jewish Scriptures, ἡ γραφή, ὁ κύριος, and ὁ θεός, with γραφή being the most significant; when he draws from the early Christian tradition it is without question ὁ κύριος who gives it authority.

We would suggest that 2 Clement represents a stage somewhere between Paul and Justin in the developing trajectory of a New Testa-

---

marked preference for Luke in certain details, and this raises the question as to whether there is any special reason for this. It is conceivable, for instance, that the *Gospel of Thomas* and Luke may have made use of a common source unknown to Matthew and Mark."

[1] *Ibid.*, p. 67.

ment canon and, if our suggestions concerning ἡ γραφή are correct, closer to Paul than to Justin. That the scripture of the primitive church was the Old Testament is clear.[1] In Paul, however, there appears alongside this norm, a new and superior norm, that of the earthly and risen κύριος. We need only examine 1 Th. 4:15; 1 Cor. 9:9,13,14 and other passages to observe that for Paul a saying of the Lord answers a question of concern as authoritatively as a quotation from the Old Testament. That these λόγοι τοῦ κυρίου ᾿Ιησοῦ take on increased importance in early Christianity is clear from 1 Clem. 13:1ff.; 46:2ff., 7ff.; 2 Pet. 3:2; Ignatius, Smyr. 7:2, as well as some of the other sources discussed previously.[2] Most likely the author of 2 Clement had access to such a "Herrenwortsammlung" and the saying found in 2 Clem. 2:4, which he introduces as γραφή, probably stems from such a collection. We see here a very early stage in which the λόγοι τοῦ κυρίου ᾿Ιησοῦ have become just as important as the Old Testament. Therefore, one is not justified in claiming that in 2 Clem. 2:4 a written synoptic gospel is placed on a par with the Old Testament. At no other point does the author of 2 Clement indicate that he is aware of the existence of a new written norm. That a reference to the words of the Lord as γραφή is not customary during the period in which 2 Clement writes can be seen from the fact that he only uses the

---

[1] Are we justified in our assumption that the Old Testament was of basic significance to the early church? Walter Bauer in his article "Der Wortgottesdienst der ältesten Christen" in *Aufsätse und Kleine Schriften* (Tübingen, 1967), pp. 155ff., denies this significance. "Es ist also mutmasslich nichts mit der gewohnheitsmässigen Vorlesung aus dem Alten Testament in den heidenchristlichen Gemeinden der apostolischen Zeit" (pp. 193-94). Bauer's support for his interpretation is not at all convincing, nor is his reply to the valid criticism that it would be difficult to imagine Paul's activity if his readers and hearers had no intimate knowledge of the Old Testament. Hans von Campenhausen has effectively refuted this position represented by Bauer in his article "Das Alte Testament als Bibel der Kirche" in *Aus der Frühzeit des Christentums* (Tübingen, 1963). Speaking of the early church he states: "... das Alte Testament ist ihre früheste völlig ausgeprägte 'Norm' " (p. 155). And further, "Auch die heidenchristliche Kirche kannte zunächst keinen Christusglauben, der sich nicht auf das Alte Testament bezogen hätte; der Glaube an Christus schloss die Anerkennung der biblischen Autorität von Anfang an mit ein, wenn er ihr—bei den jüdischen Proselyten—nicht gar vorangegangen war. Das Alte Testament als heiliges und christliches Buch der Kirche ist somit eine ursprüngliche, geschichtliche Gegebenheit und stellt bis gegen Mitte des 2. Jahrhunderts für sie als solches kaum ein Problem und jedenfalls keine Last dar" (pp. 159-60). von Campenhausen's observations are so carefully grounded in the early Christian texts, that his conclusions are well-nigh indisputable.

[2] See our discussion on pp. 56ff.

term once, and then immediately after an Old Testament text; this location probably explains the reason for the use of the term γραφή. This should not obscure the fact, however, that 2 Clement did use γραφή for a word of the Lord. The very fact that he did signifies a new stage in the trajectory which eventually results in a Christian canon, although, we would hold, a development considerably before Justin.

This may be an appropriate point to discuss Köster's suggestion that the predominance of λέγει over εἶπεν as an introductory formula substantiates the thesis "dass die synoptischen Zitate des 2. Clem. aus einer schriftlichen Quelle stammen...."[1] Köster's point is that if one is consciously quoting the historical Jesus or the historical Moses it would be natural to introduce a statement of one or the other by εἶπεν. However, as their words became part of an authoritative, written document, which is considered a present reality, then there is a shift to λέγει.[2] What makes it difficult to accept Köster's suggestion is the use of εἶπεν in 2 Clem. 4:5; 9:11 and 17:4. In the first two cases, Köster himself admits the possibility that they are dependent on a written source.[3] If this is true, the validity of his criteria for distinguishing between the use of εἶπεν and λέγει becomes less compelling. We would hold that there is no fundamental distinction in 2 Clement's use of λέγει and εἶπεν and that these introductory formulas do not, in and of themselves, offer satisfactory criteria for distinguishing whether or not 2 Clement is dependent upon an oral, non-canonical source or a written synoptic source.[4]

---

[1] Köster, *Synoptische Überlieferung*, p. 66; see also p. 65.

[2] "Herenworte werden bei ihm nicht mehr in dem Bewusstsein zitiert, dass damals der Herr so sprach, wofür εἶπεν stehen müsste, sondern sie stammen aus einer Schrift, aus der der Herr in seinen Worten gegenwärtig spricht; deshalb gebraucht 2. Clem. wie bei der Zitation der Schrift des AT das präsentische λέγει." *Ibid.*, p. 65. It might be added that in his reference to 2 Clement's introductions to the Old Testament, Köster does not present the full evidence. The introductory formula to 2 Clem. 17:4 clearly uses εἶπεν: εἶπεν γὰρ ὁ κύριος.

[3] *Ibid.*, p. 84; pp. 78ff.

[4] Both in 2 Clement and in other early Christian literature λέγει and εἶπεν can refer to a specific written quotation. It is not limited to λέγει as Köster attempts to suggest. In Barn. 5:5 a specific quotation from Gen. 1:26 is introduced with εἶπεν ὁ θεός; in Barn. 6:12 a specific quotation from Gen. 1:28 is introduced with εἶπεν κύριος. In Barn. 10:1 a quotation from Moses in introduced with Μωϋσῆς εἶπεν and in 10:11 with πάλιν λέγει Μωϋσῆς. In 1 Clem. 10:4 a quotation from Gen. 13:14-16 is introduced by εἶπεν αὐτῷ ὁ θεός. In 1 Clem. 13:2 a quotation showing signs of amalgamation of several synoptic verses

3. While we have observed slight indications for a harmonization of synoptic sources in one,[1] or possibly two quotations,[2] we find no evidence for the assertion that Justin and 2 Clement are dependent upon the same gospel harmony.

3. LITERARY AFFINITIES AND ALLUSIONS

This section will deal with traditional materials not prefaced by introductory formulas, but bearing some recognizable relationship to a known source. It is not the intention of this section to deal with literary allusions based primarily upon accidental verbal similarities, although such materials will be touched upon in a variety of different contexts in chapter three. The following texts will be examined: 2 Clem. 2:1; 6:2,9; 7:1-6; 8:2; 10:2; 11:7 (and 14:5); 13:2b; 14:1,2; 15:1 (and 19:1); 16:3,4; 17:5,7. Such an analysis should provide another indication as to the streams of tradition which influenced 2 Clement as well as reducing the number of possibly distracting technical discussions in chapter three.

2 Clem. 2:1

Εὐφράνθητι, στεῖρα ἡ οὐ τίκτουσα, ῥῆξον καὶ βόησον ἡ οὐκ ὠδίνουσα, ὅτι πολλὰ τὰ τέκνα τῆς ἐρήμου μᾶλλον ἢ τῆς ἐχούσης τὸν ἄνδρα.

The text of 2 Clem. 2:1 is identical with that of the old Greek of Is. 54:1 and Gal. 4:27. It is also found in Justin, *Apol.* 53; however this context is very different from that of 2 Clement. There is a reflection of our text in the Gospel of Philip 107:31-36. It is interesting to note that early Christianity employs Is. 54:1 liberally in discussions concerning a pre-existent church. This is reflected in Gal. 4:27, 2 Clem.

---

is introduced by οὕτως γὰρ εἶπεν. The distinctions drawn by Köster between λέγει and εἶπεν in 2 Clement are not convincing, especially since he leaves himself open to alternatives in reference to 1 Clem. 13:2: "Vielleicht schöpft der Verfasser aus irgendeiner schriftlichen Herrenwortsammlung .... Vielleicht handelt es sich auch um die Wiedergabe eines mündlichen, aber fest formulierten lokalen Katechismus" (p. 16). We might also point to Polycarp, Phil. 7:2 where a specific quotation from Mk. 14:38 // Mt. 26:41 is introduced by εἶπεν ὁ κύριος. This brief survey shows that neither the evidence from 2 Clement nor that of other sources contemporary with it warrants the view that 2 Clement is using εἶπεν or λέγει for different purposes. Rather, they appear to be used synonymously.

[1] 2 Clem. 9:11.
[2] 2 Clem. 5:2-4.

2:1 and the Gospel of Philip 107:31-36. A more precise interrelationship between these texts will be considered in the next chapter.[1]

Why is there no introductory formula to this verse which ultimately stems from the Greek of Is. 54:1 ? There are two possibilities: either it belongs to the conclusion of the preceding hymnic confession[2] or it was well known to the hearers and was thus purposely selected by the author to interpret and enlarge upon the confession. The latter is the more likely for it is one of the very few quotations which 2 Clement interprets in a systematic way.

2 Clem. 6:2

2 Clem. 6:2	Mt. 16:26	Mk. 8:36	Lk. 9:25
a) τί γὰρ	τί γὰρ	τί γὰρ	τί γὰρ
τὸ ὄφελος,	ὠφεληθήσεται	ὠφελεῖ	ὠφελεῖται
b) ἐάν τις τὸν	ἄνθρωπος, ἐὰν	ἄνθρωπον	ἄνθρωπος
	τὸν	κερδῆσαι τὸν	κερδήσας τὸν
κόσμον ὅλον	κόσμον ὅλον	κόσμον ὅλον	κόσμον ὅλον
κερδήσῃ,	κερδήσῃ,		
c) τὴν δὲ ψυχὴν	τὴν δὲ ψυχὴν αὐ-	καὶ ζημιωθῆναι	ἑαυτὸν δὲ ἀπολέ-
ζημιωθῇ;	τοῦ ζημιωθῇ;	τὴν ψυχὴν αὐτοῦ;	σας ἢ ζημιωθείς;

Part (a) of 2 Clem. 6:2 is unique, while parts (b) and (c) agree with Matthew, except that 2 Clement adds τίς in part (b) to compensate for the omission of ἄνθρωπος in part (a), and omits αὐτοῦ in part (c). One cannot with certainty assert a dependence on Matthew although that is possible. In 2 Clement this verse is placed in a dualistic context where "this world" and "the coming world" are set in opposition.

2 Clem. 6:9

"If even such upright men as these cannot save their children by their uprightness, what assurance have we that we shall enter God's Kingdom if we fail to keep our baptism pure [cf. 8:6] and undefiled ? Or who will plead for us if we are not found to have holy and upright deeds ?" One should note the overall similarity with 4 Ezra 7:102-106:

---

[1] See pp. 108-109 and 192-200 below.

[2] So Daniel Völter, *Die älteste Predigt aus Rom* (Leiden, 1908), p. 11.

"And I answered and said: If I have found favour in thy sight, show me, thy servant,
this also: whether in the Day of Judgement the righteous shall be able to intercede
for the ungodly, or to intreat the Most High in their behalf: fathers for sons, sons for
parents, brothers for brothers, kinsfolk for their nearest, friends for their dearest.
And he answered me and said: Since thou hast found favour in my sight, I will
show this also unto thee. The Day of Judgement is decisive, and displays unto
all the seal of truth. Even as now a father may not send a son, or a son his father, or
a master his slave, or a friend his dearest, that in his stead he may be ill, or sleep,
or eat, or be healed; so shall none then pray for another on that Day, neither shall
one lay a burden on another; for then every one shall bear his own righteousness
or unrighteousness."

It might very well be that this material was familiar to our author.
Perhaps it was the thought of baptism and its seal which led the
author to this passage with its reference to "the seal of truth."

2 Clem. 7:1-6

Is this section dependent upon 1 Cor. 9:24ff. ? Probably not. The
only common bond are the terms $\dot{\alpha}\gamma\omega\nu\dot{\iota}\zeta o\mu\alpha\iota$, $\sigma\tau\dot{\epsilon}\phi\alpha\nu o\varsigma$ and $\phi\theta\alpha\rho\tau\dot{o}\varsigma$.
But these are shared by the agon tradition. Further, as Pfitzner[1]
has shown, 1 Cor. 9:24ff. has a direct reference to Paul's own apostolic
ministry, and not simply to a generalized ascetic paraenesis. 2 Clement
presents us with a fusion of motifs which are found, among other places,
in 1 Cor. 9:24ff.; 2 Tim. 2:5 and Philo, Agr 120-121. As Pfitzner correctly observes, the agon motif in 2 Clement "is portrayed in a style
which is closer to that of the diatribe or Philo than to any passage
in Paul's letters."[2]

2 Clem. 8:2

The illustration of the potter is a common one, being found in Wis.
15:7; Is. 29:16; Is. 45:9; Eccl. 33:13, as well as in the rabbinic literature.[3] Especially important are the references in Jer. 18:4-6 and Rom.
9:19-21, which we will discuss momentarily.

As observed in chapter one, 2 Clement 8 is carefully constructed
and interpreted. The overall theme is "let us repent." To this end,
2 Clement uses the picture of a potter and a vessel. "If a potter makes
a vessel and it gets out of shape or breaks in his hands, he molds it over
again...." This is then interpreted: "Similarly, while we are in this

---

[1] Victor Pfitzner, *Paul and the Agon Motif* (Leiden, 1967), pp. 126ff.
[2] *Ibid.*, p. 202; see also pp. 198ff.
[3] Strack-Billerbeck, III, pp. 271ff.

world, let us too repent with our whole heart of the evil we have done
in the flesh, so that we may be saved by the Lord while we have a
chance to repent." The second half of the illustration is this: "but
if he (the potter) has once thrown it into the flames of the furnace,
he can do nothing more with it." This, too, is applied very precisely
for the sake of the readers: "For once we have departed this world
we can no longer confess there or repent any more." The primary point
of the illustration is to remind the hearers that the time to repent is
now, before it is too late, viz., before the day of judgment comes.

Paul's use of this illustration in Rom. 9:19-21 serves a different purpose. For Paul, the relation of the potter to his clay is that of creator
to creature. "But who are you, a man, to answer back to God ?" (Rom.
9:20). In 2 Clement the relationship is not one of subjection, but rather
of parallel action. Just as the potter has a chance to *re*form his clay
before he puts it in the furnace, so man has a chance to repent before
the last day arrives. Further, in 2 Clement the stress is on reshaping
a single piece of clay, whereas in Romans Paul seems to be speaking of
more than one piece of clay, although they come from the same lump,
which are designed from the outset for different vessels. In view of
this, it appears unlikely that 2 Clement was influenced by Paul's
illustration at this point.

Most probable is the suggestion that 2 Clement had Jer. 18:4 in mind:
"And the vessel he was making of clay was spoiled in the potter's
hand, and he reworked it into another vessel, as it seemed good to the
potter to do." It is this illustration which 2 Clement takes over,
expands and applies. The point of Jeremiah's illustration is identical
with that of 2 Clement: after a piece of clay has been spoiled it is
refashioned again. To this, 2 Clement adds an eschatological framework.
Although the specific points of application differ, it is significant that
the theme of repentance is also central in Jer. 18:5-12, especially in
verse 11: "Return, every one from his evil way, and amend your ways
and your doings."

2 Clem. 10:2

διώξεται ἡμᾶς εἰρήνη.

The relation of this to ζήτησον εἰρήνην καὶ δίωξον αὐτήν in the
old Greek of Ps. 33:15 is far too vague to suggest that our author was
citing this Psalm, even though Ps. 33:15 is referred to elsewhere in early

Christian literature.[1] At the very most, one might be able to argue that we are dealing with a free adaptation of this psalm; it is more likely that these words reflect an early Christian tradition. That such a thought was common in primitive Christianity can be seen from Heb. 12:14: Εἰρήνην διώκετε μετὰ πάντων.

2 Clem. 11:7 (and 14:5)

ἅς οὖς οὐκ ἤκουσεν οὐδὲ ὀφθαλμὸς εἶδεν, οὐδὲ ἐπὶ καρδίαν ἀνθρώπου ἀνέβη (11:7).

ἃ ἡτοίμασεν ὁ κύριος τοῖς ἐκλεκτοῖς αὐτοῦ (14:5).

Do we have in 2 Clem. 11:7 an allusion to the old Greek of Is. 64:3 and 65:16-17 ? That is possible, but we would have to assume a Greek text which is no longer available to us, since the differences are substantial. 2 Clem. 11:7 and 14:5, when combined, stand close to the quotation found in 1 Cor. 2:9 and 1 Clem. 34:8. It is likely that 2 Clement, 1 Cor. 2:9 and 1 Clem. 34:8 are independently citing the same Greek version of the Old Testament. That 1 Clem. 34:8 stands closer to the original might be indicated by the use of τοῖς ὑπομένουσιν (Is. 64:3: τοῖς ὑπομένουσιν). Paul may have altered his text to τοῖς ἀγαπῶσιν and 2 Clement to τοῖς ἐκλεκτοῖς. Origen[2] makes the suggestion that Paul is quoting from the apocryphal Apocalypse of Elijah. While this is an interesting possibility, Barrett correctly asserts that it "does not seem to be capable of demonstration."[3]

2 Clem. 13:2b

Οὐαὶ δι' ὃν βλασφημεῖται τὸ ὄνομά μου.

Does this quotation simply consist of (1) Οὐαὶ δι' ὃν βλασφημεῖται τὸ ὄνομά μου or does it continue on with (2) ἐν τίνι βλασφημεῖται; ἐν τῷ μὴ ποιεῖν ὑμᾶς ἃ βούλομαι to the end of verse 2 ? Funk-Bihlmeyer, Richardson, Goodspeed, Lightfoot, Graham all hold that the quotation contains only part (1), and that part (2) may be the work of the au-

---

[1] 1 Pet. 3:11; 1 Clem. 22:5.
[2] In *Matt.* 27:9; see Lightfoot, *Apostolic Fathers*, p. 106.
[3] C. K. Barrett, *The First Epistle to the Corinthians* (New York, 1968), p. 73.

thor.[1] The contrary is held by Schubert, Knopf and van Unnik. van Unnik writes: "man (soll) wohl annehmen, dass das Zitat bis βούλομαι einschliesslich geht; anders ist der Dialog unbegreiflich."[2] We will attempt to show that the words in part (2) do indeed stem from the hand of the writer of 2 Clement.

Two technical matters support the assertion that the quotation contains only part (1). Whenever our author wants to amplify, clarify or make more precise a statement he has just made, he will introduce a rhetorical question with the words ἐν τίνι. For example, in 2 Clement 3 it is stated that one must confess Jesus Christ; verse 4 begins with ἐν τίνι δὲ αὐτὸν ὁμολογοῦμεν, and is followed by the answer ἐν τῷ ποιεῖν ἃ λέγει κτλ. In 2 Clement 9 the statement is made that no one should deny the fact that the body will be judged or will be raised, and verse 2 follows: γνῶτε· ἐν τίνι ἐσώθητε, ἐν τίνι ἀνεβλέψατε κτλ. This is exactly what we have in chapter 13. First, there are statements made about blaspheming the name; then follows the question: ἐν τίνι βλασφημεῖται. The answer follows the identical pattern of chapter 3: ἐν τῷ μὴ ποιεῖν ὑμᾶς ἃ βούλομαι. This suggests that part (2) is from the hand of our author and does not belong to the quotation. Further support for this assertion is the fact that Οὐαὶ δι' ὃν βλασφημεῖται κτλ. appears in slightly varied form in other early Christian literature. In none of them do we find part (2) or even the slightest suggestion of it. In Ignatius, Trallians 8:2 we simply find: Οὐαὶ γάρ, δι' οὗ ἐπὶ ματαιότητι τὸ ὄνομά μου ἐπί τινων βλασφημεῖται. In Polycarp, Philippians 10:3 we have: Vae autem, per quem nomen domini blasphematur. In Apost. Const. I.10 we read: Οὐαὶ γάρ, φησίν, δι' οὗ τὸ ὄνομά μου βλασφημεῖται ἐν τοῖς ἔθνεσιν. And finally in Apost. Const. III.5.6 we have: Οὐαὶ δέ, φησίν, δι' οὗ ὄνομα μου βλασφημεῖται ἐν τοῖς ἔθνεσιν. In light of this evidence it is likely that ἐν τίνι βλασφημεῖται; ἐν τῷ μὴ ποιεῖν ὑμᾶς ἃ βούλομαι stems from the writer himself. The source of the first half is unknown: while it does share certain

---

[1] Funk-Bihlmeyer, Die apostolischen Väter (Tübingen, 1956), p. 77; Cyril Richardson, Early Christian Fathers (Philadelphia, 1953), p. 198; Edgar Goodspeed, The Apostolic Fathers (New York, 1950), p. 91; Lightfoot, Apostolic Fathers, pp. 241-42; Holt Graham in Grant and Graham, The Apostolic Fathers, II (New York, 1965), p. 124.

[2] W. C. van Unnik, "Die Rücksicht auf die Reaktion der Nicht-Christen" in Judentum Urchristentum Kirche (Berlin, 1964), ed. W. Eltester, p. 224, n. 10; H. von Schubert, "Der sog. zweite Clemensbrief, eine Gemeindepredigt" in Edgar Hennecke, Neutestamentliche Apokryphen (Tübingen, 1924), p. 593; R. Knopf, Die zwei Clemensbriefe (Tübingen, 1920), p. 172.

similarities with other early Christian writings,[1] it can most probably be argued that these writings are all freely adopting or reflecting the old Greek of Is. 52:5.

2 Clem. 14:1

πρὸ ἡλίου καὶ σελήνης ἐκτισμένης·

Do we have here an explicit reference to the old Greek of Ps. 71:5: καὶ συμπαραμενεῖ τῷ ἡλίῳ καὶ πρὸ τῆς σελήνης γενεὰς γενεῶν? Possible dependence of 2 Clement on Ps. 71 is difficult to assess, especially since the combination of "sun and moon" was quite common in early Christianity.[2] Yet a number of factors do suggest the possibility that Ps. 71 influenced the verse under consideration: 1) πρὸ τῆς σελήνης may be reflected in 2 Clem. 14.1; 2) a part of Ps. 71:5 is employed by Justin, *Dial.* 64, in a way similar to that of 2 Clement, except that for Justin it refers to the pre-existence of Christ while for 2 Clement it refers to the pre-existence of the church. Justin is attempting to illustrate that this Psalm proves "that this (Christ) existed before the sun...." 2 Clement is attempting to prove the same point with reference to the church.

2 Clem. 14:2

ἐκκλησία ζῶσα σῶμά ἐστιν Χριστοῦ·

We seem to have here a clear reflection of the deutero-Pauline writings. Paul himself never says that ἡ ἐκκλησία is the body of Christ. This is a "post-Pauline"[3] development which is found in Colossians and Ephesians. 2 Clem. 14:2 might well be a reflection of Col. 1:24 or Eph. 1:22-23.[4]

2 Clem. 15:1

Οὐκ οἴομαι δέ, ὅτι μικρὰν συμβουλίαν ἐποιησάμην περὶ ἐγκρατείας, ἣν ποιήσας τις οὐ μετανοήσει, ἀλλὰ καὶ ἑαυτὸν σώσει κἀμὲ τὸν συμβουλεύσαντα.

---

[1] Rom. 2:24; 2 Pet. 2:2.
[2] 1 Cor. 15:41; Barn. 15:5; 1 Clem. 25:4; Ign., Eph. 19:2.
[3] Certainly understood as Pauline by the author of 2 Clement.
[4] See also Col. 1:18.

2 Clem. 19:1

Ὥστε, ἀδελφοὶ καὶ ἀδελφαί, μετὰ τὸν θεὸν τῆς ἀληθείας ἀναγινώσκω ὑμῖν ἔντευξιν εἰς τὸ προσέχειν τοῖς γεγραμμένοις, ἵνα καὶ ἑαυτοὺς σώσητε καὶ τὸν ἀναγινώσκοντα ἐν ὑμῖν·

Perhaps a passage such as the old Greek of Ezek. 3:16-21 provided a general background for these assertions in 2 Clement. Verse 21 summarizes the intent of 2 Clement. The differences can be attributed to the fact that the Lord in Ezekiel is speaking to the prophet, while the author (the presbyter, 17:3) of 2 Clement is speaking about himself — τὸν συμβουλεύσαντα or τὸν ἀναγινώσκοντα. From Justin, Dial. 82, we know that this pericope was known in the second century. Justin argues that the prophetic gifts of the Jews are transferred to the Christians. After quoting from Ezek. 3:17-19 he concludes with this note: "And on this account we are, through fear, very earnest in desiring to converse [with men] according to the Scriptures, but not from love of money, or of glory, or of pleasure."

Another passage which must be considered in this connection is 1 Tim. 4:11-16. Verse 16 reads: ἔπεχε σεαυτῷ καὶ τῇ διδασκαλίᾳ· ἐπίμενε αὐτοῖς· τοῦτο γὰρ ποιῶν καὶ σεαυτὸν σώσεις καὶ τοὺς ἀκούοντάς σου. The similarity between this and καὶ ἑαυτὸν σώσει κἀμὲ τὸν συμβουλεύσαντα (15:1) and ἑαυτοὺς σώσητε καὶ τὸν ἀναγινώσκοντα ἐν ὑμῖν (19:1) is evident. Whether 2 Clement is directly influenced by 1 Timothy is, of course, difficult to say with certainty. 2 Clement, a presbyter (17:3), is, however, aware of the general advice given by "Paul" to Timothy concerning this office as it appears in 1 Tim. 4:13: ἕως ἔρχομαι πρόσεχε τῇ ἀναγνώσει, τῇ παρακλήσει, τῇ διδασκαλίᾳ. If we understand παράκλησις as a word of exhortation or paraenetic preaching as in Acts 13:15, the relation to 2 Clement is obvious. 2 Clement is in many ways a παράκλησις. That 2 Clement is trying to bring the correct διδασκαλία over against the κακοδιδασκαλία mentioned in 10:5 is also evident (cf. 15:1; 17:3; 19:1). The least that can be said is that the author of 2 Clement understands his role in a manner similar to that outlined by "Paul" in 1 Timothy.

2 Clem. 16:3

A

ἔρχεται ἤδη ἡ ἡμέρα τῆς κρίσεως ὡς κλίβανος καιόμενος

The old Greek of Mal. 3:19 reads: διότι ἰδοὺ ἡμέρα κυρίου ἔρχεται καιομένη ὡς κλίβανος καὶ φλέξει αὐτούς, κτλ. This citation is sufficiently different so as to suggest that our author is not quoting precisely from any known version of Malachi.

B

τακήσονταί τινες τῶν οὐρανῶν

In Is. 34:4 (MS B) we read: τακήσονται πᾶσαι αἱ δυνάμεις τῶν οὐρανῶν. Despite the fact that the τινες of Clement is well attested, Lightfoot changes τινες to δυνάμεις on the basis of MS B of Isaiah. Lightfoot's argument is based not on textual grounds, but rather on content. He argues: "Though the existing text might be explained with Harnack and Hilgenfeld by the common belief in several heavens (comp. e.g. Orig. c. *Cels.* 6:23), I can hardly think that our Clementine writer would have expressed himself in this way, even if he had believed that some of the heavens would be spared from the conflagration."[1] This fully overlooks the gnostic environment of 2 Clement and how commonplace this kind of thinking is in gnostic circles. In addition, τήκειν is such a frequent LXX word that one is in no way compelled to argue that 2 Clem. 16:3b is taken from Is. 34:4 and, then, to make a textual change in order to support this assertion.

It might even be possible that the decisive influence on 2 Clement 16:3b came from 2 Pet. 3:12 (or what is much more likely, a similar tradition), which reads: δι' ἣν οὐρανοὶ πυρούμενοι λυθήσονται καὶ στοιχεῖα καυσούμενα τήκεται. This suggestion becomes even more striking when one compares the context of 2 Peter 3 with that of 2 Clement 16. In 2 Pet. 3:9 we read: "The Lord is not slow about his promise as some count slowness, but is forbearing toward you, not wishing that any should perish (ἀπολέσθαι), but that all should reach repentance (εἰς μετάνοιαν)." This very closely resembles the opening of 2 Clem. 16:1, "So, brothers, since we have been given no small opportunity to repent (εἰς τὸ μετανοῆσαι) ...", and 17:1, "Let us, then, repent with our whole heart, so that none of us will be lost (παραπόληται)."

This matter of having time for repentance is related to the whole problem of the delay of the parousia which is expressed in similar

---

[1] Lightfoot, *Apostolic Fathers*, p. 250.

terms in 2 Peter 3 and in 2 Clement 11. In 2 Pet. 3:3 we read: "First
of all you must understand this, that scoffers will come in the last
days with scoffing, following their own passions and saying, 'Where
is the promise of his coming? For ever since the fathers fell asleep,
all things have continued as they were from the beginning of creation.'"
In 2 Clem. 11:2 we read: "For the word of the prophet says, "Wretched
are the double-minded, those who doubt in their soul and say, 'We have
heard those things long ago, even in our fathers' times, and day after
day we have waited and have seen none of them.'" And just prior to
this 2 Clem. 10:5 speaks of those who "persist in teaching evil to innocent souls."

In 2 Clem. 16:3 we read: "Understand that the day of judgment is
already on its way like a furnace ablaze, and the powers of heaven will
dissolve and the whole earth will be like lead melting in fire." Not
only does this resemble 2 Pet. 3:12, as we have indicated above, but
also 2 Pet. 3:10: "But the day of the Lord will come like a thief, and
then the heavens will pass away with a loud noise, and the elements
will be dissolved with fire, and the earth and the works that are upon
it will be burned up." Precisely because of this coming end, 2 Clem.
16:4 stresses the necessity of good actions, a theme also reflected in
2 Pet. 3:11, "Since all these things are thus to be dissolved, what sort
of persons ought you to be in lives of holiness and godliness...", and
in 3:14, "Therefore, beloved, since you wait for these, be zealous to
be found by him without spot or blemish, and at peace." In view of
these similarities, it is quite likely that 2 Clement was influenced by
a tradition similar to that now found in 2 Peter.

2 Clem. 16:4

ἀγάπη δὲ καλύπτει πλῆθος ἁμαρτιῶν

It is difficult to assume that this quotation is derived from the old
Greek of Prov. 10:12. One glance at Proverbs is sufficient to note
the striking differences: πάντας δὲ τοὺς μὴ φιλονεικοῦντας καλύπτει
φιλία.

This verse agrees word for word, as well as in the eschatological
context, with that found in 1 Pet. 4:8. It also agrees with the quotation
in 1 Clem. 49:5, but not with the immediate context. In Jas. 5:20 the
phrase appears slightly altered in the form καλύψει πλῆθος ἁμαρτιῶν.
Here in James the reference is clearly to forgiving the sins of others,
while in 1 Peter, 1 Clement and in 2 Clement it refers to the forgiveness

of one's own sins. To say that 2 Clement is dependent upon 1 Peter,
1 Clement or James is possible but at the same time one must realize
that we could be dealing with a free-floating logion, as A. Resch has
suggested.[1] Yet, on the whole, it is more likely that 2 Clement is dependent upon 1 Peter or a similar tradition, for at least three reasons:
(1) word for word agreement of the quotation; (2) a similar exegesis
of the quotation; (3) the identical eschatological context (1 Pet. 4:7:
"The end of all things is at hand, therefore...").

2 Clem. 17:5

A

καὶ ὄψονται τὴν δόξαν αὐτοῦ

This agrees with the old Greek of Is. 66:18 except that the μου has
heen changed to αὐτοῦ. This text actually serves as a further interpretation of the preceding quotation.

B

ὁ σκώληξ αὐτῶν οὐ τελευτήσει καὶ τὸ πῦρ αὐτῶν οὐ σβεσθήσεται, καὶ
ἔσονται εἰς ὅρασιν πάσῃ σαρκί.

This agrees exactly with the old Greek of Is. 66:24, as we have already
noted in our discussion of 2 Clem. 7:6. Both Mk. 9:48 and Justin,
Apol. 52, contain the identical quotation but in a shorter and slightly
altered version. This quotation serves as a further interpretation of
the preceding text taken from Is. 66:18.

2 Clem. 17:7

δόξαν διδόντες τῷ θεῷ αὐτῶν

This only very vaguely resembles the old Greek of Ps. 67:35 (δότε
δόξαν τῷ θεῷ). The same would hold true for Rev. 11:13: ἔδωκεν
δόξαν τῷ θεῷ κτλ. Perhaps we are dealing with a well known
formulation from a liturgical tradition.

---

[1] A. Resch, *Agrapha* (Darmstadt, 1967), pp. 310-11.

Summary

This survey confirms as well as expands results reached in sections one and two. On the one hand, there is the continued use of the Old Testament, particularly Isaiah (2 Clem. 2:1; 17:5) and Jeremiah (2 Clem. 8:2), although it is conceivable that 2 Clement 8 represents a thorough reworking of Romans. On the other hand, 2 Clem. 6:2 again reveals a close connection with the gospel tradition, but in a way different enough from Matthew so as to leave open the question of dependence.

What is most suggestive about this review is the indication that the author of 2 Clement was open to a wide spectrum of influences from his *Gemeindetradition*. 2 Clem. 7:1-6 take up motifs which are also found in 1 Cor. 9, 2 Clem. 11:7 and 14:5 are dependent either on Colossians or Ephesians and 2 Clem. 15:1 and 19:1 reveal affinities to aspects of congregational life as discussed in 1 Timothy. Finally, 2 Clem. 16:3-4 reveal definite relationships with traditions standing behind 1 and 2 Peter. These results display the variety and confluence of traditions present in the environment in which 2 Clement was written.

4. τὰ βιβλία καὶ οἱ ἀπόστολοι

In view of the extensive discussion above concerning the actual sources 2 Clement employed and/or alluded to, 2 Clem. 14:2 deserves our consideration: καὶ ἔτι τὰ βιβλία καὶ οἱ ἀπόστολοι τὴν ἐκκλησίαν οὐ νῦν εἶναι, ἀλλὰ ἄνωθεν. The question is this: to what do τὰ βιβλία and οἱ ἀπόστολοι refer?

The Syriac version adds τῶν προφητῶν after τὰ βιβλία. We have, however, no compelling reason to assume the originality of this addition. Lightfoot is to be followed when he states: "The Syriac translator's 'books of the prophets' is the obvious gloss of a later age."[1] Since the phrase τὰ βιβλία καὶ οἱ ἀπόστολοι is important both for the total understanding of 2 Clement as well as for the history of the canon, we must define the meaning of the terms τὰ βιβλία and οἱ ἀπόστολοι as precisely as possible. Let us begin with the former.

βιβλίον, the original diminutive form of βίβλος, has a wide range of meaning. The very context in which 2 Clement uses the term, however, suggests that it is referring to the Jewish scriptures. It is

---

[1] Lightfoot, *Apostolic Fathers*, p. 245.

often used in such a manner. Josephus, for example, frequently uses βιβλία in this way. In *Ant.* 1:15, Josephus speaks of τοῖς βιβλίοις which he has just prior (1:13) described as τῶν ἱερῶν γραμμάτων. This is also the case in *Ant.* 8:159 where Josephus speaks of ἐν τοῖς ἐπιχωρίοις ἡμῶν βιβλίοις. In the Letter of Aristeas 28 we read: "When this had been done, he ordered Demetrius to draw up a memorial with regard to the transcription of the Jewish books (βιβλία)." Also interesting in this context is the use of ἐν ταῖς βιβλίοις in Dan. 9:2, where the reference is to the prophets. Another important reference is 2 Tim. 4:13 where we read: τὰ βιβλία, μάλιστα τὰς μεμβράνας. If we keep in mind the possibility that βιβλίον referred to a roll and that μεμβράναι (skins) referred to a codex, then the suggestion of C. H. Roberts[1] is quite plausible, viz., that in 2 Tim. 4:13, Timothy is asked to bring the βιβλία (the Jewish scriptures in roll form) and especially the μεμβράναι (the apostle's own notes in codex form).[2]

These observations, as well as the immediate context in the chapter (quotations from Jeremiah and Genesis), make it probable that τὰ βιβλία in 2 Clem. 14:2 refer to the Jewish scriptures, including the Pentateuch and the Prophets.[3] That τὰ βιβλία have a wider reference than simply the prophets[4] is indicated by the fact that just immediately prior to this reference a verse from Genesis is quoted. There is little evidence, however, to answer affirmatively Köster's[5] conjectural question as to whether τὰ βιβλία in 2 Clement might include the synoptic gospels.[6]

---

[1] C. H. Roberts, "The Codex," *Proc. Brit. Acad.* 40 (1954), pp. 169ff.; also J.N.D. Kelly, *The Pastoral Epistles* (New York, 1963), pp. 215-16.

[2] See P. Katz, "The Early Christian Use of Codices instead of Rolls," *JTS* 46 (1945), pp. 63ff. The basic point is substantiated by B. Gerhardsson, *Memory and Manuscript* (Lund, 1961), pp. 157ff. On p. 201 he states: "In the Greco-Roman world the scroll enjoyed almost undisputed supremacy as the repository of literary work: a book *was* a scroll. In Judaism, too, the scroll was unchallenged as the vehicle of the written divine Word. With this in mind, it is all the more remarkable that as early as the beginning of the 2nd century—and presumably even earlier—the codex was used in the Church. Some scholars have connected this with the possibility that the gospel literature was derived from *notebooks*, which were often in codex form."

[3] Also supporting this understanding of τὰ βιβλία are Adolf von Harnack, "Über das Alter der Bezeichnung 'Die Bücher' ('Die Bibel') für die Heiligen Schrift in der Kirche," *Zentralblatt für Bibliothekswesen* 45 (1928), pp. 337ff.; and, Hans von Campenhausen, "Das Alte Testament als Bibel der Kirche" in *Aus der Frühzeit der Christentums,* pp. 154ff.

[4] Also a factor against the reading of S.

[5] Köster, *Synoptische Überlieferung,* pp. 67ff.

[6] The Oxford Committee, p. 124, comes to a similar conclusion.

To whom do οἱ ἀπόστολοι refer?[1] It is unlikely that the author of 2 Clement gave much reflection to this matter and Klein is quite right in suggesting that οἱ ἀπόστολοι has "die Funktion einer traditionsgeschichtlichen Nomenklatur...."[2] But can one be more precise in defining how the term οἱ ἀπόστολοι was used in the period when 2 Clement was written? Some helpful guidance may be found in 1 Clement 42-43, where both οἱ ἀπόστολοι and that which is recorded in ταῖς ἱεραῖς βιβλίοις are called upon to support a correct understanding of church order. In 1 Clem. 42:1, the apostles are defined as those who "received the gospel for us form the Lord Jesus Christ; Jesus, the Christ, was sent from God. Thus Christ is from God and the apostles from Christ. In both instances the orderly procedure depends on God's will. And so the apostles, after receiving their orders and being fully convinced by the resurrection of our Lord Jesus Christ and assured by God's word, went out in the confidence of the Holy Spirit to preach the good news that God's Kingdom was about to come." That "the apostles" in 1 Clement are a group wider than the Twelve is made clear, for example, in 1 Clem. 5:3 and 47:1, where Paul is definitely included in this designation.[3]

With regard to the specific context of 2 Clem. 14:1-2, one can suggest that in using τὰ βιβλία our author had Jeremiah and Genesis specifically in mind and in using οἱ ἀπόστολοι he was referring either to Col. 1:24 or Eph. 1:22-23.[4] Quite probably the author of 2 Clement also had a host of other texts in mind[5] and cited only some as specific examples. Given the whole of 2 Clement, then, we note three sources of authority: τὰ βιβλία (the Jewish scriptures), ὁ κύριος (especially with reference to the Jesus logia), and οἱ ἀπόστολοι (including Paul).[6]

---

[1] Important discussions in Köster, *Synoptische Überlieferung*, p. 68; G. Klein, *Die zwölf Apostel* (Göttingen, 1961), p. 107; von Campenhausen, *Die Entstehung der christlichen Bibel*, p. 298; W. Schmithals, *The Office of Apostle in the Early Church* (Nashville, 1969), pp. 244ff.

[2] G. Klein, *Die zwölf Apostel* (Göttingen, 1961), p. 107.

[3] See R. Grant, *The Apostolic Fathers*, II, p. 25.

[4] The references to Paul in 2 Clement would be increased if one were to understand 2 Clem. 7:1-6 and 8:2 as dependent upon 1 Corinthians and Romans respectively. See pp. 84-85 above.

[5] For example, Is. 54:1 which was quoted in 2 Clem. 2:1.

[6] There is no evidence that the term οἱ ἀπόστολοι is used by 2 Clement in the sense that they were guarantors of the "sayings of the Lord."

5. THE FUNCTION OF QUOTATIONS AND LITERARY ALLUSIONS IN 2 CLEMENT

For the most part our author does not appear to be using quotations and literary allusions in a random or haphazard manner. Rather, he inserts them into a well-defined and structured pattern. Almost every chapter in the paraenetic section of 2 Clement (chs. 3-14) begins with a major theme (1) which then carries over into paraenesis (2). Following each of these parts one usually finds either a quotation or a literary allusion. Thus, a fairly consistent pattern can be observed:

1. Paraenetic theme
   a) quotation (or literary allusion)
2. Paraenesis proper
   a) quotation (or literary allusion)

A few illustrations of this pattern must suffice. In chapter 3, verse 1 contains the theme (1) in the form of a theological summary of chapter 1. Verse 2 contains a quotation (1a) from the gospel tradition which both illustrates and supports the points previously made. The paraenesis proper (2) is found in verses 3-4 and this is followed by a quotation from Isaiah (2a), which again illustrates and supports that which precedes.

This identical pattern can be found in chapters 4, 6,[1] 11 and 13. This pattern is also observed in chapters 7, 8 and 9 except that here the first illustrative quotation (1a) is replaced by a literary allusion. In chapter 7 the allusion is to the agon motif, in chapter 8 to the potter and in chapter 9 the allusion is to the hymnic confession cited in 2 Clement 1. A variant of this pattern is found in chapter 5; however, here the second quotation (2a) is absent.

Within the ethical section of 2 Clement, this pattern is not found in chapters 10, 12 or 14. When one examines the content of these chapters the reason for the absence of this pattern becomes apparent. Chapter 10 serves as a summary and essentially nothing new is presented. Chapters 12 and 14 attempt to correct misunderstandings and therefore the quotations in question are discussed with the intent of clarifying the issue at hand.

---

[1] In chapter 6, the opening theme itself is in the form of a quotation.

There are only two points at which the author of 2 Clement takes up a quotation and gives a systematic exegesis: in chapters 2 and 12.[1] In the first case a positive argument is developed, and in the second the purpose of the exegesis is primarily negative—it attempts to "degnosticize" the quotation. Since both of these quotations are integrally related to a wider context, it will be more appropriate to discuss their individual functions in the next chapter.

What purpose do the quotations serve within the structure we have observed? To suggest that the alternative is either "illustrative" or "proof," as Thyen does,[2] is to oversimplify. In fact, a good many of 2 Clement's quotations serve a purpose somewhere in between these two designations. There are few places in 2 Clement where one can categorically claim that quotations play a purely illustrative role; further, there is no point in this address where quotations serve as proof texts in a logically thought out argument such as found in Romans 4, Galatians 3 or Romans 9-11.[3] Most of the quotations found in 2 Clement serve an illustrative and supportive function. They are illustrations of the point being made, yet, the very fact that these quotations are not simply taken from ancient worthies but carry the authority of the Jewish and early Christian traditions, allows them not only to illustrate but to support authoritatively that which is being said.

---

[1] In a minor way, interpretations are also given after the quotations in 2:4; 6:1,8; 7:6; 14:2 and 17:4.

[2] H. Thyen, *Der Stil der Jüdisch-Hellenistischen Homilie* (Göttingen, 1955), pp. 71-73.

[3] Even 4:1 and 11:2 do not function within a sustained argument. On Paul's use of the Old Testament see E. Earle Ellis, *Paul's Use of the Old Testament* (London, 1957).

CHAPTER THREE

THE INTENTION OF SECOND CLEMENT

One can describe the intention and theology of 2 Clement either within the terms of its own three-fold structure or in terms of major themes which run throughout the discourse. It is our judgment that the former approach best illuminates the different stresses of the writing as it moves from beginning to end. Also, within each section we have preferred a chapter by chapter approach rather than a thematic one, since the latter approach stands in danger both of unifying materials that originally were disparate and of insufficiently dealing with the context and argumentative structure of each chapter.

1. THEOLOGICAL (1:1-2:7)

a) *Introduction: 2 Clem. 1:1-2*

'Αδελφοί, οὕτως δεῖ ἡμᾶς φρονεῖν περὶ 'Ιησοῦ Χριστοῦ, ὡς περὶ θεοῦ, ὡς περὶ κριτοῦ ζώντων καὶ νεκρῶν·

We are here dealing with a dogmatic assertion—that we must so think of[1] Jesus Christ as God, viz., as the judge of the living and the dead. Closely related to Jesus Christ is the phrase τῆς σωτηρίας ἡμῶν (1:1). These words come immediately after the opening description of Jesus Christ and just prior to ἐν τῷ γάρ φρονεῖν ἡμᾶς μικρὰ περὶ αὐτοῦ μικρὰ καὶ ἐλπίζομεν λαβεῖν (1:2). This intimate relation between Jesus Christ and σωτηρία is further confirmed in 1:7: καὶ μηδεμίαν ἐλπίδα ἔχοντας σωτηρίας, εἰ μὴ τὴν παρ' αὐτοῦ. He who thinks lightly concerning Jesus Christ and the salvation given through Him errs, οὐκ εἰδότες, πόθεν ἐκλήθημεν καὶ ὑπὸ τίνος καὶ εἰς ὅν τόπον, καὶ ὅσα ὑπέμεινεν 'Ιησοῦς Χριστὸς παθεῖν ἕνεκα ἡμῶν (1:2).

What our author is saying in these opening verses must stand in some relationship to his hearers. Either they hold the position he is

---

[1] In the sense of holding an opinion or judgment concerning someone, as in Phil. 1:7; Isocr. 3:60; Lucian, *Dial. Mort.* 20.5; Jos., *Ant.* 12:125.

criticizing or they are being tempted to fall into such a position. The opening verses do permit us to see that our writer is dealing with an *eschatological* problem.[1] This is evident from the following statements: (1) that we must think of Jesus Christ ὡς περὶ κριτοῦ ζώτων καὶ νεκρῶν, (2) ἐλπίζομεν λαβεῖν, and, (3) εἰς ὃν τόπον. These can only be understood in an eschatological way. Let us examine each more closely.

(1) οὕτως δεῖ ἡμᾶς φρονεῖν περὶ Ἰησοῦ Χριστοῦ, ὡς περὶ θεοῦ, ὡς περὶ κριτοῦ ζώντων καὶ νεκρῶν. It would be incorrect to assert on the basis of this verse that Jesus Christ is identical with God. Rather, we have here an identity of function. Just as God is the judge of the living and the dead, in like fashion we must understand Jesus—as the judge of the living and the dead. In 2 Clement the distinction between Jesus and the Father is not blurred as is often asserted.[2] This is evident from the closing doxology, Τῷ μόνῳ θεῷ ἀοράτῳ, πατρὶ τῆς ἀληθείας, τῷ ἐξαποστείλαντι ἡμῖν τὸν σωτῆρα καὶ ἀρχηγὸν τῆς ἀφθαρσίας ... (20:5), and also when it is said in reference to Jesus ἀλλὰ ἔγνωμεν δι' αὐτοῦ τὸν πατέρα τῆς ἀληθείας (3:1). That which is being stressed in 1:1 is that Jesus Christ is the judge of the living and the dead. This concept is further elaborated in chapter 17:5: "And 'unbelievers will see his glory' and power, and they will be surprised to see the sovereignty of the world given to Jesus, and they will say, 'Alas for us, for you really existed, and we neither recognized it nor believed, and we did not obey the presbyters who preached to us our salvation.' "

Already here it becomes apparent that our author has taken up apocalyptic terminology.[3] While some of the language and thought found in 2 Clement reflects such Jewish apocalyptic texts as I Enoch,[4] it is more likely that it is dependent upon a distinctly Christian tradi-

---

[1] J. B. Lightfoot's (*The Apostolic Fathers* II, 1 [London, 1890], p. 211) suggestion that the opponents here are Ebionites has no basis in the text.

[2] See the discussion in Raymond E. Brown, "Does the New Testament Call Jesus God?" *TS* 26 (1965), p. 568.

[3] See further 2 Clem. 9:1; 10:5; 16:3; 17:6; 18:1,2; 20:4.

[4] In 1 Enoch 62:7-11 we read that the son of man is a pre-existent, divine being who is revealed at the end, a thought which finds expression in 2 Clem. 14. In 1 Enoch 69:27-29 it is stated that the son of man will ride in glory over the elect, a thought which is paralleled in 2 Clem. 17:5: "And unbelievers will see his glory and power and they will be surprised to see the sovereignty of the world given to Jesus...."

tion,[1] a tradition which shares many similarities with 1 Peter. This is suggested by the phrase κριτοῦ ζώντων καὶ νεκρῶν. This phrase has no synoptic parallel, but is found in Acts 10:42; 1 Pet. 4:5; 2 Tim. 4:1; Barn. 7:2; Polycarp, Phil. 2:1; and, in a somewhat different form, in Rom. 14:9. Two factors suggest a contact with 1 Peter or a similar tradition: (1) the probability that 2 Clem. 16:4 reflects 1 Pet. 4:8,[2] and (2) the similarity of the language and context of 2 Clem. 1:2 with that of the opening verses of 1 Peter 4. Not only do we have the identical thought in reference to judging "the living and the dead" in 1 Pet. 4:5, but in 1 Pet. 4:1 we find the same motif— Χριστοῦ οὖν παθόντος (+ ὑπὲρ ἡμῶν אc)— as in 2 Clem. 1:2: ὅσα ὑπέμεινεν Ἰησοῦς Χριστὸς παθεῖν ἕνεκα ἡμῶν.

(2) ἐλπίζομεν λαβεῖν. That this phrase refers to the future reception of the gifts of salvation is clear from the way both ἐλπίζω and λαμβάνω are used in 2 Clement. ἐλπίζω is used once again, in 2 Clem. 11:5. There (11:5) we find a clear expansion and clarification of what is meant in 1:2: ὥστε, ἀδελφοί μου, μὴ διψυχῶμεν, ἀλλὰ ἐλπίσαντες ὑπομείνωμεν, ἵνα καὶ τὸν μισθὸν κομισώμεθα. "Hoping" is related to the reception of the future eschatological reward. If one remains steadfast in hope, one will receive the future eschatological reward. That this is the basic meaning of 2 Clem. 1:2 is further confirmed by an examination of the word λαμβάνω. In 2 Clem. 8:4 we read: ὥστε, ἀδελφοί, ποιήσαντες τὸ θέλημα τοῦ πατρὸς καὶ τὴν σάρκα ἁγνὴν τηρήσαντες καὶ τὰς ἐντολὰς τοῦ κυρίου φυλάξαντες ληψόμεθα ζωὴν αἰώνιον. Here λαμβάνω has a clear future reference and that which is to be received is "eternal life." Again we observe a theme which is prominent in all of 2 Clement: to receive the final eschatological reward of salvation is dependent upon certain things which one does in this earthly life. This theme also appears in 11:7 where λαμβάνω also occurs: ἐὰν οὖν ποιήσωμεν τὴν δικαιοσύνην ἐναντίον τοῦ θεοῦ, εἰσήξομεν εἰς τὴν βασιλείαν αὐτοῦ καὶ ληψόμεθα τὰς ἐπαγγελίας. We find here not only a more precise definition of what will be received

---

[1] On the use of apocalyptic tradition in the primitive church, see especially E. Käsemann, *New Testament Questions of Today* (Philadelphia, 1969), pp. 82-37; also N. Perrin, *Rediscovering the Teaching of Jesus* (New York, 1967), pp. 164-206; Howard M. Teeple, "The Origin of the Son of Man Christology," *JBL* 84 (1965), pp. 213-50; J. Louis Martyn, *History and Theology in the Fourth Gospel*, (New York, 1968), pp. 120-35.

[2] See pp. 91-92.

(τὰς ἐπαγγελίας) but also the fact that this is conditioned by certain behavior: doing righteousness before God. That λαμβάνω refers to an eschatological factor is again confirmed in 20:3: οὐδεὶς τῶν δικαίων ταχὺν καρπὸν ἔλαβεν, ἀλλ' ἐκδέχεται αὐτόν. This section under discussion reveals a number of similarities with Hebrews which will be discussed below.

(3) εἰς ὃν τόπον (1:2). In actuality we are here dealing with topography and not eschatology. Yet the eschatological promises are intimately tied up with this topographical location. We are called from a given historical topographical location (πόθεν) to another (εἰς ὃν τόπον).[1] The purpose of 2 Clement is to deal with the Christian in between these two situations—reminding him that he has given up his past and that he must, therefore, live in a manner which will permit him to receive the future promises.

πόθεν in 2 Clem. 1:2 must be understood in a local sense—"from what place," "from where." This is supported by the parallels in the Gospel of John (e.g., 8:14) and especially Barn. 14:7, where is it used in a similar sense. Also the very use of τόπος in the same verse would make this the most natural understanding. That πόθεν cannot be understood in the sense of "from what source" or "brought about or given by whom" is ruled out by the words following directly upon πόθεν - ὑπὸ τίνος. As it sounds now we have a well-balanced phrase—from where, by whom, unto what place.

τόπος in 2 Clement can only refer to the eschatological place of salvation. This meaning of τόπος as a transcendent place to which a person's final destiny belongs is common to Hellenistic Judaism and gnosticism: for example, in Tobit 3:6, ὁ αἰώνιος τόπος, in Philo, Somn I 181 (speaking of the soul), ἀπολιποῦσα μὲν γὰρ οὐράνιον τόπον ... καθάπερ εἰς ξένην χώραν ἦλθε τὸ σῶμα, and the Gospel of Truth 40:30-42:35. Important for our purposes are the following brief selections from the Gospel of Truth (40:30-41:14): [Speaking of the Son] "For that reason, also, He sent Him in order that He (might) speak about the Place (τόπος), and about His place of repose from which He had come forth and that He might glorify the Pleroma, the greatness of His Name and the gentleness of the Father. He will speak about the place from which each one has come and the region from which he has received his essential being. He will hasten to cause (him)

---

[1] An interesting passage is Jn. 14:2-3; however, here we are dealing more with an apocalyptic, than a gnostic background. See also our discussion on pp. 160-66.

to return there once again, and to remove him from this place—the place where he (now) is—(causing him to) become attached to that place, by nourishing himself thereon and growing up therein. And his own place of repose is his Pleroma."

This gnostic concept of a place of rest— ὁ τόπος τῆς ἀναπαύσεως— found in the Gospel of Truth, the Acts of John 99, and elsewhere[1] is reflected not only here in 2 Clement 1 but also in 6:7 and 5:5: ἡ δὲ ἐπαγγελία τοῦ Χριστοῦ μεγάλη καὶ θαυμαστή ἐστιν, καὶ ἀνάπαυσις τῆς μελλούσης βασιλείας καὶ ζωῆς αἰωνίου. Rest is found in a given place —the *coming* kingdom. Important for 2 Clement, and distinctive of its "corrective" theology, is this emphasis on the future kingdom for which the Christian must prepare; contrary to the gnostic view, the Christian cannot simply ascend now to this place of rest.

The basic theme and stress of 2 Clem. 1:1-3 is an eschatological one. Jesus Christ is not only the one who has called us but he is also the one who will judge us at the end—it is then that we will receive our full salvation. In other words, our author finds it important to stress εἰς ὃν τόπον, rather than πόθεν (ἐκλήθημεν). The formula a) πόθεν ... b) ὑπὸ τίνος ... c) τόπος ... is basic to the whole discourse.[2] Important for the moment is the fact that parts (a) and (b) are dealt with in chapter 1, while the implication drawn from this, the ὁδός for getting to the τόπος, occupy the remainder of the writing. It is this latter point which our author believes imperative for his congregation to hear and to obey. It is very possible that he is dealing with a problem of realized eschatology, much in the same way as Paul is in 1 Cor. 4:8: "Already you are filled! Already you have become rich!"

The theme of "being called" to the future kingdom is a basic one in 2 Clement.[3] Parallels to this conception are found in Hebrews and the Gospel of Truth. In Heb. 9:15 we have a close connection between those who are called and the inheritance of the promises: Καὶ διὰ τοῦτο διαθήκης καινῆς μεσίτης ἐστίν, ὅπως θανάτου γενομένου

---

[1] See pp. 120-24.

[2] This formula is similar to John 8:14. G. P. Wetter, "Eine gnostische Formel im 4. Evangelium," *ZNW* 18 (1917/18), pp. 49-63, has attempted to demonstrate that we are dealing with a gnostic formula. In this he has been followed by Bultmann, *The Gospel of John* (Oxford, 1971), p. 280, and *TWNT*, I, p. 694. While similar formulations are found in gnostic texts we are not convinced that they necessarily had their origins there. The formula itself is already used in Judith 10:12 and has many points of contact with Joseph and Asenath 14 and other Jewish-Hellenistic literature.

[3] 1:2,8; 2:4,7; 5:1; 9:4-5; 10:1; 16:1.

εἰς ἀπολύτρωσιν τῶν ἐπὶ τῇ πρώτῃ διαθήκῃ παραβάσεων τὴν ἐπαγ-
γελίαν λάβωσιν οἱ κεκλημένοι τῆς αἰωνίου κληρονομίας. Interesting points of contact are found in GT 22:5: "If he is called (the Gnostic), he hears, replies and turns toward Him who calls him, in order to
reascend to Him. And he knows what he is called. Having the gnosis,
he performs the will of Him who called him. He desires to do that which
pleases Him, (and he) receives repose. (Each ?) one's name comes to him.
He who thus possesses the gnosis, knows whence he is come and where
he is going." The true gnostic is the one who responds to the one calling
him by doing His will. Such a person knows "whence he is come and
where he is going."

b) *The form of 2 Clem. 1:4-8*

Commencing with verse 4 (excepting the question in verse 5) we have
a "hymnic confession" in which the situation of the congregation
is described (ἀπολλυμένους) before God's action in Jesus Christ (ἡμᾶς
ἔσωσεν). This distinction between ἀπόλλυμι and σώζειν is firmly
rooted in New Testament Christianity (1 Cor. 1:18; 2 Cor. 2:15; 4:3ff;
John 3:16; 2 Pet. 3:9). Yet we note a difference between these assertions
and the ones in 2 Clement 1. In the New Testament there is always
an eschatological reference, and σώζεσθαι very often stands in an
eschatological future.[1] This is not the case in the confession of 2 Clement 1. Both times σώζειν appears, it appears in the aorist—ἔσωσεν—he
saved us! The action is past, not yet to come. As becomes clear from
other parts of 2 Clement, this action can only have occurred in baptism.
This is the reason for the exhortation to keep the "seal spotless"
(7:6; 8:6).

The question must be seriously entertained whether it is possible
that verses 4 through 8 represent not the theology of our author,
but the confession of his congregation. Initially this is suggested by
three factors: 1) This confession does not share the intense eschatological stress of 2 Clement. In fact, if we had only this confession to go
by, we would have to assert that salvation is a past event — it is all
over. This leads to point 2). In verses 4-8, σώζειν appears as an aorist,
with a definite past reference. This is not the case elsewhere, where

---

[1] Speaking of ἀπολλύμενοι and σωζόμενοι, Wilckens, *Weisheit und Torheit* (Tübingen,
1959), p. 22, states: "Es handelt sich um geprägte Termini der frühchristlichen Predigt
mit streng eschatologischem Sinn...."

there is a definite future implication: 8:2, ἵνα σωθῶμεν ὑπὸ τοῦ κυρίου; 13:1, μετανοήσαντες ἐκ ψυχῆς σωθῶμεν; 14:1, ἵνα σωθῶμεν; 15:1, ἑαυτὸν σώσει κἀμὲ τὸν συμβουλεύσαντα; 19:3, ἵνα εἰς τέλος σωθῶμεν. There is a distinct tension between the theological assertions in 2 Clement 1 and 2 and the remainder of the writing. 3) This tension is further exemplified in 2 Clem. 1:4 and 9:10. In 1:4 we read: ὡς πατὴρ υἱοὺς ἡμᾶς προσηγόρευσεν — he already has designated or called (aorist) us as sons; in 9:10, however, we hear: ἵνα ἡμᾶς προσδέξηται ὡς υἱούς. Here we find a subjunctive, stressing that we must repent and praise God so that he *may* accept us as sons. It appears likely that our author is taking over and reinterpreting the confession of his congregation. While he does not necessarily disagree with their assertions, he is definitely suggesting that there is vastly more involved in the Christian faith—the eschatological aspect which they have apparently neglected.

In discussing 2 Clement 1 we have often referred to verses 4-8 as a hymnic confession.[1] Is this correct? We must ask whether the verses contain either hymnic or confessional elements, or both, and if they do, whether we are really dealing with something "quoted" by our preacher. Generally speaking, the terms "confession" and "hymn" are not used very precisely in contemporary New Testament studies, and consequently not everyone means the same thing when they use these terms. In order to clarify our understanding of 2 Clement 1 as a hymnic confession, we will refer to the suggestive criteria employed by Gottfried Schille.[2]

Schille suggests that it is possible to speak accurately of a hymn only if the whole, or at least a large part of it, has been quoted. Hymns are quoted primarily either as a basis for exhortation (Phil. 2:5ff.) or for the purpose of interpretation (Heb. 1:3ff).[3] Only when one detects

---

[1] Reinhard Deichgräber's, *Gotteshymnus und Christushymnus in der frühen Christenheit* (Göttingen, 1967), also understands 2 Clement 1 to be a hymn. We know of no others who have asserted this. He also agrees that we are dealing here with a baptismal context: "Das Stück ist ganz geprägt von traditioneller Bekehrungsterminologie und mit Beziehungen auf die Taufe durchsetzt. Ich greife heraus: Die Aoriste weisen auf das Taufgeschehen; φῶς wird ebenso wie φωτίζειν und ähnliche Ausdrücke Taufterminologie sein" (p. 85). Beyond these brief suggestions, Deichgräber adds little further with reference to 2 Clement 1.

[2] Gottfried Schille, *Frühchristliche Hymnen* (Berlin, 1965).

[3] See especially G. Bornkamm's article "Das Bekenntnis im Hebräerbrief" in *Studien zu Antike und Urchristentum*, II (München, 1959), pp. 188-203.

such a relatively complete hymnic confession can one distinguish between the quotation and the theology of the one who quotes it.

We would suggest that the hymnic confession of 2 Clement 1 originally took the following form:

HYMNIC CONFESSION

δεῖ ἡμᾶς φρονεῖν περὶ 'Ιησοῦ Χριστοῦ, ὡς περὶ θεοῦ;

τὸ φῶς γὰρ ἡμῖν ἐχαρίσατο,
ὡς πατὴρ υἱοὺς ἡμᾶς προσηγόρευσεν,
ἀπολλυμένους ἡμᾶς ἔσωσεν.

πηροὶ ὄντες τῇ διανοίᾳ,
προσκυνοῦντες λίθους καὶ ξύλα καὶ χρυσὸν καὶ ἄργυρον καὶ χαλκόν,
    ἔργα ἀνθρώπων ·
καὶ ὁ βίος ἡμῶν ὅλος ἄλλο οὐδὲν ἦν εἰ μὴ θάνατος.
ἀμαύρωσιν οὖν περικείμενοι καὶ τοιαύτης ἀχλύος γέμοντες ἐν τῇ ὁράσει,
ἀνεβλέψαμεν ἀποθέμενοι ἐκεῖνο ὃ περικείμεθα νέφος τῇ αὐτοῦ θελήσει.

ἠλέησεν γὰρ ἡμᾶς καὶ σπλαγχνισθεὶς ἔσωσεν,
    θεασάμενος ἐν ἡμῖν πολλὴν πλάνην καὶ ἀπώλειαν,
    καὶ μηδεμίαν ἐλπίδα ἔχοντας σωτηρίας, εἰ μὴ τὴν παρ' αὐτοῦ.
ἐκάλεσεν γὰρ ἡμᾶς οὐκ ὄντας καὶ
ἠθέλησεν ἐκ μὴ ὄντος εἶναι ἡμᾶς.

> spacing   = descriptive "He" style
> underlined = participles

After evaluating many New Testament hymns, Schille indicates that often hymns which are quoted begin with a "Zitationspartikel" such as γάρ, δέ, ὅτι, and often end with a short summary of the whole hymn, sometimes introduced with ἄρα οὖν, μὴ οὖν τις. If we consider 2 Clem. 1:1, δεῖ ἡμᾶς φρονεῖν περὶ 'Ιησοῦ Χριστοῦ, as an introduction similar to Phil. 2:5, then the actual hymn begins with τὸ φῶς γὰρ ἡμῖν ἐχαρίσατο κτλ. Here we find, of course, the "Zitationspartikel" γάρ. A summary of the whole hymn is found in 2:7 beginning with οὕτως: οὕτως καὶ ὁ Χριστὸς ἠθέλησεν σῶσαι τὰ ἀπολλύμενα, καὶ ἔσωσεν πολλούς, ἐλθὼν καὶ καλέσας ἡμᾶς ἤδη ἀπολλυμένους.

Frequently, notes Schille, there is a difference in style between the hymn and the remainder of the letter (or in our case, discourse). In this regard, we should observe that our author does not use participles with a high degree of frequency, yet in 2 Clement 1 we find eleven participles employed within four verses—a phenomenon not found otherwise in 2 Clement. As is well known, the frequent use of participles is characteristic of the hymnic style.

Another indication of the presence of a quotation is that some elements are taken up and developed in the ensuing interpretation, while others are omitted. That a hymn is being quoted in 2 Clement which represents a theology other than that of our author seems to be suggested by the singular occurrence of such words as πηρός, νέφος, ἀμαύρωσις, ἀχλύς, ἀπώλεια, θέλησις (otherwise always θέλημα—5:1; 6:7; 8:4; 9:11; 10:1; 14:1).[1] There are certain themes and words that occur in the hymn, however, which are taken up and developed in the hortatory discourse: ἀπόλλυμι; σώζω; καλέω.

Schille also suggests that sometimes one can observe glosses in the hymn as well as, at times, a process of making it more precise. One very evident gloss in 2 Clement 1 is ὡς περὶ κριτοῦ ζώντων καὶ νεκρῶν following ὡς περὶ θεοῦ. The use of περί three times leads to a rather forced style: περὶ Ἰησοῦ Χριστοῦ ... περὶ θεοῦ ... περὶ κριτοῦ κτλ. In this gloss we note what was already observed above: the author of 2 Clement has a distinct eschatological purpose. This can also be noticed in his different understanding of σώζειν from the one found in the hymnic confession.

Let us briefly review some of Schille's more technical remarks concerning the characteristics of a hymn. He states: "Ist der Hymnus ein *Lied der Gemeinde,* so wird er den bekenntnisartigen Wir- oder den erzählend-preisenden Erstil tragen...."[2] 2 Clement 1 certainly makes use of the "we" style. But since this is used rather frequently, it hardly serves as a criterion. It is the descriptive "he" style which is significant and helps to determine the hymnic confessional character of 2 Clement 1: ἐχαρίσατο, προσηγόρευσεν, ἔσωσεν, ἠλέησεν, ἐκάλεσεν, ἠθέλησεν.

Schille's investigation suggests that since a hymn is a ὁμολογία of the congregation,[3] it can serve as a basis for ethical exhortation. Therefore, such a hymn is placed in a very prominent position, generally

---

[1] See pp. 182-91.

[2] Schille, *Hymnen,* p. 18.

[3] Schille defines this relationship between hymn and confession as follows: "Alle diese Züge erklären sich von daher, dass der Hymnus für die älteste Zeit Bekenntnis ist. 'Bekennen' meint zunächst den Lobpreis Gottes als öffentliches Eintreten für den Gepriesenen." *Ibid.,* p. 20.

at the beginning. Such is the case in Rom. 1:3ff.; Eph. 1:3ff.; Col. 1:12ff.; and Heb. 1:2ff. Both of these factors are present in 2 Clement 1: the hymnic confession is placed at the beginning and it serves as a basis for the ethical exhortation.

Another valuable aspect of Schille's work is that he attempts to subdivide the general category of "hymn" into specific types such as "Erlöserlieder," "Initiationslieder" and "Frühchristliche Epiphanie-Hymnen." Our hymnic confession in 2 Clement has its closest parallel to the "Erlöserlied" Gattung, which Schille defines as follows: "Erlöser-lieder nennen wir Hymnen, die die Taten des Erlösers im Blick auf deren Bedeutung für die Preisenden schildern."[1] This is indeed an accurate description of what we have before us in 2 Clement 1.

In addition to the general characteristics which relate it to the over-all category of "hymns," 2 Clement 1 also has some specific characteristics which made it akin to the "Erlöserlied" Gattung: 1) It is a report and confession of the action and work of the Saviour which is related in both the "he-style" characteristic of reporting the acts of someone else and the confessional "we-style." 2) A reduction to the bare essentials with its consequent short colas: τὸ φῶς γὰρ ἡμῖν ἐχαρίσατο. 3) The one whose acts are confessed is not mentioned at beginning or end; his work of salvation is described, but his name not uttered. The most probable reason for this is that the hymn is placed at a point in the liturgy where the reference to Jesus Christ is already evident. 4) An affirmative, predicate statement often stands at the opening of such a hymn. If our reconstruction of the hymn in 2 Clement along the lines of Phil. 2:5 is correct, then we have such an opening statement here too. 5) The main weight of the hymn is the conclusion, sometimes ending with a reference to the Old Testament prophecy. Both of these elements are present in 2 Clement 1. Clearly ἐκάλεσεν γὰρ ἡμᾶς οὐκ ὄντας καὶ ἠθέλησεν ἐκ μὴ ὄντος εἶναι ἡμᾶς is both a summary and a high point. Immediately following is an Old Testament quotation, although it is not likely to have been an original part of the hymn.

c) *Is. 54:1 and the* ποτὲ - νυνὶ δέ *schema*[2]

This quotation, cited exactly from the old Greek of Is. 54:1ff., is used in only two early Christian writings other than 2 Clement: Gal.

---

[1] *Ibid.*, p. 47.
[2] See also Excursus II.

4:27 and Justin, *Apol.* 53. For the moment we need spend very little time with Justin, since the basic context in which he cites Is. 54:1ff. is very different from that of 2 Clement. He is merely concerned with showing that Jesus really is "the first-born of the unbegotten God." In support of this he uses many arguments and cites certain Old Testament testimonies such as Isaiah 54.

What is the relationship, if any, between the use of Is. 54:1 in 2 Clement and Galatians 4? What is immediately striking is that the overall contexts of Galatians 3-6 and 2 Clement 1-9 are very similar. They are so alike that one receives the impression that the author of 2 Clement could have been, in fact, familiar with Galatians as well as the wider Pauline letter collection.[1]

It is indeed striking that the "hymnic confession" which precedes 2 Clement 2 has affinities with like confessional elements in Galatians 3. In 2 Clement 1 we read: "Our minds were impaired; we worshipped stone and wood and gold and silver and brass, the works of men...." But this situation is no longer true since Jesus Christ "has called us sons; he has rescued us when we were perishing .... For he called us when we were nothing, and willed our existence from nothing."

In a somewhat analogous manner Paul tells the Galatians (4:3): "When we were children, we were slaves to the elemental spirits of the universe;" and in 4:8, "Formerly, when you did not know God, you were in bondage to beings that by nature are no gods." But for Paul the Galatians are no longer children or slaves, because "God sent forth his Son...to redeem those who were under the law, so that we might receive adoption as sons." It would appear then that the basic structure which leads up to the use of Isaiah 54 is quite similar. Both Galatians 3-4 and 2 Clement 2 use what Dahl has called "das soteriologische Kontrast-Schema."[2] Both are dominated by the "then-now" (ποτὲ - νυνὶ δέ) theme, even though the "then" character of the Christians described in Galatians and in 2 Clement is different. In the Galatian heresy the Jewish element (the whole discussion of the law) is considerably more central than in 2 Clement.

This "then-now" pattern is also found in Eph. 2:11-22; 5:8; Gal. 4:8-10; Rom. 6:17-22; 7:5-6; 11:30; Col. 1:21-23; Eph. 2:1-10. We

---

[1] See pp. 93-96; 160-65.

[2] N. A. Dahl, "Formgeschichtliche Beobachtungen zur Christusverkündigung in der Gemeindepredigt," in *Neutestamentlichen Studien für Rudolf Bultmann* (Berlin, 1954), ed. W. Eltester, p. 5.

will briefly note two further examples. First, Tit. 3:3-7: Ἦμεν γάρ ποτε καὶ ἡμεῖς ἀνόητοι, ἀπειθεῖς ... ὅτε δὲ ἡ χρηστότης καὶ ἡ φιλανθρωπία ἐπεφάνη τοῦ σωτῆρος ἡμῶν θεοῦ ... κατὰ τὸ αὐτοῦ ἔλεος ἔσωσεν ἡμᾶς ... . In 1 Pet. 2:9b-10 we read: ... τοῦ ἐκ σκότους ὑμᾶς καλέσαντος εἰς τὸ θαυμαστὸν αὐτοῦ φῶς. οἵ ποτε οὐ λαὸς νῦν δὲ λαὸς θεοῦ .... This corresponds to the final summary in 2 Clement 1: ἐκάλεσεν γὰρ ἡμᾶς οὐκ ὄντας καὶ ἠθέλησεν ἐκ μὴ ὄντος εἶναι ἡμᾶς.

As the context of these texts (e.g., Gal. 3:27; Rom. 6), and sometimes the texts themselves (Tit. 3:5) indicate, the change from the situation of no faith to faith occurs in baptism. The purpose of this preaching pattern is to point out to the hearers the difference between their former existence and the blessings given to them in their new existence in Christ. Very often this ποτέ - νυνὶ δέ pattern serves as a basis for ethical exhortation. In Ephesians 2 and Col. 1:12ff. there is the exhortation to be thankful, in Galatians 4 and Colossians 2 to hold fast to the new way of life without falling back into the old (be it Jewish legalism or Gentile libertinism) and in 1 Peter 2, Tit. 3:3ff., Col. 3:3ff. we find the exhortation that the life of the Christian must be transformed in a manner worthy of the great gift he has received. In short, the Christian must bear new fruit worthy of his new existence. These same exhortations are found in 2 Clement. As we will attempt to show, 2 Clement 3-14 develops the ethical implications of the theological assertions made in 2 Clement 1-2 in a similar way.

d) *Summary*

To summarize, we assert that the author of 2 Clement has taken over a hymnic confession which is in use in his congregation. This confession serves as a basis for the hortatory address. As the discourse proceeds we observe that our author largely agrees with this confession yet finds it necessary to stress and make more precise certain theological points so as to prevent any possible misunderstanding. In all likelihood the *Sitz im Leben* of our confession is baptism. Most scholars[1] sug-

---

[1] For example, Bornkamm: "Der 'Sitz im Leben' ist für die Bekenntnisse vor allem Taufunterricht und Taufe, doch wird man daneben den Gottesdienst der Gemeinde im weiteren Sinn und die Notwendigkeit, das Evangelium gegen die Irrlehre abzugrenzen (I Joh 2,22; 4,2f) als Enstehungssituationen des Bekenntnisses, Exorzismus und - später - Martyrium als seine Bewährungssituationen ansehen müssen" (*RGG*[3], II, cols. 1002-3).

gest such a *Sitz im Leben* for the early Christian hymns, and the references to baptism in 2 Clement itself make this likely.

What kind of a congregation would utter such a confession? An examination of the text[1] reveals the decisive influence of Hellenistic Judaism and at certain points parallels appear with gnostic literature.[2] From these facts, as well as the whole environment of 2 Clement, which we have yet to explore, it would be best to suggest that we are here dealing with a Christianity heavily influenced by a speculative Hellenistic Judaism from which the later gnostic systems had fertile ground to spring.[3]

2. ETHICAL (3:1-14:5)

a) *The nature of paraenesis*

It is necessary that we make some preliminary remarks concerning the nature of paraenesis. "Paränese," holds Dibelius, "nennt man eine Aneinanderreihung verschiedener, häufig unzusammenhängender Mahnungen mit einheitlicher Adressierung."[4] While Dibelius' definition and treatment of this subject is in many ways pathbreaking,[5] it is essential to go beyond him in certain respects. Three questions must be raised: (1) do the paraenetic sections in the New Testament and in the Apostolic Fathers follow a given pattern? (2) can one define different types of paraenesis? (3) can one isolate certain paraenetic forms?

---

[1] See Excursus I.

[2] These parallels will become even more evident as we proceed, especially when we deal with 2 Clement 14.

[3] We would assert that this is true not only of chapter 1, but for the whole discourse. Our author finds himself in such an environment, takes up much of its theology, accepting, correcting and rejecting some of it.

[4] M. Dibelius, *Geschichte der urchristlichen Literatur*, II (Berlin, 1926), p. 65. For a summary of the older literature including Dibelius, see Victor Paul Furnish, *Paul's Exhortation in the Context of His Letters and Thought* (unpublished Ph. D. dissertation, Yale, 1960), pp. 6-72; see also Robert J. Karris, *The Function and Sitz im Leben of the Paraenetic Elements in the Pastoral Epistles* (unpublished Th.D. dissertation, Harvard, 1971).

[5] Especially his commentary, *Der Brief des Jakobus* (Göttingen, 1964) and his article "Zur Formgeschichte des Neuen Testaments (ausserhalb der Evangelien)," *ThRu NF3* (1931), pp. 207-42.

(1) In reference to the first question, Ferdinand Hahn[1] has suggested that there is a definite paraenetic pattern. a) The basic starting
point of Christian paraenesis is baptism; *because* of the experienced
salvation event of Jesus Christ, *therefore* certain behavior is expected.
b) The goal of Christian paraenesis is eschatological — be it the last
judgment or similar terminology. c) Between these two points, exhortations are given, the most important of which is the command to love
the brother.

(2) In group (c) just mentioned, it is further possible to distinguish
two specific types of paraenesis. For lack of better terms, perhaps we
can make a distinction between (*a*) contemporary paraenesis (*aktuell*)
and (*b*) traditional paraenesis (*usuell*). Contemporary paraenesis would
be exhortation on an *ad hoc* basis, using no, or only very few, traditional paraenetic elements since traditional elements cannot always
deal with certain new and unique situations (e.g., 1 Corinthians).

(3) Either of these types of paraenesis—contemporary or traditional
—can be expressed in the communicative plural ("we" form), in second
person direct address or in a more general way. Indeed, many of the
observations made previously with reference to ancient rhetoric are
relevant in this discussion.[2]

b) *2 Clement 3: obedience to the commands*

Chapter 3 commences with a brief summary of the confession found
in 2 Clement 1. This summary serves as a transition from the theological section (2 Clement 1-2) to the ethical section (2 Clement 3-14). It
asserts that because Jesus had mercy on the hearers they no longer
worship the dead gods and they now know (ἔγνωμεν) τὸν πατέρα τῆς
ἀληθείας.

A brief comment must be made in reference to the phrase "the
Father of Truth" which appears here and in 2 Clem. 20:5. These are
the only occurrences of the term in either the New Testament or the
Apostolic Fathers. However, it is well attested in the gnostic literature
of the second century. The term is used immediately at the outset in the
Gospel of Truth (1:1). The opening section of the Gospel of Truth

---

[1] *Göttinger Predigtmeditationen* 18 (1963-64), p. 378; see also Hahn's introduction to
the new edition of Alfred Seeberg, *Der Katechismus der Urchristenheit* (München, 1966),
especially p. xxviii.

[2] See pp. 25-36.

contains themes similar to the ones found in 2 Clement 3 and 10, although at a somewhat more developed stage: "The gospel of truth is joy to those who have received from the Father of truth the gift of knowing him by the power of the Logos, who has come from the pleroma [and] who is in the thought and mind of the Father; he it is who is called 'The Saviour,' since that is the name of the work which he must do for the redemption of those who have not known the Father."[1] The first half of this quotation expresses the same thought as 2 Clem. 3:1, except instead of "Christ" it reads "Logos"; the second half uses the identical term "Saviour" as in 2 Clem. 20:5, and the description of the function of the Saviour is common to both 2 Clement and the Gospel of Truth. The phrase "the Father of Truth" is also found in the *Hypostasis of the Archons*.[2] This secret gnostic book opens with the following words: "Upon the subject of the hypostasis of the powers in the Spirit of the Father of the Truth." The Ode of Solomon 41, entitled "Lobpreis für die Erlösung und Bekenntnis zu dem Erlöser" by Hennecke-Schneemelcher,[3] also contains this phrase (v.9). Finally, other references can be found in Heracleon's commentary on John, books 13 and 16.[4] Heracleon, a member of the Italian School of Valentinians, offers the following comment on Jn. 4:21: "So you, as the spirituals, will worship neither the creation nor the Demiurge, but the Father of Truth". The context of false worship is similar in both 2 Clement and Heracleon. In short, there can be little doubt that we are dealing with a well attested term and one found primarily in gnostic literature. This, too, may suggest that 2 Clement was written in an environment of incipient gnosticism. While taking over certain "gnosticizing" phraseology, our author is at the same time reinterpreting it.

The paraenetic section opens with a question: τίς ἡ γνῶσις ἡ πρὸς αὐτόν; The answer is given in a negative form: ἢ τὸ μὴ ἀρνρεῖσθαι δι' οὗ ἔγνωμεν αὐτόν. It is likely that the author of 2 Clement is combating a view which he believes to be in error. Perhaps it was a kind of theology which held that Jesus indeed brought gnosis about the Father, but now that they have received it the gnosis-bringer is irrel-

---

[1] Translation by Isenberg.

[2] See Jean Doresse, *The Secret Books of the Egyptian Gnostics* (New York, 1960), p. 159.

[3] Hennecke-Schneemelcher, *Neutestamentliche Apokryphen* II (Tübingen, 1964), pp. 621ff.

[4] W. Völker, *Quellen zur Geschichte der christlichen Gnosis* (Tübingen, 1932), p. 74.

evant. The historical person of Jesus and the obligation demanded
by him are not considered primary. Therefore, our author is stressing
that gnosis, in fact, includes at its very center "refusing to deny him
through whom we have come to know the Father." This view is
then supported with a Jesus logion: "He who acknowledges me before
men, I will acknowledge before my Father." Here, and in the two verses
which follow, our author is again making an eschatological correction.
οὗτος (viz. ὁμολογήσω αὐτὸν ἐνώπιον τοῦ πατρός μου) οὖν ἐστὶν ὁ
μισθὸς ἡμῶν. But this will only be a reward "if we acknowledge
him through whom we were saved (ἐσώθημεν)." He takes up the
aorist of σώζω as found in the confession and modifies it. He uses
the current language, but adds that we will only receive our reward
(μισθός always used in an eschatological sense by 2 Clement: 9:5;
11:5; 15:1; 19:1; 20:4) if we acknowledge the gnosis-bringer. This
conditional sentence is then followed by a specific exhortation in the
communicative plural, making use of positive and negative infinitives.
The specific exhortation is that we shall do what he says and not disregard his commands (μὴ παρακούειν αὐτοῦ τῶν ἐντολῶν).

This matter of keeping the commands of the Lord is an important
theme throughout 2 Clement (4:5; 6:7; 8:4; 17:1, 3, 6). The manner
in which this is stressed by the writer gives us some insight into the
position of those with whom he disagrees. These persons may in many
respects be similar to the "opponents" of Matthew and the Johannine
epistles. In Mt. 5:19, 19:17 and 28:20 we observe Matthew arguing
against Hellenistic antinomianists,[1] particularly stressing that the
commands must be kept. In 1 Jn. 2:3 we are brought yet a step closer
to 2 Clement. It is here that we can see with even greater clarity the
type of opponent 2 Clement has in mind. In verses 3 and 4 we read:
Καὶ ἐν τούτῳ γινώσκομεν ὅτι ἐγνώκαμεν αὐτόν, ἐὰν τὰς ἐντολὰς
αὐτοῦ τηρῶμεν. ὁ λέγων ὅτι Ἔγνωκα αὐτόν, καὶ τὰς ἐντολὰς αὐτοῦ
μὴ τηρῶν, ψεύστης ἐστίν, καὶ ἐν τούτῳ ἡ ἀλήθεια οὐκ ἔστιν.

Both 1 John and 2 Clem. 3:1ff. argue that he who truly knows God
is the one who keeps the commands. This is the true criterion. It is this
stress which is basic to the theology of both 1 John and 2 Clement

---

[1] For a cogent exegetical support for this understanding of Matthew see especially
G. Bornkamm's "Der Auferstandene und der Irdische" in *Zeit und Geschichte* edited
by Erich Dinkler (Tübingen, 1964), pp. 171ff. and especially p. 180 [ET: *The Future
of Our Religious Past*, ed. by James M. Robinson (New York, 1971), pp. 203-29].

as they combat a gnosticizing misinterpretation of Jesus. It is against
such a background that one must understand the ethical thrust of
2 Clement. That such false teachers were a real threat to early Christianity is abundantly clear from 2 John 6-11.

c) *2 Clement 4: acknowledgement by action*

The theme is stated in verse 1 in the form of a negative exhortation
using the subjunctive in the communicative plural. Simply calling
Jesus κύριος, it is suggested, is not sufficient for salvation. The distinctive theology of 2 Clement is apparent by the use of the future form
of the verb σώζειν: οὐ γὰρ τοῦτο (superficial acknowledgement)
σώσει ἡμᾶς. Rather, it is the doing of righteousness which is demanded.
The continuity with 2 Clement 3 is obvious and the similarity to
Mt. 7:15ff. is striking. While noting the overall similarity of context,
we are not, however suggesting a dependence on Matthew.[1] This
opening theme is then continued and supported by a quotation from
"the Lord" himself. It may be important for the total understanding
of our author's theology that in this quotation we find the verb σωθήσ-
εται, which appears neither in Matthew or Luke, and which may be
a reflection of his own theology.

The paraenesis begins with a communicative plural in verse 3. Here
the specific works, standing under the general command of love,
are listed. We find two descriptive catalogues, first listing the works to
be avoided, ἐν τῷ μὴ μοιχᾶσθαι μηδὲ καταλαλεῖν ἀλλήλων μηδὲ
ζηλοῦν, and then the works which are to be performed, ἐγκρατεῖς,
ἐλεήμονας, ἀγαθούς. Each member of these catalogues is related to
the corresponding one. This is concluded with a similar antithetical
summary: καὶ συμπάσχειν ἀλλήλοις ὀφείλομεν, καὶ μὴ φιλαργυρεῖν.

To determine with precision where our writer derived his list of
vices — μοιχάω, καταλαλέω and ζηλόω—is impossible. These terms are
common in Hellenistic Judaism (especially the Wisdom tradition) and
early Christianity. These phrases are "in the air." This being said, however, an interesting relationship exists between these terms in 2 Clement and other contemporary literature. The catalogues in Gal. 5:19ff.
also stand under the same command of love: v. 14, ἀλλὰ διὰ τῆς
ἀγάπης δουλεύετε ἀλλήλοις. In terms of content, all three vices listed
in 2 Clement 4 also appear, along with others, *twice* in the Greek (3)

---

[1] See p. 79.

Baruch Apocalypse 8:15; 13:4, a writing of the early second century. Other literature which reveals a similar thought-world includes some of the later New Testament writings and some of the Apostolic Fathers: Jas. 2:11; 3:14, 16; 4:2, 11; 1 Pet. 2:12; 1 Clem. 30; Did. 2:2; Barn. 19:4. But no dependence can be asserted on the part of the author of 2 Clement. He shared in a common tradition which, as we can see from a comparison of Barnabas 20 with Didache 5, was flexible and expanding. We are here dealing with a good example of traditional paraenesis.

As we turn our attention to the corresponding catalogue of virtues — ἐγκρατής, ἐλεήμων, and ἀγαθός — we immediately note that ἐγκρατής stands in the first position. That this is an important concept for 2 Clement is evident not only from the lead position given to ἐγκρατής in this catalogue, but also in the fact that the noun ἐγκράτεια is used as a summary for the first fourteen chapters. In 15:1 we read: Οὐκ οἴομαι δέ, ὅτι μικρὰν συμβουλίαν ἐποιησάμην περὶ ἐγκρατείας, ἥν ποιήσας τις οὐ μετανοήσει, ἀλλὰ καὶ ἑαυτὸν σώσει κἀμὲ τὸν συμβουλεύσαντα. This world and the world to come (chapters 4 and 6) represent two different ways of life. To participate in the heavenly church (ch. 14), the coming church, one must practice ἐγκράτεια. The advice which our author presents concerning ἐγκράτεια is remarkably close to that of Philo, Spec Leg IV 112:

> These two kinds of fish are symbolical, the first of a pleasure-loving soul, the latter of one to which endurance and self-control (ἐγκράτειαν) are dear. For the road that leads to pleasure is downhill and very easy, with the result that one does not walk but is dragged along; the other which leads to self-control is uphill, toilsome no doubt but profitable exceedingly. The one carries us away, forced lower and lower as it drives us down its steep incline, till it flings us off on to the level ground at its foot; the other leads heavenwards the immortal who have not fainted [comp. 2 Clem. 2:2] on the way and have had the strength to endure the roughness of the hard ascent.

ἐγκράτεια/ἐγκρατής in 2 Clement refers to a self-control with regard to sexual matters. This is evident from the corresponding term in the catalogue of vices, ἐν τῷ μὴ μοιχᾶσθαι, as well as several other exhortations not to abuse the flesh, such as in 5:5, with its derogatory reference to the world of flesh; 8:4 and 6, τηρήσατε τὴν σάρκα ἁγνήν; the great stress on not considering the flesh as a matter of little importance in chapter 9; 12:5-6, "Furthermore, 'the male with the female, neither male nor female,' means this: that when a brother sees a sister he shall not think of her sex, any more than she should think of his"; and the whole discussion of the flesh in 14:3-4, with the specific warning τηρήσατε τὴν σάρκα, ἵνα τοῦ πνεύματος μεταλάβητε.

ἐγκράτεια is a well known term in the classical tradition from Socrates on through the Hellenistic period. It was also an important virtue for the Stoics, for Plutarch (*Amat.* 767ff.), and appears frequently in Philo.[1] However, in Philo a shift in emphasis occurs, a shift also reflected in 2 Clement. "Die asketische Haltung des Philo," says Grundmann, "entspringt einem kosmologischen Dualismus, in dem die Materie abgewertet wird. Die ἐγκράτεια zielt auf Ausschaltung jeglichen leiblichen Bedürfnisse, die nicht zur Existenz notwendig sind. Es ist also gegenüber der griechischen philosophischen Ethik eine Verschiebung des Akzentes eingetreten."[2] The confirmation of this statement, as well as the proximity between Philo and 2 Clement, can be observed in the quotation previously cited from Philo.[3]

In the old Greek the term first appears in the Wisdom tradition — for example, in Sir. 18:30 and Wis. 8:21. In the New Testament its appearance is very infrequent.[4] In Gal. 5:23 it appears in the final position in a catalogue of virtues. This whole context, which is attempting to combat libertinism and the misuse of freedom, is akin to 2 Clement. In 1 Cor. 7:9, where the verbal form appears, Paul uses it in a sexual context (εἰ δὲ οὐκ ἐγκρατεύονται γαμησάτωσαν, κρεῖττον γάρ ἐστιν γαμῆσαι ἢ πυροῦσθαι) as does 2 Clement.

In 2 Pet. 1:5-6 ἐγκράτεια occurs in the following context: καὶ αὐτὸ τοῦτο δὲ σπουδὴν πᾶσαν παρεισενέγκαντες ἐπιχορηγήσατε ἐν τῇ πίστει ὑμῶν τὴν ἀρετήν, ἐν δὲ τῇ ἀρετῇ τὴν γνῶσιν, ἐν δὲ τῇ γνώσει τὴν ἐγκράτειαν, ἐν δὲ τῇ ἐγκρατείᾳ τὴν ὑπομονήν .... There is a striking proximity in language between these verses and 2 Clement: not only do they share the term ἐγκράτεια, but also ἀρετή (2 Clem. 10:1), γνῶσις (2 Clem. 3:1), εὐσέβεια (2 Clem. 19:1) and ἀγάπη

---

[1] Spec Leg I 149; IV 112; Leg All III 18; Quod Omn; Virt 182.

[2] Grundmann, *TWNT*, II, p. 339. On the basis of this terminology Rendell Harris argued that the encratite Julius Cassianus was the author of 2 Clement, "The Authorship of the So-called Second Epistle of Clement," *ZNW* 23 (1924), pp. 193-200. This position was effectively refuted by Hans Windisch, "Julius Cassianus und die Clemenshomilie," *ZNW* 25 (1926) pp. 258-62. One observation made by Windisch is worth noting at this point: "Anderseits ist unser II Clemens doch nicht eigentlich ein Traktat περὶ ἐγκρατείας. Die Enthaltsamkeit, in geschlechtlichem wie in weiterem Sinne, wird zwar stark betont, aber im ganzen ist die Homilie doch nicht eigentlich ein Traktat περὶ ἐγκρατείας, eher eine Homilie περὶ μετανοίας" (pp. 259-60).

[3] p. 115.

[4] Among the Apostolic Fathers both 1 Clement and Hermas use ἐγκράτεια and derivatives frequently: 1 Clem. 30:3; 35:2; 38:2; 62:2; 64:1; Hermas Vis. 2:9; 3:8; Mand. 1, 6, 8; Sim. 5:1; 9:15.

(2 Clem. 12:1; 15:2; 16:4). Both writers draw upon the same Hellenistic background and seem to be dealing with related problems. 2 Pet. 1:3ff. shares many similar thoughts with 2 Clem. 1:4ff. and both are equally concerned with correcting eschatological misconceptions. They both warn false teachers, although in 2 Clement this stands more at the periphery (10:5), while in 2 Peter it plays a far more significant role (2:1ff.).[1]

The paraenesis in chapter 4 is concluded with a supportive quotation. This quotation was obviously selected with care, and one should, therefore, keep in mind the stress on "doing the law" and the rebuke which the ἐργάται ἀνομίας receive. This fits in well with the theological intention of 2 Clement.

It was previously suggested[2] that Christian paraenesis contains at least three elements: a) baptism as the starting point; b) eschatology as the goal; and c) exhortations dealing with love for the brother lying between these two points. These three elements can be found in 2 Clement 4: a) the catalogue of vices draws the line by indicating what kind of behavior is not acceptable to the new life in Christ; b) the catalogue of virtues describes the kind of behavior expected if one is to

---

[1] The final two terms used in the catalogue of virtues, are ἐλεήμων (compassionate, merciful) and ἀγαθός (kind). ἐλεήμων appears only in Mt. 5:7 and Heb. 2:17 in the New Testament. In the Apostolic Fathers it appears in 1 Clem. 60, P. Phil. 6:1 and with ἀγαθός in Did. 3:8. Perhaps 2 Clement is here using cathechetical material based on the Sermon on the Mount which is also common to the Didache. More probable, however, particularly in light of the strong Hellenistic and Jewish-Hellenistic influence already observed in 2 Clement, is that 2 Clement took over this term from such a Jewish-Hellenistic tradition. The Stoics used it as well as the LXX (eg. Prov. 11:17), Epictetus II.21. 3,5,6; Corp. Herm. 1:22; Jos. Ant. 10:41; Test. Sim. 4:4 as well as numerous times in Philo (eg. Somn I 94). ἀγαθός is a term so widely used in the tradition of the early church that it is impossible to define it any further. The concluding exhortation in the communicative plural is συμπάσχειν (in the sense of "to have sympathy with") and μὴ φιλαργυρεῖν. This last theme recurs in the catalogue found in 2 Clem. 6:4 with the use of the term φιλαργυρία. The theme is also found in 2 Clem. 20:4, but neither of these two terms is used. In the New Testament φιλαργυρέω (φιλαργυρία, φιλάργυρος) is found only in Lk. 16:14, 1 Tim. 6:10 and 2 Tim. 3:2 (cf. also Heb. 13:5 and 1 Tim. 3:3). Among the Apostolic Fathers it is a common term in Polycarp's Epistle to the Philippians (2:2; 4:1,3; 6:1). The background of this terminology is definitely from Hellenistic and Jewish Hellenistic circles. It is used in 2 Maccabees, 4 Maccabees, Test. Levi. 17:11, Philo; in the Greek and Hellenistic tradition it is found in Diogenes Laertius VI 50; Epicurus; Bion the Borysthenite (in Stobaeus, Eclog III. 417.5H); Epictetus II. 9, 12, 16, 45; Seneca de. Clem. 2:1; and Pseudo-Phocylides 42.

[2] See pp. 110-11.

receive the eternal reward. This is also strengthened by the eschatological quotation; c) by putting into practice these virtues one does
not only secure his future reward, but he concretely manifests his
concern and love for the brother. As we have tried to show, our author
has taken over many of these traditional paraenetic elements from the
sphere of Jewish-Hellenistic and Hellenistic ethics. Yet even though
Stoic preachers and 2 Clement could use similar terms, we must not
overlook the fact that the Christian preacher was always speaking to
a community while the "Wanderprediger" was not. This is certainly
one reason why 2 Clement makes such frequent use of the communicative plural.

d) 2 Clement 5: the Christian as sojourner

Chapter 5 serves as both a summary and conclusion to chapters
3 and 4. Yet it also sharpens what was previously stated. κατα-
λείψαντες τὴν παροικίαν τοῦ κόσμου τούτου κ.τ.λ. is best translated
with Lightfoot as follows: "let us forsake our sojourn in this world and
do the will of Him that called us, and let us not be afraid to depart out
of this world."[1] Knopf has suggested that we are here dealing with an
exhortation to martyrdom.[2] This is unlikely; ἐξελθεῖν ἐκ τοῦ
κόσμου need not suggest martyrdom,[3] but rather refers to the dualism
between this world and the next. Only the one who is obedient here
shall receive the future rewards. This is exactly what the last part of
the quotation teaches: ἀλλὰ φοβεῖσθε τὸν μετὰ τὸ ἀποθανεῖν ὑμᾶς
ἔχοντα ἐξουσίαν ψυχῆς καὶ σώματος τοῦ βαλεῖν εἰς γέενναν πυρός.
This is the reason why οὐ δεῖ ἡμᾶς φοβεῖσθαι τοὺς ἀνθρώπους μᾶλλον,
ἀλλὰ τὸν θεόν (4:4). That verses 5:1-5 are simply indicating the opposition between two ways of life is supported in the paraenetic section.
In verses 6 and 7 we read: "What, then, must we do to get these things,
except to lead a holy and upright life and to regard these things of
the world as alien to us and not to desire them? For in wanting to
obtain these things we fall from the right way." This is not the kind

---

[1] Lightfoot, Apostolic Fathers, p. 308.

[2] R. Knopf, Die zwei Clemensbriefe (Tübingen, 1920), pp. 159ff: "Hier ist es, wie
schon 4:4 leise angedeutet hatte, das Martyrium, was deutlich gefordert wird, obwohl
die Weisung, aus der Welt zu gehen, keineswegs nur auf das Martyrium beschränkt wird,
vgl. 5:6, 6:1ff. Die Aufmunterung zum Martyrium kann mit veranlasst sein durch die
Polemik gegen die Gnosis, die an verschiedenen Stellen der Predigt deutlich ist."
However, one would expect a polemic to be less veiled and more explicit.

[3] This is also confirmed by the usage of this phrase in 8:3.

of exhortation one expects in connection with martyrdom. The point is that the one who does God's will receives "rest" and "eternal life" and will not "be cast into the flames of hell." There is little in this chapter to suggest the context of martyrdom.

Some of the terms or phrases used to describe "this world" in 2 Clement include παροικία, in the sense of a sojourn in a strange place or foreign country: ἡ ἐπιδημία ἡ ἐν τῷ κόσμῳ τούτῳ τῆς σαρκός and τὰ κοσμικὰ ταῦτα ὡς ἀλλότρια ἡγεῖσθαι. These terms all stem from a dualism prevalent in Hellenism and gnosticism. πάροικος, παροικία and παροικεῖν are used frequently in the LXX, primarily meaning a sojourn in one geographical location or another. In Philo, and likewise in 2 Clement, we note a basic shift in meaning. παροικία no longer refers to any one given geographical location as opposed to another; it now refers to "the physical world" *per se*. There is a clear dualism between this world and the next. Thus, the sojourner who dwells on this earth should really be thinking of and striving for his heavenly home. This thought is often expressed by Philo,[1] especially in Conf 77-80. This passage not only shares similar terminology with 2 Clement, but also at many points has similarities with its theology:

> This is why all whom Moses calls wise are represented as sojourners (παροικοῦντες). Their souls are never colonists leaving heaven for a new home. Their way is to visit earthly nature as men who travel abroad to see and learn. So when they have stayed awhile in their bodies, and beheld through them all that sense and mortality has to shew, they make their way back to the place from which they set out at the first. To them the heavenly region, where their citizenship lies, is their native land; the earthly region in which they became sojourners is a foreign country. For surely, when men found a colony, the land which receives them becomes their native land instead of the mother city, but to the traveller abroad the land which sent him forth is still the mother to whom also he yearns to return.... And just as natural are the words of the Practiser Jacob, when he laments his sojourn (παροικίαν) in the body."

In the same way the writer of 2 Clement can exhort his readers "not to be afraid to leave this world," or, "our stay in this world of flesh is slight and short," because one finds "rest in the coming Kingdom and in eternal life."

As used by Philo and 2 Clement, παροικία has the meaning of non-citizenship; the Christians are sojourners, and not citizens on

---

[1] Cher 120; Ebr. 121; Mut 209. See also Diognetus 5-6.

this earth. They dwell here as aliens, ξένοι, παρεπίδημοι, πάροικοι — a conception also found in 1 Peter (1:17; 2:11) and Hebrews (11:13).[1] Since 2 Clement shares this conception we can understand why it asserts that ἡ ἐπιδημία ἡ ἐν τῷ κόσμῳ τούτῳ τῆς σαρκὸς ταύτης μικρά ἐστιν καὶ ὀλιγοχρόνιος and why it advises τὰ κοσμικὰ ταῦτα ὡς ἀλλότρια ἡγεῖσθαι.

The gifts of ὁ μέλλων αἰών (6:3) are ἀνάπαυσις and ζωῆς αἰωνίου. 2 Clement tells its hearers how to obtain this: ποιήσομεν τὸ θέλημα τοῦ καλέσαντος ἡμᾶς. This means nothing εἰ μὴ τὸ ὁσίως καὶ δικαίως ἀναστρέφεσθαι. If we do not do this, but desire this world we hear that ἀποπίπτομεν τῆς ὁδοῦ τῆς δικαίας. These thoughts have familiar echoes in the Gospel of Truth and Hebrews: GT 22:9ff. reads, "Since he has knowledge, he does the will of him who called him (cf. 2 Clem. 3:1,2). He desires to please him and he finds rest (ἀνάπαυσις)."[2] In Hebrews there is a clear connection between disobedience and failing to enter into the "rest." In 3:12ff. we read: "Take care, brethren, lest there be in any of you an evil, unbelieving heart, leading you to fall away from the living God ... And to whom did he swear that they should never enter his rest, but to those who were disobedient? So we see that they were unable to enter because of unbelief."

ἐπαγγελία is an important concept in 2 Clement and first appears here in chapter 5. The promise of Christ is described as great and marvellous. The content of the promise is "rest in the coming Kingdom and in eternal life." In 10:3 ἐνθάδε ἀπόλαυσις contrasted is with μέλλουσα ἐπαγγελία and in 10:4 we have the same contrast. In 11:1 we read: "Let us therefore serve God with a pure heart and we shall be upright. But if, by not believing God's promises (ἐπαγγελία), we do not serve him, we shall be wretched." This contrasted is with the opposite behavior in verse 7: "If, then, we have done what is right in God's eyes, we shall enter his Kingdom and receive the promises...." In chapter 11, the content of the promise is not discussed. However, there can be no doubt from chapter 5 and 6:7 (ποιοῦντες γὰρ τὸ θέλημα τοῦ Χριστοῦ εὑρήσομεν ἀνάπαυσιν) that the specific content of this promise is ἀνάπαυσις in the future kingdom. Before we discuss

---

[1] Also important in this connection is Parable 1 of the Shepherd of Hermas, especially v. 7.

[2] Translation by Isenberg.

the meaning of ἀνάπαυσις we must first add some further remarks on the meaning of ἐπαγγελία in 2 Clement.

From the above observations it is apparent that for 2 Clement ἐπαγγελία has a purely eschatological significance; it will be fulfilled in the coming age. The content of the promise is rest in the Kingdom. Moreover, it is only because God has revealed himself in Christ and given man knowledge of Himself, that one is able to pursue this goal. Indeed, this whole conception of ἐπαγγελία, and particularly its relation to the term "rest," finds a close parallel in Hebrews.[1]

2 Clement specifically states that "Christ's promise ... means rest (ἀνάπαυσις) in the coming Kingdom and in eternal life." What is the context of this term "rest" as used in 2 Clement? That the Old Testament cannot serve as a precise background has been demonstrated by Gerhard von Rad.[2] In the Old Testament the concept of "rest" has a "this worldly" reference—such as rest from the attacks of the enemy. An illustration of this would be Josh. 21:43-44. In comparing the conception of "rest" found in Hebrews with that of the Old Testament, von Rad concludes: "Allerdings ganz neu ist das Verständnis der Ruhe als eines jenseitigen Heilsgutes, dessen die Gläubigen erst nach diesem Leben teilhaftig werden dürfen."[3] While von Rad mentions the fact that Hebrews combines the Sabbath-rest speculation of Gen. 1-2:4a with that of κατάπαυσις as an eschatological location toward which the people of God are moving, it was really Käsemann in his suggestive little volume, Das wandernde Gottesvolk, who moved the investigation of the κατάπαυσις speculation in Hebrews a step further. Especially helpful is Käsemann's definition of the term κατάπαυσις as it is used in Hebrews. "Es sollte eigentlich klar sein, dass sie ein rein himmlisches Gut ist ... Die 'Ruhe' ist schlechterdings eine rein lokale Grösse, eine himmlische Ortsbezeichnung ... so ist die göttliche Ruhe nichts anderes als der himmlische κόσμος selbst."[4]

If the Old Testament does not offer a satisfactory explanation for this κατάπαυσις/ἀνάπαυσις speculation, does Philo? While Philo

---

[1] See Ernst Käsemann, Das wandernde Gottesvolk (Göttingen, 1961), pp. 11-19. For a critique of Käsemann, see Ottfried Hofius, Katapausis: Die Vorstellung vom endzeitlichen Ruheort im Hebräerbrief (Tübingen, 1970).

[2] G. von Rad, "Es ist noch eine Ruhe vorhanden dem Volk Gottes" in Gesammelte Studien zum Alten Testament (München, 1961), pp. 101-108.

[3] Ibid., p. 106.

[4] Käsemann, Das wandernde Gottesvolk, p. 41.

uses both terms frequently,[1] and even at points combines κατάπαυσις with σαββατισμός[2] as in Hebrews, he does not share the same developed understanding of κατάπαυσις / ἀνάπαυσις as a heavenly locality. This same observation holds true for the Wisdom literature.[3]

Important for our consideration is the way in which the Jewish-Hellenistic writing known as Joseph and Asenath uses the term κατάπαυσις/ἀνάπαυσις.[4] Joseph's prayer on behalf of Asenath in chapter 8 not only uses the term under consideration, but also reveals some striking similarities to the thought of 2 Clement.[5] This prayer describes God in a way analogous[6] to 2 Clement, and both writings closely relate the concepts of "rest" and "eternal life" to one another. In each case these terms represent future promises to be fulfilled in the heavens. This is evident from chapter 15 where, speaking of Asenath we hear: καὶ [πάντας τοὺς μετανοοῦντας] τόπον ἀναπαύσεως παρέξαι ἐν τοῖς οὐρανοῖς.[7]

Kilpatrick[8] and J. Jeremias[9] both suggest that Joseph and Asen-

---

1 For example, Fuga 174; Somn I 174; Post 24; Leg All III 77; Cher 87; Congr. 45-48.

2 For example, in Quod Deus 12 and Abr 28-30.

3 The term "rest" appears frequently in the Wisdom tradition—Wis. 4:7; Sir. 6:28; 11:19; 20:21; 22:13; 24:7; 28:16; 30:17 and elsewhere. The one reference which might be of interest, Sir. 30:17 (ἀνάπαυσις αἰῶνος), is textually uncertain and is omitted in manuscripts B, S. and A.

4 I hold Joseph und Asenath to be a pre-Christian writing, stemming from speculative Jewish-Hellenistic circles. See the recent studies by C. Burchard, *Untersuchungen zu Joseph und Aseneth* (Tübingen, 1965) and Marc Philonenko, *Joseph et Aséneth* (Leiden, 1968).

5 Κύριε ὁ θεὸς τοῦ πατρός μου ᾿Ισραήλ, ὁ ὕψιστος καὶ δυνατὸς θεός, ὁ ζωοποιήσας τὰ πάντα καὶ καλέσας ἀπὸ τοῦ σκότους εἰς τὸ φῶς, καὶ ἀπὸ τῆς πλάνης εἰς τὴν ἀλήθειαν, καὶ ἀπὸ τοῦ θανάτου εἰς τὴν ζωήν, σὺ καὶ τὴν παρθένον ταύτην εὐλόγησον, καὶ ζωοποίησον καὶ ἀνακαίνισον αὐτὴν τῷ πνεύματί σου τῷ ἁγίῳ, καὶ φαγέτω ἄρτον ζωῆς σου καὶ πιέτω ποτήριον εὐλογίας σου, καὶ συγκαταρίθμησον αὐτὴν τῷ λαῷ σου ὃν ἐξέλεξας πρὶν γενέσθαι τὰ πάντα, καὶ εἰσελθέτω εἰς τὴν κατάπαυσίν σου ἣν ἡτοίμασας τοῖς ἐκλεκτοῖς σου, καὶ ζησάτω ἐν τῇ αἰωνίᾳ σου ζωῇ εἰς τὸν αἰῶνα χρόνον (Battifol; see p. 189, n.1).

6 God "calls from the darkness to the light and from error to truth and from death to life."

7 Significant for an understanding of 2 Clement are the words of Asenath to the angel a little further on in this chapter: ᾿Ευλογητὸς κύριος ὁ θεός σου, ὁ ἐξαποστείλας σε τοῦ ῥύσασθαι με ἐκ τοῦ σκότους (Battifol). Compare, for example, 2 Clem. 20:5.

8 G. D. Kilpatrick, "The Last Supper," *ExpT* 64 (1952), pp. 4-8.

9 J. Jeremias, "The Last Supper," *ExpT* 64 (1952), pp. 91-92.

ath was written in the first century B.C. K. G. Kuhn[1] suggests a date not later than the first century A.D. Burchard in his recent study comes to the following conclusion: "JA wird also, grob gesprochen, irgendwann zwischen 100 v. Chr. und 100 n. Chr. entstanden sein."[2] If this suggested time-span is correct, we have another example of the influence of Hellenistic Judaism on the theology of 2 Clement.[3]

We need not dwell long on the importance of ἀνάπαυσις in gnosticism, since this has been carefully analysed by Philip Vielhauer in his article, "*ΑΝΑΠΑΥΣΙΣ*: Zum gnostischen Hintergrund des Thomasevangelium."[4] On the basis of Clement of Alexandria, *Paed.* 1.29, the Ode of Solomon 26:12 and other texts, Vielhauer makes this assertion: "Gnosis auf Grund von Offenbarung ist Voraussetzung und Anfang der 'Ruhe'; die 'Ruhe' wird verstanden als verbürgtes Ende und letztes Ziel der Gnosis."[5] In 2 Clement there is also a connection between "knowledge" and "rest." In chapter 3 we are told that it is Christ who has brought the γνῶσις concerning the Father. In fact it was the Father who sent him "to manifest the truth and the heavenly life" (20:5). Therefore, γινώσκετε, ἀδελφοί … ἡ δὲ ἐπαγγελία τοῦ Χριστοῦ μεγάλη καὶ θαυμαστή ἐστιν, καὶ ἀνάπαυσις τῆς μελλούσης βασιλείας καὶ ζωῆς αἰωνίου.

Vielhauer observes that very often ἀνάπαυσις is an eschatological gift involving a specific locality, viz., the divine sphere. Such is the case in the Acts of John 99, Acts of Philip 148 and especially in GT 22:10; 36:38; 40:33; 41:13, 29; 43:1 and the Gospel of Thomas 60. Of all these texts, the closest to 2 Clement is the Gospel of Truth. In this early Valentinian writing, much of the later speculation concerning the heavenly world is absent. In GT 40:30ff. one finds summarized in one sentence thoughts expressed at a variety of places in 2

---

[1] K. G. Kuhn, "The Lord's Supper and the Communal Meal at Qumran" in K. Stendahl, ed., *The Scrolls and the New Testament* (London, 1958), pp. 65-93.

[2] Burchard, *Joseph und Aseneth*, p. 146.

[3] While we would approach the problems concerning Joseph and Asenath in a different way than Burchard, we fully agree with his final observation (p. 152): "Die Beschäftigung des Neutestamentlers mit JA läuft so grundsätzlich darauf hinaus, einen Gesichtspunkt zu unterstreichen, den die Forschung der letzten Jahre überhaupt stärker zu beachten angefangen hat: die Bedeutung der hellenistisch-jüdischen Voraussetzungen des NT. JA ist ein Zeugnis eines hellenistisch-jüdischen Denkens und Redens, das das werdende Christentum tiefer geprägt hat, als man es oft sieht."

[4] Phillipp Vielhauer, *Aufsätze zum Neuen Testament* (München, 1965), pp. 215-34.

[5] *Ibid.*, p. 216.

Clement: "For that reason, also, He sent Him in order that He (might) speak about the Place (τόπος), and about His place of rest from which He had come forth...."

Our discussion of the concept of "rest" leads to this conclusion: that 2 Clement stands in a stage of development between a speculative Hellenistic Judaism (especially Joseph and Asenath) and the Gospel of Truth and later gnosticism. While in many ways 2 Clement stands close to the Gospel of Truth, it must be acknowledged that the Gospel of Truth belongs at a point further along the gnostic trajectory.

e) 2 Clement 6: keeping baptism pure and undefiled

Man cannot serve two masters: ἔστιν δὲ οὗτος ὁ αἰὼν καὶ ὁ μέλλων δύο ἐχθροί. This assertion brings to mind such New Testament references as Col. 1:4; 2 Cor. 4:4; Jas. 4:4; 1 Jn. 2:15ff. and others. Even a passage such as 1 Jn. 2:15ff., which is perhaps closest to 2 Clement at this point, does not express the same radical cosmological and ethical dualism which is present in 2 Clement. Here in 2 Clement the two aeons are "enemies" — opposed to one another in the sharpest possible sense. "This world" is filled with μοιχεία, φθορά, φιλαγυρία and ἀπάτη. One is reminded of the similarities to certain phrases in the Corpus Hermeticum: ὁ γὰρ κόσμος πλήρωμά ἐστιν τῆς κακίας and ἀπὸ τῆς τοῦ κόσμου ἀπάτης.

The paraenesis urges that one must give up this world so that the other may be obtained. In fact, one is "to hate this world" (ὅτι μικρὰ καὶ ὀλιγοχρόνια καὶ φθαρτά) and "to love" the other world because it contains τὰ ἀγαθὰ τὰ ἄφθαρτα. Therefore verse 7 stresses that only by doing the will of Christ—which means keeping his laws—will one find ἀνάπαυσις in ὁ αἰὼν ὁ μέλλων. Again it is made clear that these heavenly gifts are to be received in the future, and that their reception is contingent upon ποιοῦντες γὰρ τὸ θέλημα τοῦ Χριστοῦ. At the same time those who disobey the commands will receive eternal punishment. We have here a very brief form of the blessings and curses motif which is greatly expanded in chapters 15-18.

To support this paraenesis with its blessing and curses motif, a supportive quotation is cited from Ezekiel in somewhat altered and expanded form. Perhaps the use of the verb ῥύομαι in verses 7 and 8 led to its selection. The question is then raised: "If even such upright men as these cannot save their children by their uprightness, what assurance have we that we shall enter God's Kingdom if we fail to keep our baptism pure and undefiled ? Or who will plead for us if we are not found to have holy and upright deeds ?" The point is that there is nothing automatic concerning salvation. In the last analysis the decisive question is not whether one's father was a righteous giant such as Noah, Job, or Daniel, or even whether one has been baptized ! The crucial matter is to keep τὸ βάπτισμα ἀγνὸν καὶ ἀμίαντον (6:9). It is possible, and this is supported at other points in 2 Clement, that our author is trying to refute a point of view which claims that at baptism the climax of salvation is reached. Over against this position he urges that one will not enter into God's Kingdom unless one keeps baptism pure and undefiled.

This exhortation concerning baptism can only be fully understood when it is viewed in relation to other similar statements made in chapters 7, 8, and 14. In chapter 7:6 we read: "For in reference to those who have not guarded the seal (τὴν σφραγῖδα), it says, 'Their worm shall not die and their fire shall not be quenched, and they shall be a spectacle to all flesh.'" In 8:6 we hear the exhortation: τηρήσατε τὴν σάρκα ἀγνὴν καὶ τὴν σφραγῖδα ἄσπιλον, ἵνα τὴν αἰώνιον ζωὴν ἀπολάβωμεν. Related to these are two statements: 14:3, τηρήσατε τὴν σάρκα, ἵνα τοῦ πνεύματος μεταλάβητε, and 14:5, τοσαύτην δύναται ἡ σὰρξ αὕτη μεταλαβεῖν ζωὴν καὶ ἀφθαρσίαν κολληθέντος αὐτῇ τοῦ πνεύματος τοῦ ἁγίου, οὔτε ἐξειπεῖν τις δύναται οὔτε λαλῆσαι, ἃ ἡτοίμασεν ὁ κύριος τοῖς ἐκλεκτοῖς αὐτοῦ.

σφραγίς in 2 Clement can only refer to the baptismal seal. Thus, the words βάπτισμα and σφραγίς are used synonymously.[1] Speaking of 2 Clement, G.W.H. Lampe advocates the same view: "In this homily Baptism is directly equated with the 'seal.'"[2] That Paul and the Pauline school related "sealing" to baptism is clear from 2 Cor. 1:22, Eph. 1:13 and 4:30. In 2 Cor. 1:22 we read that "he has put his seal (σφραγισάμενος) upon us and given us his Spirit in our hearts as a guarantee." In 1 Cor. 12:13 we learn that Paul associates the gift of the Spirit with baptism: "For by one Spirit we were all

---

[1] Note the parallelism of the phrases τηρεῖν τὸ βάπτισμα (6:9) and τηρεῖν τὴν σφραγῖδα (8:6). Erich Dinkler, *Signum Crucis* (Tübingen, 1967), p. 109, makes the same suggestion: "In 2 Clem 7,6; 8,6 ist ebenfalls die Gleichung Versiegelung = Taufe eindeutig." The identification of the seal with the baptismal water is made explicit in Hermas, Sim. 9:16—ἡ σφραγίς τὸ ὕδωρ ἐστίν. See also P. Benoit, *Le Baptême chrétien au deuxième Siècle* (Paris, 1953).

[2] G. W. H. Lampe, *The Seal of the Spirit* (London, 1967), p. 103.

baptized into one body—Jews or Greeks, slaves or free—and all were made to drink of one Spirit." Eph. 4:30 further develops these thoughts: "And do not grieve the Holy Spirit of God, in whom you were sealed for the day of redemption."

For 2 Clement, the flesh can be viewed positively because it shares the Spirit. It is this gift of the Spirit which in fact redeems the flesh and permits it to participate in heavenly things (cf. 14:5, τοσαύτην δύναται ἡ σάρξ αὕτη μεταλαβεῖν ζωὴν καὶ ἀφθαρσίαν κολληθέντος αὐτῇ τοῦ πνεύματος τοῦ ἁγίου...). The flesh is the antitype of the Spirit only insofar as it already shares in the Spirit. For this reason 2 Clement frequently exhorts that the flesh must be guarded—it must be kept pure and blameless—so that it can continue to share the Spirit, and eventually participate in the fullness of the spiritual church.[1]

Each of the baptismal references in 2 Clement has a strong eschatological emphasis. This is also the case in 2 Cor. 1:22, and especially in Eph. 1:13ff., "In him you also ... were sealed with the promised Holy Spirit, which is the guarantee of our inheritance until we acquire possession of it, to the praise of his glory;" also Eph. 4:30, "And do not grieve the Holy Spirit of God, in whom you were sealed for the day of redemption." The "already—not yet" pattern is clear. Already now the Christian has been sealed in the presence and activity of the indwelling Spirit of God, but he has not yet received the final redemption which comes only at the parousia.[2] For 2 Clement final redemption is only received at the parousia if one's flesh, baptism and seal are kept pure and spotless and if one obeys the commandments of the Lord.

Why has our author found it necessary to deal so extensively with the eschatological dimension of baptism and "the flesh" within so short an address? As we shall see more fully in our discussion of chapter 9, it is likely that the author of 2 Clement is opposing a particular group of Christians who advocated that at baptism the consummation of salvation had been attained.[3] They probably asserted that

---

[1] See 8:4,6; 14:3.

[2] There is no reason to believe that the author of 2 Clement has in mind an external sign or mark when he speaks of the seal. While this comes to the fore in the second century we find no compelling reason for attributing this to 2 Clement. As for Paul, we are here dealing with an internal sealing. The usage would be similar in certain respects to Philo's use, when he speaks of a seal stamped upon the human soul in Plant 18.

[3] See Irenaeus, *Adv. Haer.* 1.21.4 and Clement, *Excerpts* 77.1-3.

there was no need for a future resurrection, or for a future eschatology. That this problem is already present during New Testament times is suggested by Paul and the Pauline school. It is significant that when Paul discusses baptism in Romans 6 he explicitly refers to the futurity of the resurrection (Rom. 6:5, εἰ γὰρ σύμφυτοι γεγόναμεν τῷ ὁμοιώματι τοῦ θανάτου αὐτοῦ, ἀλλὰ καὶ τῆς ἀναστάσεως ἐσόμεθα; and in v. 8, εἰ δὲ ἀπεθάνομεν σὺν Χριστῷ, πιστεύομεν ὅτι καὶ συζήσομεν αὐτῷ). The resurrection is a promised hope because of our baptism into His death—but it is clearly a future event.[1] In the Deutero-Pauline epistles, however, reference to the resurrection is made in the aorist (Col. 3:1, Εἰ οὖν συνηγέρθητε τῷ Χριστῷ, τὰ ἄνω ζητεῖτε, and Eph. 2:6, [ὁ θεὸς] καὶ συνήγειρεν καὶ συνεκάθισεν ἐν τοῖς ἐπουρανίοις ἐν Χριστῷ Ἰησοῦ). When 2 Tim. 2:18 speaks of those "who have swerved from the truth by holding that the resurrection is past already," it may be that a similar position is being attacked. Such views which held that salvation was received in its totality at baptism were frequent in the first and second centuries. This is affirmed by Irenaeus when he speaks of the gnostic Menander, a student of Simon Magus: "for his disciples obtain the *resurrection* by being baptized into him, and can die no more, but remain in the possession of immortal youth."[2] Hippolytus testifies to the same phenomenon: "This Nicholas ... driven by an alien spirit, was the first to affirm that the resurrection had already come; meaning by 'resurrection' the fact that we believe in Christ and have received baptism; but he denied the resurrection of the body."[3]

It is likely that 2 Clement's congregation did not realize the full dimension and implications of baptism and resurrection; they may have overstressed the "already" and neglected the "not-yet" character of the Christian life. Due to this kind of eschatological misunderstanding, the author of 2 Clement finds it necessary to exhort his

---

[1] The same position is asserted by Paul in 1 Cor. 15.3.

[2] *Adv. Haer.* 1.23.5.

[3] Fragment I, *De Resurrectione*, preserved in Syriac, ed. Achelis, p. 251. G. W. H. Lampe has pointed out the significant role which the concept of the seal played in gnosticism. He states that for the gnostic the seal "protects him against the evil influence of the heavenly powers, affords him a passport to carry him safely through the spheres of the 'Archontes', and guarantees him redemption from the material world, and the promise of future blessedness" (*Seal*, p. 121). Lampe's basic support for this assertion is found in Clement, *Excerpts* 70, 81 and 86; Acts of Philip 38; and Pistis Sophia 86, 103, 108, 111.

congregation on such basic matters as baptism, the seal, the flesh, and resurrection.

f) 2 Clement 7: competing for the heavenly prize

The outward form of both chapter 7 and 8, at first glance, seems to differ from the preceding one. However, this is only partially true. The basic pattern is the same, except that in place of the first supportive quotation, we have the illustration (v. 1b); paraenesis (vv. 3-5); supportive quotation (v. 6).

One is immediately impressed by the strong rhetorical effect produced by the frequent repetitions of στέφανος/στεφανόω (ten times) and ἀγών / ἀγωνίζομαι (five times). The influence of ancient rhetoric can be recognized not only at this point, but also in the selection of the illustration dealing with an athletic contest.[1] Instructive is a similar illustration found in Seneca, *Epistulae Morales*, 78.16.

> What blows do athletes receive on their faces and all over their bodies! Nevertheless, through their desire for fame they endure every torture, and they undergo these things not only because they are fighting but in order to be able to fight. Their very training means torture. So let us also win the way to victory in all our struggles, —for the reward is not a garland or a palm or a trumpeter who calls for silence at the proclamation of our names, but rather virtue, steadfastness of soul, and a peace that is won for all time ....

Here, too, just as in 2 Clement, the reference to an athletic contest is given a moral application.[2]

The basic theme of chapter 7 is stated in the first verse: "So, my brothers, let us enter the contest, recognizing that it is at hand...." 2 Clement's understanding of this contest is further expanded in 20:2: "We are engaged in the contest of the living God and are being trained by the present life in order to win laurels in the life to come." In a real sense the title which Käsemann gave to his study on Hebrews, *Das wandernde Gottesvolk*, could very aptly be applied to 2 Clement's understanding of the church. The period after baptism is a contest

---

[1] "Unendlich oft setzt die Diatribe die Tugendübung mit der Athletik in Parallel." Paul Wendland, *Die urchristlichen Literaturformen* (Tübingen, 1912), p. 357, n. 4.

[2] Philo makes a passing reference to athletic contests in Leg All III 47ff., and deals with them very extensively and very critically in Agr 110-123. In both his positive and negative evaluations, the moral and ethical application is always clear. See also our previous discussion on p. 84.

in which the Christian prepares himself for the heavenly rewards. At the very outset the author warns that "we shall not lose heart like women in labor" (2:2). It was for this reason that the people of the Old Testament did not receive the promised "rest."[1]

The actual paraenesis begins with verse 2, using the form of the communicative plural in the subjunctive. "Let us, then, compete so that we may all be crowned. Let us run the straight race, the incorruptible contest; and let many of us sail to it and enter it, so that we too may be crowned." As we have already noted, the reward of the incorruptible contest is ἀνάπαυσις in the heavenly kingdom. "And if we cannot all be crowned, let us at least come close to it." This third verse is difficult and puzzling. Previous commentaries on 2 Clement have often avoided giving any interpretation. The intention is to suggest that even those who do not make first place will receive recognition for their striving. Philo makes a similar point:

> So these athletes prevail over their opponents, but they are also competing among themselves for the highest place. For they do not all win the victory in the same way, though all deserve honour for overthrowing and bringing down most troublesome and doughty opponents. Most worthy of admiration is the one who excels among these, and, as he receives the first prizes, no one can grudge them to him. Nor let those be downcast who have been held worthy of the second or third prize. For these, like the first, are prizes offered as a reward for the acquisition of virtue, and those who cannot reach the topmost virtues are gainers by the acquisition of the less lofty ones, and theirs is actually, as is often said, a more secure gain since it escapes the envy which ever attaches itself to preeminence.[2]

g) 2 Clement 8: the necessity of repentance

The theme of 2 Clement 8 is a very brief one: Ὡς οὖν ἐσμὲν ἐπὶ γῆς, μετανοήσωμεν.[3] This theme, which is introduced here for the first time, plays a significant role in the remainder of 2 Clement.[4] Both H. Windisch[5] and R. Knopf[6] argue that the theme of repentance in chapter 8 marks a break with the preceding chapters and stands in contradiction to them. "Da man nicht gern annehmen möchte, dass die

---

[1] See 2 Clem. 2:3; Heb. 3:7-4:10; 1 Cor. 10:1-13.

[2] Agr 120-121.

[3] The reader is also referred to the previous discussion of this chapter on pp. 84-85.

[4] μετανοέω — 8:1,2,3; 9:8; 13:1; 15:1; 16:1; 17:1; 19:1; μετάνοια — 8:2; 16:4.

[5] Hans Windisch, *Taufe und Sünde im ältesten Christentum bis auf Origenes* (Tübingen, 1908), pp. 329-40.

[6] Rudolf Knopf, *Zwei Clemensbriefe*, pp. 164ff.

beiden so stark widersprechenden Anschauungen unmittelbar neben-
einanderstehen, 8:1f. hinter 7:6, so empfiehlt sich, μετανοήσωμεν
(und entsprechend 9:7f.) möglichst weit zu fassen, so dass es auf alle
Menschen und nicht auf die Christen geht: dass Ungetaufte, Kate-
chumenen und Gäste, unter den Hörern angenommen werden dürfen,
ist sicher.... II Clem. verknüpft also zwei Mahnungen miteinander,
die altchristliche Taufparänese und den kirchlichen Bussruf."[1]

Windisch argues that the assertions made about baptism in 2 Clement 1 are inconsistent with the exhortations to repentance in the remainder of 2 Clement. If the Christian already has been saved and
cleansed from sin, asks Windisch, why must he still repent? It is
unlikely, however, that chapter 1 stands in opposition to the remainder
of 2 Clement in the way Windisch suggests. As we have observed, our
author has taken over a hymnic confession in use in his congregation.
He is aware of its possible misinterpretation, and therefore makes
certain eschatological corrections and amplifications throughout his
address. We would assert against Windisch that if one is to speak of
a "contradiction" between chapter 1 and the remainder of 2 Clement,
it is not a "contradiction" within the preacher's own theology, but
between that of an already given confession and that of the author.
However, it is probably more accurate to say that our preacher
essentially accepts much of the theology of the confession but feels
that it is necessary to balance it by stressing the eschatological dimension of the Christian life.

A general understanding of the theology and situation of 2 Clement
is sufficient to refute the interpretation of Knopf and Windisch. The
author is trying to preach to a congregation in which certain libertinistic tendencies have become manifest. These persons base their
actions on what they believe to be a correct understanding of their
baptismal confession. 2 Clement acknowledges the congregation's baptismal confession, and proceeds to state its logical consequence: to
keep the seal undefiled and the flesh pure so that salvation may be

---

[1] *Ibid.*, pp. 164-65. Hans Windisch, *Taufe und Sünde*, pp. 332-33, moves in the same
direction: "So sind Missions- und Christenparänese hier zusammengeschlossen. Die Un-
bekehrten mahnt der Prediger, die Bussfrist zu nützen, die Getauften, das Taufwessen
zu bewahren." He continues on pp. 337-38, "Der Kontrast des empirischen Christen zu
dem Idealbild, wie es die Theorie zum Ausdruck bringt, ist kaum in einer andern Schrift
so grell zu sehen wie in der Clemenspredigt."

granted on the last day. However, some in the congregation have not been faithful to the totality of their baptismal covenant and consequently they must be asked to repent. Since Christians are not yet living in the new aeon, there is a constant temptation to sin (cf. 2 Clement 18). While they are expected to keep their baptism pure and undefiled, it is certainly possible that some may falter. Therefore, they are urged to repent while there is still a time for repentance. The thought of 2 Clement is similar to that of 1 Jn. 2:1-7, especially v. 1: "My little children, I am writing this to you so that you may not sin; but if any one does sin, we have an advocate with the Father, Jesus Christ the righteous." Noteworthy, too, is the common use of παρά-κλητος in 1 Jn. 2:1 (only here in 1 John) and in 2 Clem. 6:9 (only here in 2 Clement). There is a difference, though. In 2 Clement the role of the παράκλητος is essentially eschatological—he will plead for us on the last day. If we sin we must repent by doing certain works of repentance: in 1 John, if we sin we can call on the παράκλητος *now*, in the present.

A number of factors point to the continuity of thought between chapters 7 and 8. To begin with, there is little evidence, if any, for the view that 2 Clement 8 is addressed to non-Christians and that this chapter is an example of "Missionsparänese." If 2 Clement 6 and 7 are addressed to baptized Christians, then surely the opening words of 2 Clem. 8:4, "Thus, brothers...," have the same referent. Also, the illustration of the potter, "if a potter makes a vessel and it gets out of shape or breaks in his hands, he molds it over again..." is best understood as referring to the Christian who was newly formed in baptism and then, at a later point, sins again. But, if one has not only defiled the seal but also not repented while he still had a chance, then the second half of the illustration applies: "but if he has once thrown it into the flames of the furnace, he can do nothing more with it." This interpretation is also supported by 7:6 which is addressed to the baptized Christian: "For in reference to those who have not guarded the seal, it says, 'Their worm shall not die and their fire shall not be quenched, and they shall be a spectacle to all flesh.'"

Further weight is given to this understanding by the other references to "repentance" in 2 Clement. Both 13:1 and 16:1 connect the call to repentance with the address "brother," which is certainly a designation for Christians and not for the unconverted world. Hermas, too, indicates that the exhortation to keep the seal undefiled is not incongruent with the call to repentance:

> Now, sir, explain to me what sort of person one of those who have given up their
> sticks is, and where they live, in order that those who have believed and have
> received the seal, and have broken it, and have not kept it whole, when they hear
> it may realize what they have done and repent ....[1]

2 Clement, then, applies a prophetic understanding of repentance to the "lapsed" Christian. This is done in a manner similar to Rev. 2:5, "Remember then from what you have fallen, repent and do the works you did at first. If not, I will come to you and remove your lampstand from its place, unless you repent." On the whole, then, there is no evidence to suggest that 2 Clem. 8:1, "So while we are on earth, let us repent," is addressed to non-Christians.

After the story of the potter[2] has been used to illustrate the basic theme, $\mu\epsilon\tau\alpha\nu o\acute{\eta}\sigma\alpha\mu\epsilon\nu$, it is paraenetically applied to the present situation of the congregation. Once again the theme of the flesh is stressed, and the congregation is specifically asked to repent from the sins of the flesh so that they might be saved on the last day. If the flesh is not kept pure, there can be no ultimate salvation. Repentance must take place now during this earthly life, $\H{\epsilon}\omega\varsigma$ $\H{\epsilon}\chi o\mu\epsilon\nu$ $\kappa\alpha\iota\rho\grave{o}\nu$ $\mu\epsilon\tau\alpha\nu o\acute{\iota}\alpha\varsigma$. Once the Christian leaves this world it will no longer be possible "to confess" or "to repent."

How should $\dot{\epsilon}\xi o\mu o\lambda o\gamma\epsilon\hat{\iota}\sigma\theta\alpha\iota$ be interpreted? According to Knopf it means "das öffentliche Bekenntnis, das einmal vor der Taufe und dann ständig von den Gläubigen im Gemeindegottesdienst abgelegt wird...."[3] Recalling our previous discussion of 2 Clement 1, there are a number of reasons which make Knopf's suggestion attractive. Yet it is difficult to hold that our writer is thinking of a baptismal confession at this point. It is more likely that he is thinking of the confession of post-baptismal sins.[4] All the author of 2 Clement is attempting to say is that once Christians have left this world they can no longer confess their post-baptismal sins or make repentance for them.

Important for 2 Clement's concrete situation is the exhortation in verse 4: "Thus, brothers, by doing the Father's will and by keeping

---

[1] Sim. 8:6. Bernhard Poschmann, *Paenitentia Secunda* (Bonn, 1940), p. 133, is fully correct when he states: "Der zweite Clemensbrief lehrt also so klar und nachdrücklich wie möglich, dass es für den Christen, solange er auf Erden lebt, eine Busse gibt, die ihm das verlorene Heil wiederverschafft."

[2] See our previous discussion on pp. 84-85.

[3] Knopf, *Zwei Clemensbriefe*, p. 165.

[4] See Jas. 5:16; 1 Clem. 51:3; Did. 4:14 (Barn. 19:2).

the flesh pure and by abiding by the Lord's commands, we shall obtain eternal life." The phrase ποιήσαντες τὸ θέλημα τοῦ πατρός, or slight variations thereof, occurs frequently in 2 Clement.[1] It always appears, as in this context, in connection with the gifts related to eternal life. θέλημα is the more general concept which is then specified by τὰς ἐντολὰς τοῦ κυρίου φυλάξαντες. This phrase, too, is very frequent in 2 Clement[2] and is close to the usage found in the Gospel of John (14:15; 15:10) and, especially, 1 John (2:3; 3:22). Both 2 Clement and 1 John use the term ἐντολή over against a libertinistic front[3] and both are concerned about the relationship of γινώσκειν θεόν to ἐντολή (1 Jn. 2:3-6; 2 Clem. 3:1-4). What is the content of these "commandments"? When 1 John speaks of the "commandments" he means love to the brethren; in 2 Clement one is never entirely sure what is meant by the term. One can surmise from 2 Clem. 4:3 that the writer has something similar in mind, but it is not stated with the same degree of precision as in 1 John.

This relationship between doing the commandments and eternal life is followed by a supportive quotation. The argument is then summarized in the form of an imperative, which also serves as a transition to the further discussion of σάρξ in chapter 9: τηρήσατε τὴν σάρκα ἁγνὴν καὶ τὴν σφραγῖδα ἄσπιλον, ἵνα τὴν αἰώνιον ζωὴν ἀπολάβωμεν (8:6).

h) 2 Clement 9: resurrection of the flesh

This chapter opens with a firm warning: Καὶ μὴ λεγέτω τις ὑμῶν, ὅτι αὕτη ἡ σάρξ οὐ κρίνεται οὐδὲ ἀνίσταται. The three key terms are σάρξ[4], κρίνω, and ἀνίστημι. Our author is anxious to ward off two possible misunderstandings: 1) that the flesh will not be judged; and, 2) that the flesh will not be raised. That 2 Clement's eschatological corrective in this chapter is carried out in close connection with the hymnic confession of chapter 1 is obvious by the use of phrases (ἐν τίνι

---

[1] 5:7; 6:7; 8:4; 9:11; 10:1; 14:1. This terminology is frequent in both the LXX and the New Testament; it is very similar to Mt. 7:21; 12:50 and Jn. 6:40.

[2] 3:4; 4:5; 6:7; 8:4; 17:1,3,6.

[3] As Schrenk (TWNT, II, p. 551) very succinctly states: "Die gnostische Bewegung nötigt zum Unterstreichen des Elementaren." See also Schnackenburg, Die Johannesbriefe (Freiburg, 1965), pp. 94ff.

[4] σάρξ appears six times in this chapter alone and twenty times in all of 2 Clement.

ἐσώθητε, ἐν τίνι ἀνεβλέψατε[1] and ἐν τῇ σαρκὶ ἐκλήθητε) which contain the same three key verbs as in the confession.

In order to interpret this chapter adequately, it will be helpful to gain a broader perspective on the problem of the resurrection in the first two Christian centuries. The basic conflict during this period is between a Hellenistic and a "mainstream" Christian view of salvation. This point is effectively developed by Oscar Cullmann's study, *Immortality of the Soul or Resurrection of the Dead?*[2] Although Cullmann is essentially concerned with the New Testament period, his monograph gives valuable suggestions as to the nature of the problem in the second century as well.

> Indeed for the Greeks who believed in this immortality of the soul it may have been harder to accept the Christian preaching of the resurrection than it was for others. About the year 150 Justin (in his *Dialogue*, 80) writes of people, 'who say that there is no resurrection from the dead, but that immediately at death their souls would ascend to heaven.' Here the contrast is indeed clearly perceived.[3]

We will begin our survey with the second century. Very illuminating is the work of Justin's student Tatian, *Discourse to the Greeks*. Here we have not so much an apology for the Christian faith, as a vehement polemic against the whole Greek culture. In chapter 6 he deals with the Christians belief in the resurrection and he asserts: καὶ διὰ τοῦτο καὶ σωμάτων ἀνάστασιν ἔσεσθαι πεπιστεύκαμεν μετὰ τὴν τῶν ὅλων συντέλειαν.... In chapter 13 there is a specific discussion of the relation of soul and body: "If, indeed, it (the soul) knows not the truth, it dies, and is dissolved with the body, but rises again at last at the end of the world with the body, receiving death by punishment in immortality. But, again, if it acquires the knowledge of God, it dies not, although for a time it be dissolved." This passage stresses the fact that the body and the soul rise together at the end of the world. This close connection between the two is again affirmed in chapter 15: "... nor does the flesh (σάρξ) rise again without the soul."

---

[1] Used only here and in 1:6.

[2] London, 1962. See also the significant study by George W. Nickelsburg, Jr., *Resurrection, Immortality, and Eternal Life in Intertestamental Judaism* (Cambridge, Mass., 1972) which contains a critique (pp. 177-80) of Cullmann's *Immortality or Resurrection*, and Georg Kretschmar, "Auferstehung des Fleisches," in *Leben Angesichts des Todes*, Helmut Thielicke zum 60. Geburtstag (Tübingen, 1968), pp. 101-37.

[3] Cullmann, *Immortality or Resurrection*, p. 59.

According to Eusebius, Theophilus was the sixth bishop of Antioch in Syria. In 180 A.D., or shortly thereafter, he composed *Ad Autolycum* which is a defense of Christianity against the objections raised by his pagan friend Autolycus. In a discussion of immortality in 1.7, Theophilus wishes to assert that which is distinctively Christian over against the pagan world: Ἀνεγείρει γάρ σου τὴν σάρκα ἀθάνατον σὺν τῇ ψυχῇ ὁ θεός. The difficulty of such an assertion concerning the resurrection of the flesh is recognized in 1.8: "But you do not believe that the dead are raised. When the resurrection shall take place, then you will believe, whether you will or no; and your faith shall be reckoned for unbelief, unless you believe now." A number of illustrations follow which are intended to convince Autolycus. How important this subject is can be seen again in 1.13 where Theophilus returns to the theme of the resurrection with even more examples. Referring to Autolycus, Theophilus begins: "Then, as to your denying that the dead are raised...."

The very affront which the Christian doctrine of the resurrection caused the pagan world is clearly demonstrated by Eusebius.[1] He discusses the persecution of the Christians during the reign of Marcus Aurelius (161-180), illustrating this with quotations from the letter of the churches of Lyons and Vienne:

> Thus the bodies of the martyrs, after having been exposed and insulted in every way for six days, and afterwards burned and turned to ashes, were swept by the wicked into the river Rhone which flows near by, that not even a relic of them might still appear upon the earth. And this they did as though they could conquer God and take away their rebirth in order, as they said, 'that they might not even have any hope of resurrection, through trusting in which they have brought in strange and new worship and despised terrors, going readily and with joy to death; now let us see if they will rise again, and if their God be able to help them and to take them out of our hands.'

From this account it is apparent that to the pagan world Christianity is identified as a religion of the resurrection. To make this doctrine more understandable to the non-Christian world is an important responsibility of the Christian apologist in the second century. Justin, for example, is very much concerned to show how the resurrection is possible, and tries to suggest various heathen analogies to this Christian doctrine (*Apol.* 19-21). In like manner, chapter 5 of Pseudo-Justin, *On the Resurrection*, begins: "But again, of those who maintain that

---

[1] *H.e.* 5.1.62-63.

the flesh has no resurrection, some assert that it is impossible...."
After some preliminary arguments, a whole chapter (6) is devoted to
demonstrating that the resurrection is in fact consistent with the
opinions of the philosophers. Likewise, Athenagoras is his *A Plea for
the Christians* (ch. 36), tries to argue "that it is not our belief alone that
bodies will rise again, but that many philosophers also hold the
same view ...." This is then followed by a complete treatise on *The
Resurrection of the Dead*.

When one turns to Irenaeus, *Adv. Haer.* 5.1-18, the picture
changes somewhat. Irenaeus is not involved in a simple defense of
the Christian doctrine of a resurrection in the flesh; rather his remarks
are specifically directed against certain heretics—particularly the
Valentinians. "Vain therefore are the disciples of Valentinus who put
forth this opinion, in order that they may exclude the flesh from salvation, and cast aside what God has fashioned."[1] Irenaeus is opposing
those "who despise the entire dispensation of God, and disallow the
salvation of the flesh, and treat with contempt its regeneration,
maintaining that it is not capable of incorruption."[2] He argues that
"our bodies ... shall rise at their appointed time, the Word of God
granting them resurrection to the glory of God, even the Father, who
freely gives to this mortal immortality, and to this corruptible incorruption."[3] To support his contention, Irenaeus is primarily dependent on
a eucharistic theology which has some connection with Ignatius, but
is quite unlike the argumentation of Paul, 1 or 2 Clement.

In 2 Clement 9 there is a noteworthy stress on the verb σώζειν
as illustrated in the question, "In what state were you saved ?" It is
likely that Irenaeus has similar opponents in mind when he writes:
"Among the other (truths) proclaimed by the apostle, there is also
this one, 'That flesh and blood cannot inherit the kingdom of God.'
This is (the passage) which is adduced by all the heretics in support
of their folly, with an attempt to annoy us, and to point out that the
handiwork of God is not saved."[4] These references in Irenaeus are
sufficient to suggest that the resurrection provided difficulty not only
to the pagan world, but also to the Christian community itself. Need-
less to say there are countless others involved in this anti-heretical

---

[1] *Adv. Haer.* 5.1.
[2] *Ibid.*, 5.2.
[3] *Ibid.*, 5.2.
[4] *Ibid.*, 5.9.

battle. Tertullian, in his treatise *On The Resurrection of the Flesh*, attempts to demonstrate that "in proving that the flesh shall rise again we *ipso facto* prove that no other *flesh* will partake of that resurrection than that which is in question...."[1]

It was the concept of a bodily resurrection which, among other things, divided "orthodox" Christianity from the gnostics.[2] Even a person like Clement of Alexandria who tries to refute gnosticism by developing a type of Christian gnosticism, firmly holds to the Christian conception of the resurrection. In *Paedagogus* I he asserts that "the end is reserved till the resurrection of those who believe; and it is not the reception of some other thing, but the obtaining of the promise previously made."[3] In *Paedagogus* II he refers to Psalm 150: "Praise with the timbrel and the dance, τὴν ἐκκλησίαν λέγει τὴν μελετήσασαν τῆς σαρκὸς τὴν ἀνάστασιν ἐν ἠκοῦντι τῷ δέρματι."[4]

Before some of the gnostic documents are examined, it must be recognized that a great tension existed between the church's traditional teaching about the resurrection and the gnostics' re-interpretation of it. This tension is very evident in a document such as the *Epistula Apostolorum* which Hornschuh dates within the first half of the second century.[5] Here is a document influenced by a type of gnostic thought, yet at crucial points rejecting cardinal elements of this gnosticism. The reality of Christ's body and the resurrection in the flesh is strongly maintained over against Cerinthus and Simon. In the Ethiopic text of chapter 21 we read: "Truly I say to you, as the Father awakened *me* from the dead, in the same manner *you* also will arise in the flesh...." In chapter 22 the following question is raised: "After he had said this to us, we said to him, 'O Lord, is it really in store for the flesh to be judged (together) with the soul and spirit, and will (one of these) rest in heaven and the other be punished eternally while it is (still) alive?'" The response in chapter 24 is: "He answered and said to us, 'Truly

---

[1] Chapter 55.

[2] We are fully aware that there is no clear line of demarcation between "orthodoxy" and "heresy." For a discussion of this subject see the suggestive work of Walter Bauer, *Rechtgläubigkeit und Ketzerei im ältesten Christentum* (Tübingen, 1964) and Helmut Koester, "ΓΝΩΜΑΙ ΔΙΑΦΟΡΟΙ: The Origin and Nature of Diversification in the History of Early Christianity" in *HTR* 58 (1965), pp. 279-318. A different perspective is offered by H. E. W. Turner, *The Pattern of Christian Truth* (London, 1954).

[3] 6.28.

[4] 4.41.

[5] Manfred Hornschuh, *Studien zur Epistula Apostolorum* (Berlin, 1965), pp. 116ff.

I say to you, the flesh of every man will rise with his soul and his spirit.' " This discussion is confirmed in chapter 26: "Truly I say to you, the flesh will rise alive with the soul, that they may confess and be judged with the work they have done, *whether it is good or bad*, in order that it may become a selection and exhibition for those who have believed and have done the commandment of my Father who sent me."[1]

By far the most comprehensive treatment to date of the gnostic understanding of the resurrection is provided in the Letter to Rheginus, a part of the Jung Codex. Quispel and others hold it to be a writing of Valentinus himself.[2] On the one hand, the Epistle to Rheginus gives a sufficiently clear conception of the gnostic understanding of the resurrection to help one realize why the Fathers had such little patience with it. On the other hand, there are certain factors which add complexity to our understanding and certainly prohibit attempts at oversimplification.

From the outset one observes that a realized eschatology permeates the whole Epistle.[3] On p. 43, l. 35f., those who still seek their "rest" are ridiculed: "which we have received through our Saviour, our Lord Jesus Christ, which we received when we came to know the truth and found our rest therein." "Rest" is a reality which can be received now—it is not reserved for the future. This is also the case with the resurrection: "many indeed do not believe it, but few find it" (p. 44, l. 9f.). This present character of the resurrection is stressed beyond all doubt on p. 49, l. 15f. "... already ($\check{\eta}\delta\eta$) thou hast the resurrection ($\dot{a}\nu\dot{a}\sigma\tau a\sigma\iota s$)." This understanding is further elaborated on p. 45, l. 24ff.: "But then as the Apostle said, we suffered with him, and we arose with him, and we went to heaven with him .... We are drawn upward by him like the beams by the sun, without being held back by anything. This is the spiritual ($\pi\nu\epsilon\nu\mu a\tau\iota\kappa\acute{\eta}$) resurrection ($\dot{a}\nu\dot{a}\sigma\tau a\sigma\iota s$) which swallows up the physic ($\psi\nu\chi\iota\kappa\acute{\eta}$) alike ($\dot{o}\mu o\acute{\iota}\omega s$) with the fleshly ($\sigma a\rho\kappa\iota\nu\acute{\eta}$)."

We now approach those parts of the treatise which are quite paradoxical. On p. 47, l. 4f. we read: "For if thou wert not in (the) flesh

---

[1] Translation from Hennecke-Schneemelcher-Wilson, *New Testament Apocrypha*.

[2] Gilles Quispel, "The Jung Codex and Its Significance" in *The Jung Codex* (London, 1955), ed. by F. L. Cross, pp. 35-78. On p. 56 Quispel asserts that "we may suppose, with even more confidence than in the case of the *Gospel of Truth*, that it is by Valentinus himself."

[3] Throughout we refer to the text and translations by Malinine, Puech, Quispel, Till, *De Resurrectione* [Epistula ad Rheginum] (Zürich, 1963).

(σάρξ) thou didst take on flesh (σάρξ) when thou didst come into this world (κόσμος). Wherefore shouldst thou not take on the flesh (σάρξ) when thou goest up into the aeon (αἰών)? That which is better than the flesh (σάρξ) is for it the cause (αἴτιος) of life." First, there is no mention of a future resurrection. The text only says that when one goes up into the aeon, then one also takes the flesh along. This conception seems to be completely contradicted by the following lines. In line 17ff. we read that the "afterbirth of the body (σῶμα) is old age, and thou art corruption. For thee absence (ἀπουσία) is an advantage. For thou wilt not give up what is better if thou shouldst depart." And further, line 36ff.: "Let none be doubtful concerning this ... the members (μέλος) which are visible (but) dead will not be saved for it is (only) the living (members) that are within them which were to rise again."

To offer a solution to this paradox is not easy. It is interesting, though, that a somewhat similar situation appears in the Gospel of Philip. In 104:26-34 the author appears to be attacking the concept of a resurrection in the flesh, and in 105:9ff. he seems to be defending it. Wilson is probably correct in his suggestion that the authors of the Epistle to Rheginus and the Gospel of Philip "were grappling, not altogether successfully, with the Pauline doctrine as presented in the Corinthian epistles...."[1] However, is Wilson's specific attempt to solve the paradox in the Gospel of Philip correct? The key for him is a saying of Jesus spoken after his resurrection found in the Apocryphon of James (Jung Codex 14:35-36): "from now I shall unclothe myself in order that I may be clothed." From this, Wilson makes the following suggestion for a solution: "The idea may be that the Gnostic must rise in the flesh in order to be stripped of the garment of flesh and clothed in his heavenly robe; in which case 104.26-34 may be an attack on those who maintain a resurrection of the flesh *and no more*, who are thus bound to the things of this world; and 105.9ff. may be directed against the 'Greek' view that only the soul (or the spirit) is immortal. Both are wrong ...."[2] Wilson's interpretation of the passage from the Letter of James is quite plausible, and is paralleled in the Gospel of Thomas (21 and 37). It is apparent that what the true gnostic really desires is to strip off the body and to leave the world, a conception

---

[1] *The Gospel of Philip* (London, 1962), ed. R. M. Wilson, p. 88.
[2] *Ibid.*, p. 89.

which Paul refutes in 2 Cor. 5:4. However, it is unlikely that this is
the conception underlying either the Gospel of Philip or the Epistle
to Rheginus.

Might it be that in both of these writings we are dealing with a
play on the word "flesh"? GP 104:26-32 asserts: "Some are afraid lest
they rise naked. Because of this they wish to rise in the flesh, and
they do not know that those who bear the flesh [it is they who are]
naked; those who ... themselves to unclothe themselves [it is they who
are] not naked."[1] As it stands now, the train of thought is not very
clear. The clue may be in that which follows. " 'Flesh [and blood
shall] not inherit the kingdom [of God]. What is this which will not
inherit? This which we have.' " This can only mean our earthly, mortal
flesh—that which in reality in nakedness. "But what is this which
will inherit? That which belongs to Jesus with his blood. Because
of this he said: He who shall not eat my flesh and drink my blood has
no life in him. What is it? His flesh is the logos, and his blood is
the Holy Spirit. He who has received these has food and drink and
clothing." Our flesh in conjunction with the flesh and blood of Jesus
is "transformed" flesh; he who unclothes himself of his mortal flesh
is not naked because he has received "food and drink and clothing."
Therefore, when the writer continues, "For myself, I find fault with
the others who say that it will not rise," he is clearly talking about
the flesh in its transformed state, that flesh "which belongs to Jesus
with his blood."

Perhaps the suggestion of a "transformed flesh" may enable us to
find a solution to the line in Rheginus which reads: "Wherefore shouldst
thou not take on the flesh ($\sigma\acute{\alpha}\rho\xi$) when thou goest up into the aeon
($\alpha\grave{\iota}\acute{\omega}\nu$)?" This is immediately qualified: "That which is better than the
flesh ($\sigma\acute{\alpha}\rho\xi$) is for it the cause ($\alpha\ddot{\iota}\tau\iota\sigma$) of life." "For it" can only
refer to $\sigma\acute{\alpha}\rho\xi$. The words which follow can only refer to "the cause of
life": "What comes into being for thy sake, is it not thine? What is
thine, is it not with thee?" The suggestion that we are here dealing
with the conception of a "transformed flesh" appears to be confirmed
a bit further on (48:32ff.) where it has just been stated that the resurrection is not an illusion; rather, "it is the truth, that which stands
firm, and it is the revelation of that which is and the transformation
of things, and a transition ($\mu\epsilon\tau\alpha\beta\sigma\lambda\acute{\eta}$), into a new existence. For in-

---

[1] See Wilson's further comments on pp. 87-89.

corruptibility descends upon the corruption, and the light flows down upon the darkness, to swallow it up, and the Pleroma makes perfect the deficiency." This concept of a "transformation of things" and a "transition into a new existence," as well as the statement that "the members (μέλος) which are visible (but) dead will not be saved for it is (only) the living (members) that are within them which were to rise again," permit us to gain a better understanding of the words in Rheginus, "Wherefore shouldst thou not take on the flesh (σάρξ) when thou goest up into the aeon?" What is here meant is a "transformed" flesh which has already undergone "a transition into a new existence."

Before returning to 2 Clement, we must give attention to the other Apostolic Fathers and the New Testament with regard to their understanding of resurrection. At several points Ignatius' letter to the Smyrnaeans criticizes docetism, as in 2:1, "And he genuinely suffered, as even he genuinely raised himself. It is not as some unbelievers say, that his Passion was a sham." This is followed by a stress (3:1ff.) on the nature of Jesus after the resurrection: "For myself, I am convinced and believe that even after the resurrection he was in the flesh.... Moreover, after the resurrection he ate and drank with them as a real human being, although in spirit he was united with the Father." In 5:2 the position of the opponents is refuted: "What good does anyone do me by praising me and thus reviling my Lord by refusing to acknowledge that he carried around live flesh?" In 7:2 Ignatius advises that such people be avoided: "Rather pay attention to the prophets and above all to the gospel. There we get a clear picture of the Passion and see that the resurrection has really happened." For Ignatius, a docetic Christology must be avoided because it refuses to recognize the reality of Christ's resurrection.

Polycarp in his letter to the Philippians faces similar opponents. In 7:1 we hear: "For 'whosoever does not confess that Jesus Christ has come in the flesh is antichrist'; and whosoever does not confess the testimony of the cross 'is of the devil'; and whosoever perverts the sayings of the Lord to suit his own lusts and says there is neither resurrection nor judgment—such a one is the first-born of Satan." Again it can be observed how a docetic Christology leads to the denial of a future resurrection and judgment.

1 Clement 23-27 deals at some length with the problem of resurrection. While a precise description of the opponents does not emerge, nevertheless it becomes clear from the context that Clement of Rome is dealing with persons who deny a *future* resurrection *in the flesh*.

This is suggested in 1 Clem. 24:1: "Let us consider, dear friends, how the Master continually points out to us that there will be a future resurrection (τὴν μέλλουσαν ἀνάστασιν ἔσεσθαι)."[1] It is important to note that Clement can affirm without further elaboration that God "made the Lord Jesus Christ the first fruits by raising him from the dead (24:1)." This is not the problem—the problem is that of the *future* resurrection. The goal of 1 Clement's examples and illustrations is not just to support the resurrection of the dead, but to support the *futurity* of such a resurrection. Those whom he is opposing are most likely representatives of a realized eschatology.

As one turns to the New Testament, there are several relevant texts which must be examined. One of them is 2 Tim. 2:18, where we learn about Hymenaeus and Philetus οἵτινες περὶ τὴν ἀλήθειαν ἠστόχησαν, λέγοντες ἀνάστασιν ἤδη γεγονέναι. Perhaps it is such a misunderstanding which lies at the root of the problem in 1 Clement. Certainly the position of Hymenaeus and Philetus is near to that observed in the gnostic texts above.[2]

These same elements criticized in 2 Timothy are already present in Colossians and Ephesians. In Col. 2:12 we read: "... and you were buried with him in baptism, in which you *were* also raised (συνηγέρθητε; cf. 3:1) with him through faith in the working of God, who raised him from the dead." And in Eph. 2:6 we learn that Christ "*raised* us up (συνήγειρεν) with him, and made us sit with him in the heavenly places in Christ Jesus." Any sense of eschatological reservation is lost in these texts. Because of trends such as these, Paul expresses himself most carefully and precisely in Rom. 6:5: "For if we have been united with him in a death like his, we *shall* (ἐσόμεθα) certainly be united with him in a resurrection like his." Paul's "eschatological reservation" is not accidental. He is very conscious of those Christians who stressed the ἤδη of the resurrection and the consummation of salvation in the baptismal event.[3]

---

[1] Perhaps it is not insignificant to note in this context that in 26:3, 1 Clement has σάρξ for Job's (LXX) δέρμα: Καὶ ἀναστήσεις τὴν σάρκα μου ταύτην τὴν ἀναντλήσασαν ταῦτα πάντα.

[2] See pp. 138-41

[3] For an illuminating discussion concerning the interrelation of these texts, see the article by James M. Robinson, "Kerygma and History in the New Testament," in *The Bible in Modern Scholarship* (Nashville, 1965), ed. by J. Philip Hyatt, pp. 114-50, especially pp. 121ff.

The final New Testament text to be discussed is 1 Corinthians 15, which can only be correctly interpreted when placed in the context of the whole letter. This chapter poses the immediate question as to the identity of those who deny the resurrection, and further, what they mean when they assert ἀνάστασις νεκρῶν οὐκ ἔστιν (1 Cor. 15:12). In reference to the latter question, Hans von Soden makes this suggestion: "Ebenso handelt es sich m. E. 1 Kor. 15 nicht um Leugnung der Auferstehung—so formuliert Paulus von seinem eschatologischen Verständnis der Auferstehung aus—, sondern um die Behauptung, dass die Auferstehung schon erfolgt sei (in der γνῶσις, im πνεῦμα). Geleugnet wird in Korinth der somatische und eschatologische (beides gehört wesentlich zusammen) Charakter der Auferstehung."[1] In support of this position a number of brief points may be made. To begin with, verse 46 is most important: ἀλλ' οὐ πρῶτον τὸ πνευματικὸν ἀλλὰ τὸ ψυχικόν, ἔπειτα τὸ πνευματικόν. Paul must stress this point because his opponents have argued that the spiritual resurrection has already taken place. Paul says "no"—first the physical resurrection and *then* the spiritual. Right now we still bear the image of the man of dust, but "we *shall* also bear the image of the man of heaven." We do not yet bear this heavenly image ! Paul must urge against the spiritualizers that "flesh and blood cannot inherit the kingdom of God, nor does the perishable inherit the imperishable" (v. 50). Thus, it is impossible that they have already been resurrected. Paul is saying all through this chapter, wait a moment, not so fast ! "Lo ! I tell you a mystery ... we *shall* (!) all be changed ... the dead *will* (!) be raised imperishable, and we *shall* (!) be changed .... *When* the perishable puts on the imperishable, and the mortal puts on immortality, *then* ....." That the Corinthians had totally confused the time order is again stressed in verses 23ff., "But each in his own order: Christ the first fruits, *then* at his coming those who belong to Christ. *Then* comes the end, when he delivers the kingdom to God ...."

These suggestions appear to be confirmed by the larger setting of the letter. One of the basic problems with which Paul must deal throughout is the spiritual superiority of the Corinthians. Typical may be the attitude which Paul ridicules in 4:8: "Already you are filled !

---

[1] Hans von Soden, "Sakrament und Ethik bei Paulus" in *Urchristentum und Geschichte*, I (Tübingen, 1951) ed. by H. von Campenhausen, pp .259-60, n. 28. This general understanding has recently also been accepted by James Robinson, "Kergyma and History," pp. 123ff.

Already you have become rich !"[1] Both in terms of this larger setting
as well as the specific points raised in chapter 15, it is likely that Paul's
opponents in 1 Corinthians 15 are spirit-filled enthusiasts who believed
that there was no need of a future resurrection of the dead since salvation was already consummated. They conflated the gift of a future
resurrection with the baptismal event. Thus, the whole chapter
serves at least one major purpose: to provide a correct eschatological
time-table. Conzelmann puts the matter succinctly: "Throughout
Paul maintains the futurity of the resurrection. His anti-enthusiastic
thrust is clear."[2]

It was this Pauline view of the resurrection which served as the
basis for further discussion in the early church. Paul's understanding
was either accepted, defended and amplified by the Apostolic Fathers
and others in the second century; or it was rejected as absurd by
those influenced by the Greek view of the immortality of the soul; or
it was modified by those moving in a gnosticizing direction.[3] Basically
there were four factors which militated against the Pauline view of
the resurrection: 1) the concept of the immortality of the soul; 2)
the delay of the parousia (e.g., 1 Th. 4); 3) realised eschatology (e.g.,
Col. 2:12); and 4) a docetic Christology (Ign. Smyr. 2; 3; 5). It is
surely not accidental that each of these factors is dealt with in 2
Clement.

The basic assertion in 2 Clem. 9:1 concerning the resurrection is
this: Καὶ μὴ λεγέτω τις ὑμῶν, ὅτι αὕτη ἡ σὰρξ οὐ κρίνεται οὐδὲ

---

[1] See C. K. Barrett, *The First Epistle to the Corinthians* (New York, 1968), pp. 108-109,
and Hans Conzelmann, *Der erste Brief an die Korinther* (Göttingen, 1969), pp. 106-107.

[2] Hans Conzelmann, *An Outline of the Theology of the New Testament* (New York,
1969), p. 188. We have modified Bowden's translation at this point. Instead of trans-
lating "durchweg" as "continually," we have translated it as "throughout" which better
captures the sense of the German word in this context.

[3] The strength and attractiveness of the gnostic position was its ability to use Christian resurrection terminology in a way that sounded "orthodox" when in reality the
content of its understanding of resurrection was quite different. In this connection, we
find helpful some of Hermann Langerbeck's suggestions, *Aufsätze zur Gnosis* (Göttingen,
1967), edited by Hermann Dörries, which our own study partially confirms. His one
statement, while not true of all gnosticism, does contain an element of truth in reference
to the gnostic movement: "Gemeinsames Motiv ist also lediglich: τὸ σπουδάζειν συνιέναι
τὰ χριστιανισμοῦ, die christliche Verkündigung zu verstehen" (p. 28). Also in reference
to our immediate discussion, we find this thought very suggestive: "Nur an einem Ort,
in einem geistigen Umkreis, in dem die Septuaginta, der Timaios und die paulinischen
Briefe zugleich in jedermanns Hand sind, ist die Entstehung eines so vielschichtigen
Gebildes wie etwa der valentinianischen Gnosis überhaupt vorstellbar" (p. 25).

ἀνίσταται. What type of person does our author have in mind when he says: καὶ μὴ λεγέτω τις ὑμῶν ... ? When one keeps in mind the problem of baptism dealt with in chapters 6-8, the strong eschatological stress of chapter 10 and the discussion of the spiritual church in chapter 14, there can be little doubt that the writer is dealing with a similar phenomenon as was Paul in 1 Corinthians 15 and the author of 2 Timothy in chapter 2:18. He is dealing with pneumatics who have pushed the credo of chapter 1 to its ultimate limit—"we have been saved," and thus the future is of no consequence. To meet these enthusiasts on their own terms he asks: ἐν τίνι ἐσώθητε, ἐν τίνι ἀνεβλέψατε? Answer—in the *flesh*, and you dare not think little of it, you dare not neglect it: δεῖ οὖν ἡμᾶς ὡς ναὸν θεοῦ φυλάσσειν τὴν σάρκα. The author of 2 Clement takes up precisely that phrase about the temple of God which Paul uses almost exclusively in his Corinthian correspondence.[1] He then refers back to the confession and expands it: ὃν τρόπον γὰρ ἐν τῇ σαρκὶ ἐκλήθητε, καὶ ἐν τῇ σαρκὶ ἐλεύσεσθε. The flesh in which man was called will be the very flesh in which he will receive his reward. It is likely that the author of 2 Clement has 1 Corinthians 15 in mind; if so he has not completely understood Paul, or at least has not presented the totality of Paul's understanding. Paul not only stresses the continuity, as does 2 Clement, but also the discontinuity. For Paul this σάρξ does not equal that σάρξ in the hereafter. Rather, the perishable is raised imperishable; the mortal nature must put on immortality. Paul could never have made the assertion which is found in 2 Clement. But why does the author of 2 Clement argue the way he does? Very possibly the gnostic threat is greater. Perhaps he is even trying to suggest what Paul really meant over against those who are misinterpreting him.[2] For 2 Clement man will be raised in the *same* flesh. He will be raised in the same flesh and he will receive his rewards in the same flesh; therefore, it is imperative that he keep his flesh pure and spotless. These observations are followed by a paraenetic section in the communicative plural using traditional materials, urging his readers to repent while there is still time for repentance. Only in this way can they finally be received as sons. The tension between this assertion and chapter 1 is evident and has already been discussed.[3]

---

[1] 1 Cor. 3:16,17; 6:19; 2 Cor. 6:16. See also 2 Th. 2:4.

[2] See 2 Pet. 3:16.

[3] See pp. 103-107.

In short, then, 2 Clement is asserting the reality of a resurrection of the flesh in the future. This is stated not only in opposition to the more general Hellenistic mentality concerning immortality of the soul, but specifically against the gnosticizing interpretation that was being given by many to Paul's understanding of the resurrection. To refute this latter movement, the writer of this discourse ignores the tension involved in Paul's view of the resurrection of the body ($\sigma\hat{\omega}\mu\alpha$) and adopts a rather simplistic, crude and one-dimensional view which equates the future resurrection of the flesh ($\sigma\acute{\alpha}\rho\xi$) with that possessed by the individual during his present life. For the writer of 2 Clement and the church of his time this appeared to be the only way to preserve that which for them was integral to the Christian faith.

i) *2 Clement 10: false teachers*

The overall form of chapter 10 is different from the preceding chapters because it contains no supportive quotations.[1] Perhaps this is due to its summary character and its warning against the false teachers. Since the false teaching (10:5) probably deals with the resurrection/eschatology problem, this is indeed a fitting place for this particular excursus. Yet chapter 10 is not "formless"; it has a unique construction, relying rather heavily on the principles of antithesis. First, verse 1a states what is expected of the Christian: "So, my brothers, let us do the will of the Father who called us, so that we may have life; and let our preference be the pursuit of virtue." Then verse 1b states in antithetical fashion what the Christian should avoid: "Let us give up vice as the forerunner of our sins, and let us flee impiety, lest evils overtake us." This same principle is employed in

---

[1] We have suggested that 2 Clement 10 does not have the same overall form as the preceding chapters, essentially because it does not contain supportive quotations or illustrations. There is one way that one could maintain that such quotations are present. That would be to follow the suggestion of Holt Graham, *The Apostolic Fathers* (New York, 1965) by Robert M. Grant and Holt M. Graham, p. 121, concerning 2 Clem. 10:2: "Rather, he turns in the succeeding verse to a summary of the thought of Psalm 33:11-14, already drawn upon for similar purposes in 1 Peter 3:10-12 ...." I cannot really imagine, though, that our author has this Psalm in mind. The decisive verse for Graham is Ps. 33:15; yet the accent is different from that of 2 Clement. 2 Clement states that peace will pursue us; Ps. 33 that we are to pursue peace! For 2 Clem. 10:5, Graham draws our attention to possible parallels: Mt. 18:6; Rom. 1:32; Ezek. 3:18 and 33:8. The point of 2 Clem. 10:5 is that the false teachers *and* their followers will have their sentence doubled.

verse 3 where the "pleasures of the present" are contrasted with "promises of the future" and again in verse 4 where the phrase "what great torment the pleasures of the present bring" is contrasted with "what delight attaches to the promises of the future." A similar use of this antithetical principle is found in a number of New Testament paraenetic sections[1] as well as in the Testaments of the Twelve Patriarchs.[2]

"For if we are eager to do good, peace will pursue us" is a conditional sentence and it bears some similarity to the casuistic section of Ex. 21:1-11 and to such New Testament texts as Mt. 18:15-17 and Lk. 17:3. This form, which is also used frequently elsewhere,[3] is a wisdom form which does not give specific commands but rather, general rules about life; therefore its non-specific character: "If we are eager to do *good*." But what is "good"? This can only be determined from the larger context of the chapter.

Chapter 10 is also of interest because it illuminates our earlier suggestion concerning a common early Christian paraenetic pattern.[4] It was proposed that the basic starting point of Christian paraenesis is baptism. That this is the case here is indicated by the reference to the Father as τοῦ καλέσαντος ἡμᾶς, καλέω having specific reference to the baptismal context of chapter 1. *Because* of the experienced salvation event of Jesus Christ, *therefore* certain behavior is expected. The characteristics of that behavior are clearly outlined throughout the chapter. It was further suggested that the goal of Christian paraenesis is eschatological. This aspect is present in verse 5 where 2 Clement refers to the false teachers: οὐκ εἰδότες, ὅτι δισσὴν ἕξουσιν τὴν κρίσιν, αὐτοί τε καὶ οἱ ἀκούοντες αὐτῶν. Finally it was suggested that the proper context for ethical exhortations is between these two poles of baptism and last judgment, and that the most important of these exhortations is love of the brother. In the first verse of this chapter there is a reference to baptism, in the last verse a reference to the last judgment, and in between there are exhortations which include the infinitive ἀγαθοποιεῖν.

---

[1] Rom. 12:9b, 21; 13:12; 2 Cor. 6:14-16; 2 Tim. 2:22; 1 Tim. 6:11.

[2] T. Benj. 8:1; T. Dan. 6:10; T. Gad. 6:2; T. Dan. 6:1-2a; T. Benj. 5:2; T. Naph. 8:4 and 6; and in CD 1 2ff.

[3] eg. T. Dan. 4:1-7; T. Gad 6:3-7:6; also, Prov. 1:10-11:15 and Prov. 23:1.

[4] See pp. 110-11.

One of the opening exhortations in 2 Clement 10 is: καὶ διώξωμεν μᾶλλον τὴν ἀρετήν. ἀρετή here means "moral virtue." This gives another indication as to the provenance of the preacher's theology since ἀρετή is a prominent word in Hellenistic Judaism. Here in 2 Clement ἀρετή and κακία are opposites. One notes the same phenomenon in the Pseudo-Aristotelian (1st cent. B.C.) writing περὶ ἀρετῶν καὶ κακιῶν.[1] There is also a popular writing called "Two Women"— (ἀρετή and ἡδονή).[2] ἀρετή is used so frequently in Philo that Leisegang needs over seven pages in his index to cite all the references.[3] It is also used in the Hermetic writings (9:4; 10:9), Wisd. 8:7; 2, 3, 4 Maccabees. In the New Testament it is used only in Phil. 4:8; 1 Pet. 2:9 and 2 Pet. 1:3, 5 and very frequently by Hermas among the Apostolic Fathers.[4]

In our chapter ἀρετή and κακός are set over against one another. In a sense, one could understand the whole of this chapter as an interpretation of these terms. ἀρετή represents the promise of the future and κακός represents the pleasures of the present. The consequences of these pleasures and promises are further defined in verse 4: "For they do not realize what great torment the pleasures of the present bring, and what delight attaches to the promises of the future." Only he who pursues virtue will receive life and inherit the promises. Here again one can observe how 2 Clement uses the apocalyptic schema of "this world" and "the world to come." While sharing aspects of what might be called a vertical dualism with a heavenly world above, aspects of which have been revealed in this world by Jesus Christ, the preacher recognizes that this type of dualism can lead to "gnosticizing" misinterpretations—"there is no resurrection," "there is no future judgment!" To counter this our author employs also the horizontal schema of apocalytic—this world and then the world to come. Although the heavenly world above is the same as the future world to come, one should not be misled into thinking that just because the assertion is true that "'the only invisible God,' the Father of truth, who dispatched to us the Saviour and prince of immortality, through whom he also disclosed to us the truth and the heavenly life...," one can therefore participate fully in this heavenly life in the present—as some

---

[1] Aristotle, ed. I. Bekker (Berlin, 1831-70), II, pp. 1249ff.
[2] Sacr. AC. 32.
[3] Ionnes Leisegang, *Philonis Alexandrini* (Berlin, 1963), vol. 7.
[4] Mand. 1; 6:2; 10:3; Sim. 6:1; 8:10.

held—and that consequently there is no future hope. On the contrary, urges the writer, only as one pursues ἀρετή will one inherit the *future* promises.

This chapter can be best understood as a polemic against a gnost-icizing direction toward which 2 Clement's congregation was moving. Hans Jonas in his illuminating study of the term ἀρετή brings to our attention the fact that Plotinus severely criticizes the gnostics because they have no λόγος περὶ ἀρετῆς.[1] "Von einer Wartung (θεραπεύειν) und Reinigung der Seele durch Ausbildung ihrer verschiedenen ἀρεταί wüssten sie nichts zu sagen. Sie begnügten sich vielmehr mit der Auf-forderung 'Blicke zu Gott hin' ...."[2] Radical gnosticism viewed the world so negatively that is was impossible to practice "virtue" in it. For 2 Clement, however, salvation in the world to come could only be obtained if one had practiced virtue in this world. Speaking of "rest in the coming Kingdom" the writer asks: "What, then, must we do to get these things, except to lead a holy and upright life and to regard these things of the world as alien to us and not to desire them" (5:6). Virtue for 2 Clement is loving one another, refraining from adul-tery, backbiting and jealousy, and being self-controlled, compassionate, kind (4:3). κακός means "adultery, corruption, avarice and deceit" (6:4).

2 Clement 10 closes with the following warning: "If they did these things by themselves, it might be tolerable. But they persist in teaching evil (κακοδιδασκαλοῦντες) to innocent souls, and do not realize that they and their followers will have their sentence doubled." Although our author does not exactly specify the natuie of this false teaching in chapter 10, he has given clues throughout the whole discourse. At least one of the characteristics of this teaching is given in 2 Clem. 10:3: they "prefer the pleasures of the present to the promises of the future." Apparently these false teachers had a wrong conception of eschatology—"there is no future;" "already *now*," they assert, "we have been saved, we have been given light and we see again" (cf. 2 Clement 1). Therefore, they misunderstand the ethical demands of baptism (ch. 6-8), the futurity of the resurrection (ch. 9), and the relationship of the future promises to the kingdom (ch. 11 and 12). Already now they claim to be participants in the "first Church, the spiritual one, which was created before the sun and moon" (14:1).

---

[1] *Gnosis und Spätantiker Geist* (Göttingen, 1964) II, pp. 24ff.
[2] *Ibid.*, p. 24.

This teaching is related to that of the false teachers in 2 Peter (as we shall see immediately in our discussion of chapter 11); also, the warning against them in 2 Clement is somewhat similar to the warning made by Ignatius in Eph. 16:1-2: "Make no mistake, my brothers: adulterers will not inherit God's Kingdom. If, then, those who act carnally suffer death, how much more shall those who by wicked teaching corrupt God's faith for which Jesus Christ was crucified. Such a vile creature will go to the unquenchable fire along with anyone who listens to him."

j) *2 Clement 11: the double-minded*

Chapter 11 deals with eschatology and follows the pattern which we have thus far observed in the ethical section of 2 Clement. The theme (1) is stated in verse 1: "Let us therefore serve God with a pure heart and we shall be upright. But if, by not believing God's promises, we do not serve him, we shall be wretched." Then follows a supportive quotation (1a) in verses 2-4. The next two verses contain paraenesis (2), followed by a supportive quotation (2a) in verse 7.

The point of the quotation, which has been discussed above,[1] is expressed in the first line: Ταλαίπωροί εἰσιν οἱ δίψυχοι, οἱ διστάζοντες τῇ καρδίᾳ οἱ λέγοντες. The term δίψυχος should be translated simply as "doubt," thus, "wretched are those who doubt ...." The term itself appears only in James (1:8; 4:8), 1 Clement 23 and Hermas (over forty times).[2] Yet the use of the term is not the same throughout. Only in 1 and 2 Clement does it have a specific eschatological reference; in both James and Hermas it refers to moral behavior. In Mand. 9:1 we read: " 'Cast off doubt from yourself,' he said to me, 'and do not hesitate at all to ask God for anything, or say in yourself, 'How can I ask anything from the Lord and receive it, when I have sinned so much against him?" This, as well as what follows, is very similar to Jas. 1:5-8. Thus, that which is unique to 1 and 2 Clement is that they both use the word in a quotation and in this quotation it refers to those who deny a future eschatology.

---

[1] See pp. 52-53 above.

[2] For a further discussion of this term see the articles by Oscar J. F. Seitz, "Relationship of the Shepherd of Hermas to the Epistle of James," *JBL* 63 (1944), pp. 131-40; and, "Antecedents and Signification of the Term ΔΙΨΥΧΟΣ," *JBL* 66 (1947), pp. 211-19. See also Irenaeus, *Adv. Haer.* 3.1-3 where Irenaeus accuses the gnostics of saying one thing "with their mouth" and thinking another "in their heart."

When the context beyond 2 Clement 11 is examined, one notices
that the elements which precede and follow this section on doubt
about the future are almost identical to a pattern which is found in
2 Peter and 1 Clement: (1) a reference to false teachers (2 Clem. 10:5;
2 Pet. 2:1ff. and 17ff.; 1 Clem. 21:5);[1] (2) a discussion of the eschatological problem (2 Clem. 11; 2 Pet. 3; 1 Clem. 23); and (3) a reference
to the nearness of the kingdom (2 Clem. 12:1; 2 Pet. 3:10; 1 Clem.
23:5). The suggestion would be near at hand that all three are sharing
a common pattern. Not only do these three early Christian writings
have these three elements in common, they also seem to share the
same general eschatological problem. The problem is well summarized
by the question of the scoffers in 2 Pet. 3:4ff: "Where is the promise
of his coming? For ever since the fathers fell asleep, all things have continued as they were from the beginning of creation." All three writings
attempt to deal with this eschatological misunderstanding.

The suggestion that these books might share a common pattern
does not mean, however, that the problems which they are facing are
not actual ones. For the author of 2 Clement it is indeed an acute problem that there are some who deny God's future. For him this is a
basic denial of the Christian faith because Christians are people
living by promise and these promises will only be fulfilled at the
end of the age. The Christian must live patiently in hope. For this
reason, it is perhaps not insignificant that 2 Clement introduces its
first supportive quotation concerning eschatology with the phrase
λέγει γὰρ καὶ ὁ προφητικὸς λόγος. That the use of this phrase is
not accidental is suggested by two factors: it is unique in 2 Clement
and the same quotation in 1 Clement is simply introduced as "scripture." It is possible that 2 Clement uses this introductory phrase for
polemical reasons. Precisely against those who may claim to be the
spirit-filled prophets and who claim to have experienced the entire
salvation reality now, 2 Clement states, "but the prophetic word says...."
That this interpretation has some degree of plausibility is probable
in light of 2 Pet. 1:19ff. where the same phrase—προφητικὸς λόγος—is
used in a polemical context, especially against false teaching.[2]

---

[1] In reference to this verse in 1 Clement, Knopf, *Zwei Clemensbriefe*, p. 83, correctly
holds that "5 ist ein deutlicher Hinweis auf die Führer des Streites ...."

[2] Ernst Käsemann, "An Apologia for Primitive Christian Eschatology," *Essays
on New Testament Themes* (London, 1964), pp. 187-88, in referring to the matter of
prophecy in relation to 2 Pet. 1:19ff. makes a statement which also has relevance to our

However, this can only be a conjecture and it may be that 2 Clement is simply using the term "the prophetic word" as a synonym for the Old Testament[1] or scripture.

Before we proceed to chapter 12, a point of clarification must be made. We have indicated that the nature of 2 Clement 11 is eschatological. But according to the outline given, this chapter falls within the ethical section and not within the eschatological section of blessings and curses which only begins with chapter 15. Is this correct? It is, since chapter 11 is primarily concerned with presenting a correct view of eschatology so that the congregation might fulfill the ethical implications inherent in the Christian life. Chapters 15-18 are much more concerned with the eschatological sanctions of ethical behavior in terms of blessings and curses, threats and promises. The threatening character present in 2 Clement 15-18 is essentially absent from 2 Clement 11.

k) 2 Clement 12: the coming of the kingdom

The anti-gnostic thrust which has been observed at several points in 2 Clement is also to be found in this chapter. In 2 Clement 12 we find an answer of Jesus to the question when the kingdom would come: "When the two shall be one, and the outside like the inside, and the male with the female, neither male nor female." Our author is quite serious when he states that "we must be on the watch for God's Kingdom hour by hour ...." However, it is likely that some in his congregation did not hold this position, but claimed rather that the true gnostic could already participate in the kingdom, and they used this quotation for their defense. Our author takes up this quotation and proceeds to give what he holds to be the correct interpretation,

---

context and which will be further discussed below in our exegesis of 2 Clement 17. "We might well wonder," asserts Käsemann, "why all mention of primitive Christian prophecy has disappeared. But there is a simple solution to this problem. It is very evident that primitive Christian prophecy was one of the most dangerous instruments, if not indeed the determining factor, in the increasing hold which Gnosticism was gaining on the Church. It was in order to meet this danger that the Church adopted the Jewish institution of the presbyterate, of which the monarchical episcopate grew. A ministry conferred by ordination is bound to be the natural opponent both of Gnosis and of primitive Christian prophecy. Thus it was no accident that the latter either died out gradually within the ranks of orthodoxy or was crowded out into the sects."

[1] See Philo, Plant 117; Justin, Dial. 56:6.

namely, that the kingdom is not a present spiritual phenomenon, but that it is future and the Father's kingdom will only come "when you do these things."

There is a noticeable similarity between this quotation in 2 Clement 12 and logion 23 in the Gospel of Thomas, as we previously noted.[1] Langerbeck is probably correct in asserting that these quotations are further developments of certain Pauline (and Johannine) thoughts in a gnostic direction.[2] J. Doresse suggests that we are dealing with a further development of such New Testament texts as Jn. 17:11, 20-23; Rom. 12:4-5; 1 Cor. 12:27; and Eph. 2:14-18.[3] Even closer is the suggestion of Grant in citing Gal. 3:28: "There is neither Jew nor Greek, there is neither slave nor free, there is neither *male nor female.*"[4] Making reference to this saying in the Gospel of Thomas, Grant suggests that this "kind of unity looks back to the first creation story in Genesis, where 'man' is male and female .... The original state of creation is to be reached through spiritual union. Man is not to be man, woman is not to be woman ...."[5] A very similar position, according to Hippolytus (Ref. 5), is held by the Naassenes, who rejected sexual intercourse as leading to death since the first man was androgynous.

Bertil Gärtner interprets logion 23 of the Gospel of Thomas from the Valentinian understanding that the souls of the elect proceed into the Pleroma as brides of the angels, and not as bridegrooms. He concludes that "the final unity does not come about until man's heavenly goal is united with his 'angel' in heaven, when it can enter the Pleroma. But when man has become enlightened on earth, through gnosis, and then already belongs to the company of the saved, the resulting state of unity is manifested, *inter alia*, in the 'neutralisation' of the sexual life ...."[6]

In light of our discussion concerning the meaning of this quotation in gnostic circles, the particular exegesis which our writer gives stands out the more strikingly. He "de-gnosticizes" this text in terms which are completely on the moral and ethical plane. Thus the phrase "When

---

[1] See pp. 73-77.

[2] *Aufsätze zur Gnosis*, pp. 25ff.

[3] *Les Livres secrets des gnostiques d'Égypte* (Paris, 1958), pp. 155-56.

[4] Translated literally the English should read: "there is not male and female."

[5] Robert M. Grant and David Noel Freedman, *The Secret Sayings of Jesus* (Garden City, 1960), p. 141. The Valentinians often use sexual terminology metaphorically i.e., male = pneumatic, female = psychic (cf. Clement, *Excerpts* 21.1ff.).

[6] *The Theology of the Gospel of Thomas* (London, 1961), p. 256.

the two shall be one ..." is interpreted in a most ungnostic manner: "when we tell each other the truth and two bodies harbor a single mind with no deception."[1] The phrase "the outside like the inside" is interpreted to mean: "Just as your body is visible, so make your soul evident by your good deeds." And finally the phrase "the male with the female" is interpreted to mean this: "that when a brother sees a sister he should not think of her sex, any more than she should think of his." Cyril Richardson is correct when he asserts that these "terms refer, not to family, but to Christian, relations."[2] We are dealing here with an inner-church situation where, among otheɪ things, indiscriminate sexual behavior was occurring. Therefore, it must be stressed that only when the flesh is kept pure, *then* the kingdom will come and only *then* will one be able to participate in it fully. This is the message our preacher is trying to communicate to his congregation.[3]

A word must be said about the phrase τὴν ἡμέραν τῆς ἐπιφανείας τοῦ θεοῦ in verse 1. This description of the parousia is very Hellenistic and in addition to 2 Clem. 12:1 and 17:4 it is found only in the Pastoral Epistles (1 Tim. 6:14; 2 Tim. 1:10; 4:1,8; Tit. 2:13) and once in Paul — 2 Th. 2:8.[4] Again we have an indication of 2 Clement's milieu.

l) 2 Clement 13: on not blaspheming the Name

The central theme of this chapter is concisely stated in verse 1: "And we must not seek to please men or desire to please only ourselves, but by doing what is right to please even outsiders (τοῖς ἔξω ἀνθρώποις), so that the Name (ὄνομα) may not be scoffed at on our account." Two important factors are involved here, "the outsiders" and "the Name." Their behavior as seen through the eyes of the outsider, the non-Christian, must be such that the Name will not be blasphemed.[5]

---

[1] We must consider below whether the reference to "two bodies" can refer to two different groups in the congregation. If this is so, it may shed valuable light on the historical setting of 2 Clement.

[2] Richardson, *Early Christian Fathers*, p. 198, n. 42.

[3] Thus K. Mueller, *Die Forderung der Ehelosigkeit aller Getauften in der alten Kirche* (Tübingen, 1927), p. 16, misses the point when he cites this text in defense of his position that baptism in the church obligated the believers to the celibate life.

[4] For a discussion concerning the Hellenistic background of the term ἐπιφάνεια see M. Dibelius, *Die Pastoralbriefe* (Tübingen, 1955), p. 77, and Dieter Lührmann, "Epiphaneia" in *Tradition und Glaube* (Göttingen, 1971), ed. by G. Jeremias, H.-W. Kuhn and H. Stegemann, pp. 185-99.

[5] The theme of "the outsider" has received careful study by van Unnik, "Die

The reference to οἱ ἔξω ἄνθρωποι is not new with 2 Clement, but is found at a number of points in the New Testament: in 1 Th. 4:11-12 Paul advises the Thessalonians "to aspire to live quietly, to mind your own affairs, and to work with your hands, as we charged you; ἵνα περιπατῆτε εὐσχημόνως πρὸς τοὺς ἔξω καὶ μηδενὸς χρείαν ἔχητε; in Col. 4:5 we read, Ἐν σοφίᾳ περιπατεῖτε πρὸς τοὺς ἔξω. Similar thoughts are also expressed in 1 Cor. 10:32ff.; Phil. 2:15; 1 Tim. 3:7, and elsewhere. From just these brief references it can be seen that concern for the outsider, the non-Christian, played a significant role in the early Christian paraenetic tradition.[1]

To what or whom does "the Name" refer as found in verses 1 and 4 ? Richardson understands it to mean the name "Christian,"[2] and Knopf urges that "ὄνομα ist wegen des gleich folgenden Zitates als der Name Christi zu fassen ...."[3] The general theological context of 2 Clement also would suggest, with Knopf, that the statement "so that the Name may not be scoffed at on our account" refers to none other than Jesus Christ. An important concern of 2 Clement is that the person of Jesus neither be underestimated nor blasphemed. The opening of the discourse asserted that "we ought to think of Jesus Christ as we do of God" (1:1) and that "we ought not ... to belittle him." This is, of course, amply supported by the credo which follows. In 3:1 the question is raised "what is knowledge in reference to him, save refusing to deny him through whom we came to know the Father ?" It is then asked, "But how do we acknowledge him ?" (3:4). The answer, having explicit reference to Christ, is: "By doing what he says and not disobeying his commands; by honoring him not only with our lips, but with all our heart and mind." This is the very problem which the writer raises toward the end of chapter 13—the dichotomy between words and action. Because the actions of his congregation do not coincide with their confession, they blaspheme the Name, viz., Jesus Christ.

We have already had opportunity to observe the proximity of 2 Clement's environment to that of Valentinian gnosticism at several

---

Rücksicht auf die Reaktion der Nicht-Christen als Motiv in der altchristlichen Paränese," in *Judentum Urchristentum Kirche* (Berlin, 1964) edited by W. Eltester, pp. 221-34, and we are largely indebted to him in the following remarks.

[1] For a full discussion of the relevant texts see the article by van Unnik, "Reaktion der Nicht-Christen."

[2] *Early Christian Fathers*, p. 198.

[3] *Zwei Clemensbriefe*, p. 172.

points. It is therefore interesting to note that the Gospel of Truth not only shares a similar understanding of the relation of Jesus to the Father, but also uses the term "Name" to signify Jesus Christ. Since the discussion which follows is based on GT 38:7-41:19, it will be helpful to have the complete text before us.

> It is He who, in the principle, gave a name to Him who came forth from Him and who was Himself, and whom He engendered as a Son. He gave him His Name which belonged to Him—He, the Father, to whom belong all things which exist around Him. He possesses the Name; He has the Son. It is possible for them to see Him. But the Name, on the contrary, is invisible, for it alone is the Mystery of the Invisible destined to penetrate to the ears which are completely filled with It. For, indeed one does not pronounce the Name of the Father; but He reveals Himself through a Son. Thus, then, the Name is great. Who, then, could have pronounced a name for Him, this great Name, if it is not He, alone, to whom the Name belongs, and the sons of the Name in whom reposed the Name of the Father, (and who), themselves, in their turn, reposed in His Name. Since the Father is unengendered, it is He alone who engendered it for Him as a Name before He had produced the Eons, in order that the Name of the Father should be over their heads as a Lord, that which is the authentic Name, firm in its authority (and) in its perfect power. For this Name does not belong to the (category of) words, nor to the (category of) appellations (does) His Name (belong); but it is invisible. He gave the Name to Him alone, being the only one able to see It (and) being alone capable of giving Him the Name. For, indeed, the Unengendered has no Name. For what Name could one give to Him who did not come into existence? On the contrary, he who did come into existence, came into existence with his Name. And He is the only one who knows It and it was to him alone that the Father was to give a Name. The Son is His Name. He did not, therefore, hide it secretly, but the Son existed: He alone was given the Name. The Name, then, is that of the Father just as the Name of the Father is the Son. For where, indeed, would Mercy find a Name, if not near the Father? But doubtless someone will say to his neighbor: "Who can give a Name to someone who existed before himself, as if, indeed, children did not receive a name from those who gave them birth." That which we must do, then, above all, is to meditate on this point: "What is the Name?" It is the authentic Name; it is, indeed, the Name which came from the Father, for He is the Proper Name. It is not as a loan that He received the Name, as in the case of others, according to the particular manner in which each one of them is produced. But this the Proper Name. There is no other person to whom He has given It. But it was unnameable (and) ineffable till the moment when He, alone, who is perfect, pronounced It and it was He (alone) who had the strength to pronounce His Name and to see It. When it pleased Him, then, that His well-beloved Son should be His Name, and (when) He gave this Name to Him, He who came forth from the Depths spoke of His secrets, knowing that the Father is absolute Goodness. For that reason, also, He sent Him in order that He (might) speak about the Place, and about His place of repose from which He had come forth and that He might glorify the Pleroma the greatness of His Name and the gentleness of the Father. He will speak about the place from which each one has come and the region from which he has received

his essential being. He will hasten to cause (him) to return there once again, and to remove him from this place—the place where he (now) is—(causing him to) become attached to that place, by nourishing himself thereon and growing up therein. And his own place of repose is his Pleroma.

In 40:23ff. we read: "When it pleased Him, then, that His well-beloved Son should be His Name, and (when) He gave this Name to Him, He who came forth from the Depths ($\beta\acute{a}\theta\text{os}$) spoke of His secrets, knowing that the Father is absolute Goodness. For that reason, also, He sent Him in order that He (might) speak about the Place ($\tau\acute{o}\pi\text{os}$)...." We are dealing here with what Daniélou calls "an apophatic theology of the divine incomprehensibility."[1] This ineffable essence of the Father is revealed through His Son to whom He gave His Name. So we read in 38:7ff., "It is He who, in the principle, gave a name to Him who came forth from Him and who was Himself, and whom He engendered as a Son. He gave Him His Name which belonged to Him ...," or again in line 21ff., "For, indeed, one does not pronounce the Name of the Father; but He reveals Himself through a Son. Thus, then, the Name is great." It is clear from these texts that the Son not only was given the Name, but in fact is the Name. Further, according to the Gospel of Truth, this Name shares in the divine nature, and the divine nature reveals itself through it, yet it is distinct from the Father. Finally, both Daniélou and Quispel stress that the Name is here used as a mediator of revelation, and not as an instrument of creation: "the Name is indeed a Divine Manifestation, an independent hypostasis, which functions as a mediator of revelation."[2]

The Gospel of Truth and 2 Clement share a similar frame of reference. The doctrine of the invisible God common in gnosticism generally, and in the Gospel of Truth specifically, is also reflected in 2 Clement 20:5, "To the only invisible God, the Father of Truth ...." The language used to describe God's revelation in 2 Clement, He "dispatched to us the Saviour and prince of immortality, through whom he also disclosed to us the truth and the heavenly life ...," is strikingly close to that used in the Gospel of Truth. Or, speaking of Jesus, in 2 Clem. 3:1, it is said that "through him (we) have come to know the Father of truth ...." These close relationships between the Gospel of Truth and 2 Clement seem to make it even more possible that both are

---

[1] *The Theology of Jewish Christianity* (London, 1964), p. 158.
[2] G. Quispel, "Gnosticism and the New Testament," *VC* 19 (1965), p. 75.

using the term "Name" in a rather similar way. Precisely those who claim to have gnosis concerning the Father fail to realize that the dichotomy between their confession and their actions leads to a denying and blaspheming of the One to whom the Father has given His Name. "But when they see that we fail to love not only those who hate us, but even those who love us, then they mock at us and scoff at the Name" (13:4). The point is that they mock us, viz., Christians, and therefore scoff at the Name, viz., Jesus Christ. This verse also strongly supports the interpretation given that the "Name" refers to Jesus Christ.[1]

---

[1] From what source did the Gospel of Truth and 2 Clement take over this conception of the "Name?" Daniélou and Quispel discuss the matter in detail, yet we are not convinced they have clearly demonstrated their case for a Jewish or heterodox Jewish background. While we would certainly agree that heterodox Judaism provided the general milieu for such an understanding, it is only this heterodox Judaism in conjunction with Christology which provides any kind of an adequate explanation of what occurs in 2 Clement and Valentinus.

The Old Testament references—Ex. 23:21; Deut. 12:11; Tob. 8:5, etc.,—are too vague to be of any help. 1 Enoch 69:14 refers to the Name in relation to creation and not redemption. Even Qumran (CD 15:3; 1 QM 11:2,3; 18:6,8 etc.) speaks frequently of the Name, but primarily as an expression of the power of Yahweh. What is of interest here, though, is the Apocalypse of Abraham (probably early second century A.D., according to R. Meyer, RGG³ I, 72) which seems to be a further development of what is found in Qumran (cf. Quispel, "Gnosticism," pp. 20ff.). Speaking of the angel Jaoel, Quispel asserts that "it is also clear that this figure is the Mediator and Bringer of Revelation since He is in possession of the ineffable Name.... This proves that the speculations of Judaism about the Name as a mediator of revelation were very ancient and pre-Christian." At a stage earlier one finds a thought in Philo (Conf 146) which is remarkably close to that of 2 Clement and the Gospel of Truth: "But if there be any as yet unfit to be called a Son of God, let him press to take his place under God's First-born, the Word, who holds the eldership among the angels, their ruler as it were. And many names are his, for he is called, 'the Beginning,' and the Name of God ($\H{o}νομα$ $θεοῦ$) and His Word, and the Man after His image...." Here it is explicitly said that the logos is the Name of God. This parallels the Gospel of Truth far more closely than the Apocalypse of Abraham where we read in Chapter 10: "I am called Jaoel by Him Who moveth that which existeth with me on the seventh expanse upon the firmament, a power in virtue of the ineffable Name that is dwelling in me." (Translated by G. H. Box, The Apocalypse of Abraham [London, 1919]). The point that should not be overlooked here is that the Name only dwells, but is not identical with, the person. Now even if Box's (p. xxv) conjecture is correct that Jaoel is properly the Name itself, it is still more likely that it was the type of thought represented by Philo which influenced both 2 Clement and the Gospel of Truth, first because it is earlier in time, and secondly because the whole thought world is so much closer than that of the Apocalypse of Abraham.

In terms of the New Testament itself, the most that we can say is that it helped prepare

There is a passage in 1 Clem. 47:6ff. which must be noted: "It is disgraceful, exceedingly disgraceful, and unworthy of your Christian upbringing, to have it reported that because of one or two individuals the solid and ancient Corinthian Church is in revolt against its presbyters. This report, moreover, has reached not only us, but those who dissent from us as well. The result is that the Lord's name is being blasphemed because of your stupidity, and you are exposing yourselves to danger." There is a remarkable proximity here to 2 Clement 13. In each case the paraenesis points out: 1) the poor behavior of the Corinthians; 2) the relation of this behavior to the outsiders; and, 3) the fact that the Name is ridiculed. It is worth raising the question whether both 1 and 2 Clement might be referring to the same situation in which the revolt against the presbyters in Corinth caused the Name to be blasphemed.[1]

---

for that which is found in the Gospel of Truth, but its reflection about the name moves at a simpler level. Christ is never explicitly called the "Name." At most we find Old Testament quotations which because of the context possibly refer to Christ (e.g., Is. 52:5 in Rom. 10:12). Even in Jn. 17:6 Christ is not explicitly identified with the Name; rather, Christ manifests the name of the Father. In Jas. 2:7 we read: "Is it not they who blaspheme that honorable name by which you are called ?" Here, as in many of the passages in the Shepherd dealing with the Name, what is meant is the name "Christian," not "Christ." As Dibelius puts it, *Der Brief der Jakobus* (Göttingen, 1964), p. 175, "Wenn man das Volk Israel als Gottes Eigentum bezeichnen will, so sagt man, dass Jahves Name über ihnen genannt sei Dt 28:10 (Am 9:12) Jer 14:9 Jes 43:7 2 Chron 7:14 2 Makk. 8:15 Ps Sal 9:18 (9) u. a. "Even Daniélou admits that the Name refers to a context larger than merely Christ: "The Name ... does not stand here for the Person of the Word only ..." (p. 150). A bit further on Daniélou makes a sober assessment of the New Testament usage of the term Name when he states that "the term is applied to the Son, in a way that provides an incentive to theological speculation along these lines."

While a discussion of the concept of Name in the Shepherd of Hermas would no doubt be illuminating, it would go beyond the range of this study. Hermas, however, never refers to Christ as the Name in an absolute manner. Mostly he speaks of "The Name of the Son of God" (Sim. 9) or he speaks about "bearing the Name."

[1] That 2 Clement 13 is dealing with a real situation of conflict and not simply passing on traditional paraenesis may also be suggested by the use of the word ἄνοια in verse 1. This word is very infrequent in early Christian texts. However, in 2 Tim. 3:8-9 it is used in the context of false teaching: "As Jannes and Jambres opposed Moses, so these men also oppose the truth, men of corrupt mind and counterfeit faith; but they will not get very far, for their folly (ἄνοια) will be plain to all, as was that of those two men." As we shall see, it is not unlikely that our author has his opponents directly in mind throughout this whole chapter. See also our discussion on pp. 1-13 and 172-77.

m) *2 Clement 14: the spiritual church*

The chapter opens with these words: "So, my brothers, by doing the will of God our Father we shall belong to the first Church, the spiritual one (τῆς πνευματικῆς), which was created before the sun and the moon." The theme of doing the will of the Father is a prominent one in 2 Clement[1] and in every case, including this one, the statement about "doing the will" is made in relation to the eschatological gift of salvation. The preacher is combating a libertinistic attitude caused by an excessive stress on realized salvation. It is this latter attitude which is under fire in 14:1. There are some who hold that they already belong to the spiritual church, and therefore "doing the will of the Father" in this earthly life is unimportant. Against this view 2 Clement tells his hearers that "*we shall* (ἐσόμεθα) belong to the first Church" only if we do the will of the Father. He stresses that obedience to the Father is a prerequisite to future participation in the spiritual church.

The concept of a spiritual church which existed from the beginning is again repeated in verse 2 and has close parallels with gnostic literature. Heracleon also used the term "spiritual (πνευματική) Church"[2] and the general conception of the church found in 2 Clement is extremely close to that of the recently found *Tripartite Tractate* at Nag Hammadi.[3] What is particularly noteworthy is that this document speaks not only of a pre-existent church, but a pre-existent church which is in close association with the pre-existent Son. On page 57,1. 35 we read: "Not only does the Son exist from the beginning, but the Church also exists from the beginning;" and on page 58, 1. 30 a "Church that exists before the aeons" is discussed.[4] The incisive remarks by Puech and Quispel must be noted: "If we understand it rightly, the Church is born from all time, in a state of permanence without beginning

---

[1] 5:1; 6:7; 8:4; 9:11; 10:1.

[2] *Comm. John* 13.51.

[3] The older designation for this document was the *Treatise of Three Natures*. H. C. Puech and G. Quispel, "Le quatrième écrit gnostique du Codex Jung," *VC* 9 (1955), pp. 94-102, attributed it to Heracleon; however, this suggestion should be regarded with extreme caution.

[4] This English translation is from Jean Daniélou, *Jewish Christianity*, p. 304, who is himself dependent upon the information supplied by Puech and Quispel in the article cited. It is at present impossible to confirm the accuracy of the translation since the Coptic text is still unavailable.

or end, from the act by which the Son conceives himself as such, from the embrace that unites the Son to the Father .... In any case it certainly seems as if the generation of the Church, like that of the Son, is prior to the generation of the aeons and distinct from it. Most probably as the Spouse of the Son, this Ἐκκλησία is, without doubt, the pre-existent Church, the first or primordial Church, which, at about the same period, the homily known as *II Clement* conceived in its turn as 'spiritual', 'originating from on high', 'created before the Sun and the Moon.' "[1]

2 Clement proceeds: "But if we fail to do the Lord's will, that passage of Scripture will apply to us which says, 'My house has become a robber's den.' " The reference here is obviously to this earthly church. If disobedience is the condition of this earthly church, then it cannot possibly hope to inherit the spiritual church. Therefore the preacher says, "we must choose to belong to the Church of life in order to be saved." But in order to belong to this "Church of life," an expression parallel to "the first Church, the spiritual one ...," we must do the will of the Father.

What follows in verses 2-4 has a paraenetic intent and everything is subservient to this goal. "I do not suppose that you are ignorant," asserts the writer, "that the living 'Church is the body of Christ.' " Although he is probably referring to Eph. 1:22-23, this is not the crucial point; what is important is that our author begins with a given, something which he can assume his congregation knows. The assertions made about Christ and the church which follow all serve the major paraenetic goal of the chapter: "This, then, is what it means, brothers: Guard the flesh so that you may share in the spirit. Now, if we say that the Church is the flesh and Christ is the spirit, then he

---

[1] Puech and Quispel, "Codex Jung," p. 97; English translation from Daniélou, *Jewish Christianity*, p. 304. How does one understand the reference to the church in Hermas (Vis. 2:4) which reads: "She was created before all things .... and for her sake the world was framed...." We are not dealing with the same phenomenon as in 2 Clem. 14:1. The contexts are very different: Hermas stands closer to Jewish apocalyptic; 2 Clement closer to a gnosticizing Christianity. There is a cosmological dualism present in 2 Clement which is by and large not the case in the Shepherd of Hermas. Vernon Bartlett reviews some of the sharp differences between Hermas and 2 Clement with reference both to their views on Christology and repentance in "The Origin and Date of 2 Clement," *ZNW* 7 (1906), pp. 123-35. Reference should also be made to the recent contribution of Lage Pernveden, *The Concept of the Church in the Shepherd of Hermas* (Lund, 1966).

who does violence to the flesh, does violence to the Church. Such a person, then, will not share in the spirit, which is Christ." It becomes evident that our author is trying to establish a relationship between Christ and the church. Therefore, he who does violence to the church here and now, cannot receive Christ who is the Spirit. There was probably a group in the congregation who asserted that they had already been saved and that already they were participating in the spiritual church. It is such a conception, viz., that the earthly church and the heavenly Christ are unrelated, which our author is combatting. Let us now examine by what means he refutes this view.

Already in the quotation which states that the "Church is the body of Christ" it is apparent that our preacher is trying to stress the close relationship which exists between Christ and the church. It is likely that this reference to the relationship between Christ and the church as his body is taken from the Christian tradition, particularly Eph. 1:23ff., although one should not overlook the frequency of similar statements in the New Testament.[1] Following this comes another quotation based on Gen. 1:27 which is meant as a further clarification of what has been said. This quotation, "God made man male and female," is then interpreted by 2 Clement in this manner: "The male is Christ, the female is the Church." Here again our author is concerned with the intimate and undeniable relationship between Christ and the church. Were 2 Clement to stop at this point, it would have been quite likely that some would argue, as some actually did, that this is true, but that it is true only on the historical level, viz., because of the historical appearance of Christ there is also a church, but that this church has no connection with the spiritual church. This church is only for the psychics, while the pneumatics already participate in the spiritual church. It would seem then that the opponents of 2 Clement saw no connection between the physical church and the spiritual church. To counter this notion our author continues: "The Bible moreover, and the Apostles say that the Church is not limited to the present (νῦν), but existed from the beginning (ἄνωθεν)." ἄνωθεν can here only be understood horizontally as referring to time, and not vertically as is often the case in the Gospel of John.[2] Only in this way can

---

[1] Rom. 12:5; 1 Cor. 10:16ff.; 12:27; Col. 1:18,24; 2:19; 3:15; Eph. 2:16; 4:4, 12-16; 5:30.

[2] e.g., Jn. 3:31.

one understand its relationship to νῦν.[1] But his opponents could ask, what is the relationship of this church to the present church? "For it was spiritual, as was our Jesus," continues our writer, "and was made manifest in the last days to save us. Indeed, the Church which is spiritual was made manifest in the flesh of Christ ...."[2] Therefore, this present church is related to the spiritual church, precisely because this spiritual church was manifested in the flesh of Christ. Let us summarize for a moment the logic and progression of 2 Clement's thought: 1) both Christ and the church are one in the same manner as God originally made man male and female; 2) both Jesus used (synonymously with Christ) and the church existed from the beginning and both were spiritual; 3) both, once spiritual, were made manifest in the last days to save us and, concretely, this occurred in the flesh of Christ.

Because the church has been manifested in the flesh of Christ, the preacher can proceed to exhort his hearers in this way: "if any of us guard it (the Church) in the flesh and do not corrupt it, he will get it in return by the Holy Spirit." Therefore proper participation in the present church is essential to participation in the spiritual church. The present church cannot be bypassed. Why? "Now, if we say that the Church is the flesh and that Christ is the spirit, then he who does violence to the flesh, does violence to the Church. Such a person, then, will not share in the spirit, which is Christ." Since the author of 2 Clement has already made his point about the indissoluble relation between Christ and the church, he can now switch to another image: church = flesh; Christ = spirit. The difference between Christ and the church is this. Christ who was first spirit, was manifested in the flesh, but now because of his resurrection and ascension he is again in the spiritual relam. Not so the church. She too was first spirit and then manifested in the flesh, but now she remains in the flesh until the parousia.[3] Having explained the progression of 2 Clement's thought,

---

[1] If our understanding is correct, then one cannot cite Ptolemy as a parallel despite the external similarity in language when he speaks of "the Church on high (ἄνω)"—see Irenaeus, Ad. Haer., 1.5.6.

[2] That ἐκκλησία is properly the subject of ἐφανερώθη has been convincingly argued by G. Krüger, "Zu II Klem. 14.2," ZNW 31 (1932), pp. 204-205. Also, Richardson, Early Christian Fathers, p. 199.

[3] This whole conception is based on the Platonic distinction between the non-material reality and the copies thereof found in this world. This same thought is present in Philo, Leg All I 43ff., esp. 45: "Well then, God sows and plants earthly excellence for the race of the mortals as a copy and reproduction of the heavenly." See also Heb. 9:24.

we must now take a further look at the background of 2 Clement 14. One of the remarkable elements in this chapter is the conception of a preexistent marriage between Christ and the church,[1] which is remarkably close to the syzygy thought in Valentinian gnosticism.[2] Each of these syzygies is composed of male and female elements. The first in the pleroma is that between Abyss (male) and Ennoia (female). Ennoia produced and brought forth Mind (m.). The partner of Mind was Truth (f.). Then came Word (m.) and Life (f.) and then Man and Church (f.). These comprised the original Ogdoad of the Pleroma. After a crisis occurred in the Pleroma, a new pair, Christus and Holy Spirit (f.), emanated from the Father in order to restore it.[3] Already it is possible to discern an affinity between 2 Clement 14 and Valentinian thought.

This affinity might even be closer if Daniélou's suggestion that the two couples, Word and Life, and Man and Church, are a duplication of an original couple, Christ and Church.[4] Daniélou bases his conjecture on an account in Irenaeus in which Irenaeus attempts to demonstrate how the Valentinians perverted the scriptures in order to support their own conceptions. The subject of discussion is the couple Christ-Holy Spirit, and Irenaeus asserts: "They declare also that Paul has referred to the conjunctions within the Pleroma, showing them forth by means of one; for, when writing of the conjugal union in this life, he expressed himself thus: 'This is a great mystery, but I speak concerning Christ and the Church.' "[5] If Danielou's suggestion is correct it is possible to trace a progressive development from Ephesians through 2 Clement to the Valentinians.

Concerning the origin of these conceptions in 2 Clement 14, it is difficult to agree with Schlier when he makes the following assertion about 2 Clement: "So aber zeigt er deutlich, dass ihm der Mythos vom mannweiblichen Anthropos nicht unbekannt war."[6] The much more

---

[1] That this is of central importance for the gnostics is clear from Irenaeus' description of the Marcosians in *Adv. Haer.* 1.18.2: "Some of them also hold that one man was formed after the image and likeness of God, masculo-feminine, and that this was the spiritual man; and that another man was formed out of the earth."

[2] See the discussion by Robert Grant, *After the New Testament* (Philadelphia, 1967), especially chapter 13, "The Mystery of Marriage in the Gospel of Philip," pp. 183-94.

[3] See Irenaeus, *Adv. Haer.* 1.11.1.

[4] Daniélou, *Jewish Christianity*, p. 302.

[5] *Adv. Haer.* 1.8.4

[6] Schlier, *Christus und die Kirche im Epheserbriefe* (Tübingen, 1930), p. 67.

likely background is, in fact, Ephesians. In chapter 1:22ff. it is stated that God "has put all things under his (Christ) feet and has made him the head over all things for the church, which is his body ...." Similarly, Col. 1:18 affirms that Christ "is the head of the body, the church ...." Now it could be objected that this reference to Ephesians is not precise enough since in 2 Clement the relationship of Christ to the church is that of male to female, while in Ephesians it is between Christ as the head and the church as the body. However, the author of Ephesians stresses this same point in 5:25ff.: "Husbands, love your wives, as Christ loved the church and gave himself up for her .... Even so husbands should love their wives as their own bodies. He who loves his wife loves himself. For no man ever hates his own flesh, but nourishes and cherishes it, as Christ does the church, because we are members of his body. 'For this reason a man shall leave his father and mother and be joined to his wife, and the two shall become one.' This is a great mystery, and I take it to mean Christ and the church."[1] These materials were then taken up by gnosticizing circles and further developed and expanded.

Finally, we would suggest that the quotation in 2 Clement 12 concerning the coming of the kingdom, "When the two shall be one, and the outside like the inside, and the male with the female, neither male nor female," originally may have had a connection with the speculation involved in chapter 14. "The two shall be one," in its gnostic context, may have meant when the present church and the spiritual church shall be one again, viz., as a spiritual church; "the outside like the inside" may have meant when physical men become spiritual men, or perhaps, like the spiritual man, Jesus;[2] and "neither male nor female"

---

[1] In this connection one ought not to overlook the passage in 1 Cor. 6:15-16: "Do you not know that your bodies are members of Christ? Shall I therefore take the members of Christ and make them members of a prostitute? Never! Do you not know that he who joins himself to a prostitute becomes one body with her? For, as it is written, 'The two shall become one flesh.' " A word must also be added about the use of Gen. 1:27. That 2 Clement refers to Gen. 1:27 in a context so strongly filled with the thought of pre-existence is quite understandable when one recalls the very speculative interpretations which were given to the opening chapters of Genesis in Hellenistic Judaism, and especially by Philo. One need only think of the soteriological function which was attributed to Adam in such writings as the Life of Adam and Eve, or in 2 Esdras and 2 Baruch, not to mention the numerous other sources cited by Egon Brandenburger, *Adam und Christus* (Neukirchen, 1962), pp. 68ff.

[2] This would be supported by Zosimus, who probably is drawing on much earlier

may have referred to the elimination of the separation between Christ
and His church. If this should be the case, one receives a clear impression of how our author takes up and interprets gnosticizing materials present in his congregation in order to express his major ethical
and eschatological purpose. In chapter 12 he "de-gnosticizes" the
material to make his point; in chapter 14, he takes up gnostic conceptions in a positive way and by further elaboration is able to have
them serve his central theme: "by doing the will of God our Father
we shall belong to the first Church, the spiritual one ...."

3. ESCHATOLOGICAL (15:1-18:2)

a) *Introduction*

The third and final part of the hortatory discourse known as 2
Clement is the eschatological section. In suggesting that chapters
15 through 18 comprise an eschatological section, it must once again
be stressed that we do not wish to deny that eschatology plays an
important role in the theological and ethical section of 2 Clement.
Rather, what makes this section unique is that the eschatological
sanctions of blessing and curses are dominant. The primary focus of
section one was the theological assertions about God's revelation in
Jesus Christ and that of section two was paraenesis; here in section
three there is a specific discussion of the separation which will take
place on the day of judgment and the fact that this judgment will
be determined by one's present behavior. The reality of the day of
judgment is the unique emphasis of this section.

Holt Graham, in his commentary on 2 Clement, notes a distinction
in emphasis between chapters 14 and 15 and suggests that there
"is something of a break between chapters 1-14 and chapters 15-
20 ...."[1] However, this correct observation is not carried through
consistently. While Graham asserts a break between chapters 14 and 15,
he combines chapter 15 in a section entitled "Repentance and faithful
obedience in gratitude and in hope" (13:1-15:5) and combines chapter
16 in a section entitled "While we have time, then, let us repent,

---

tradition. (See Brandenburger, *Adam und Christus*, p. 81). Here ἔσω ἄνθρωπος refers
to the πνευματικός ἄνθρωπος and ἔξω ἄνθρωπος refers to the σάρκινος Ἀδάμ.

[1] Graham, The *Apostolic Fathers*, 2, p. 127.

using present opportunities to prepare for the judgment to come"
(16:1-20:5).[1] How consistent is it to argue for a sharp break between
chapters 14 and 15 and then to include them in the same section?

Some of the differences in vocabulary between chapters 1-14 and
chapters 15-20 cited by Graham include the following:[2]

	Chapters 1-14	*Chapters 15-20*
σάρξ —	19 times	once (17:5); means "mankind"
πνεῦμα —	6 times	once (20:4); means "person"

On the basis of these divergences, Graham concludes: "These differences
do not necessarily suggest that 2 Clement consists of two separate
documents, but they may imply that the author later added chapters
15-20 to his earlier sermon, chapters 1-14."[3] This conclusion is not
warranted. The difference can be accounted for completely by the
fact that prior to chapter 15 our author is dealing primarily with
ethical exhortations and after chapter 15 primarily with the eschatological sanctions of blessings and curses. For example, why is it that the
word πνεῦμα is used only prior to 2 Clement 15? Because in the only
two chapters where it is used, 2 Clement 9 and 14, it appears in a
context of illustrations and ethical warnings against the pneumatics.
Since 2 Clement 15-18 has a totally different intent there is no reason
to expect the appearance of πνεῦμα. In short, while Graham's instinct

---

[1] *Ibid.*, p. 111.

[2] *Ibid.*, p. 128. Although Graham also uses πνευματικός and ψυχή, we are not convinced that one can make a significant comparison between the two sections in question
on the basis of these two words. πνευματικός appears *only* in 2 Clement 13 and therefore
to base any judgment on this meagre evidence is methodologically wrong. Further,
Graham's comparison based on ψυχή is equally questionable since the term appears in
the context of quotations in at least four of its occurrences. Further, to make a distinction
between ψυχή as "good" in 10:5, for example, and as perishing in 15:1 and 17:1 as an
indication for a break in meaning is unallowable. The word ψυχή in these three situations
is neutral, and it is the *context* which can give positive or negative meanings to it. In
10:5 our writer is talking about the false teachers who "persist in teaching evil to innocent
souls...." In 15:1 he indicates that "no small reward attaches to converting an errant and
perishing soul ..." and in 17:1 he raises the question "how much more is it wrong for the
soul which already knows God to perish?" There can be little question that we are dealing with the same "souls" throughout; they have been misled, therefore they are now
perishing and must be saved.

[3] *Ibid.*, p. 128.

concerning a difference in stress between what comes before and after chapter 15 is correct, his explanation is not. A more plausible explanation of these different nuances in 2 Clement is the recognition that this discourse follows a basic form, and that each of the three sections in it has a different focus.

b) *2 Clement 15: the great promise—blessing or curses*

The opening words of this section, "Now I do not think that I have given you any small counsel about self-control ...,"[1] make it evident that the author has concluded the presentation of the major points of his ethical exhortation. The remarks which now follow are guided and concluded by the theme explicitly expressed in 18:2, "I am afraid of the judgment to come."

In 15:3ff. we read: "Consequently, we must remain true to our faith and be upright and holy, so that we may petition God in confidence, who says, 'Even while you are speaking, I will say, 'See, here I am.' Surely this saying betokens a great promise; for the Lord says of himself that he is more ready to give than we to ask. Let us, then, take our share of such great kindness and not begrudge ourselves the obtaining of such great blessings." First, there is the exhortation to "remain true to our faith and be upright and holy ..."; this is followed by a quotation from Is. 58:9 which is described by 2 Clement as "a great promise" and a "great blessing." If one remembers the many chapters of ethical exhortations which precede this quotation, then one finds that the selection from Is. 58:9 is indeed, upon closer examination, an appropriate one. Westermann identifies Is. 58:1-12 as a "Mahnrede";[2] it is an indictment against Israel: "Behold, in the day of your fast you seek your own pleasure, and oppress all your workers. Behold, you fast only to quarrel and to fight and to hit with wicked fist. Fasting like yours this day will not make your voice to be heard on

---

[1] My translation: Richardson, *Early Christian Fathers*, p. 199, translates ἐγκράτεια as "continence" which is somewhat too restrictive. The reader is referred to the previous discussion of the term ἐκράτεια (pp. 115-16) as well as the phrase about saving "himself and me his counsellor" (p. 89). The only further point that should be noted here is the proximity of 2 Clement, and especially this eschatological section, to 4 Maccabees in its use of "self-control" (1:2; 1:19; 5:23,34; 7:23; etc.), the concept that at death men receive the reward of the punishment due for their deeds (9:8,32; 10:11,15; 12:19; 13:15,17; 17:4,18; 18:5,13,22) and the concept of εὐσέβεια.

[2] Claus Westermann, *Das Buch Jesaja* (Göttingen, 1966), p. 242.

high" (Is. 58:3-4). When righteousness is again present in the personal and corporate life of the people, then the promise of God's protecting presence will be fulfilled. The nature of this promise is amplified in verses 11ff.: "And the Lord will guide you continually, and satisfy your desire with good things, and make your bones strong...." That 2 Clement has this chapter of Second Isaiah, as well as its larger context, in mind might possibly be suggested by the reference to the creator God (2 Clem. 15:2) and the remarks concerning the conversion of errant and perishing souls (15:1), both of which are important themes in Second Isaiah.[1]

The last verse summarizes the main point of the chapter, as well as introducing what will be an important theme in 2 Clement 16 and the dominant theme of chapter 17: "For these sayings hold as much pleasure in store for those who act on them, as they do condemnation for those who disregard them." The use of the term ἡδονή in this verse deserves comment. It is of interest for at least two reasons: 1) it is used infrequently in the New Testament;[2] 2) in the New Testament, Philo, Wisdom, 4 Maccabees and in Stoicism the term is always used in a negative and derogatory sense, yet 2 Clement uses it positively. Perhaps this unusual usage can be explained in the following way. The author of 2 Clement begins chapter 15 with a reference to his previous remarks about ἐγκράτεια, which had been contrasted with various abuses of the flesh and other libertinistic tendencies. These practices could well be summarized by the Greek term ἡδονή. What our preacher is trying to say is that true ἡδονή is not to be found in the pleasures of the flesh, but in the promises of God.

c) 2 Clement 16: the day of judgment

That the ethical exhortations are not the central interest in the first part of chapter 16 is suggested by the fact that the writer simply refers to previously discussed motifs in a most summary fashion. For example, the first phrase, "So, brothers, since we have been given no small opportunity to repent, let us take the occasion to turn to God who has called us, while we still have One to accept us," is a summary of 2 Clem. 8:12 and 9:7. Verse 2 also takes up the "pleasure" theme

---

[1] For example, Is. 42:5-6; 45:22-23.
[2] Lk. 8:14; Tit. 3:3; Jas. 4:1,3; 2 Pet. 2:13.

which had been previously discussed in 2 Clem. 6:3ff. and 10:3ff. What is of particular interest in this verse is the use of the term ἡδυπάθεια, which is unique to 2 Clement[1] among the Apostolic Fathers and does not occur in the New Testament. It does appear, however, in Plutarch's *Moralia* 132c, and the heavily Stoic 4 Maccabees (2:2,4). Following this reference to the abandonment of "these pleasures" comes the important and central thought of the last judgment in verse 3: "Understand that 'the day' of judgment is already "on its way like a furnace ablaze,' and 'the powers of heaven will dissolve' and the whole earth will be like lead melting in fire. Then men's secret and overt actions will be made clear." What was implicit in verses 1 and 2, is here made explicit—the threat of the last judgment.[2]

What is the function of verse 4 in this chapter? "Charity (ἐλεημοσύνη), then, like repentence from sin, is a good thing. But fasting (νηστεία) is better than prayer (προσευχής) and charity than both. 'Love covers a multitude of sins,' and prayer, arising from a good conscience, 'rescues from death.' Blessed is everyone who abounds in these things, for charity lightens sin." This is the only combination of the terms charity, fasting and prayer in the New Testament or the Apostolic Fathers. What is the intention of 2 Clement? Perhaps the writer is opposing a tradition similar to that of logion 14 in the Gospel of Thomas: "Jesus said to them: If you fast, you will beget for yourselves a sin, and if you pray, you will be condemned, and if you give alms, you will do harm to your spirits." And in logion 5 we read: "His disciples asked him and said to him: Do you want us to fast? and in what way shall we pray and give alms? And what observances shall we keep in eating? Jesus said: Do not speak falsely, and what you hate, do not do. For all things are revealed before heaven. For there is nothing hidden which will not be manifest, and there is nothing which is covered which will remain without being uncovered." Robert Grant correctly observes that prayer, charity and fasting are pointless and sinful for the gnostics since they regard the kingdom as present and not future.[3] This is confirmed in logion 101: "But when the bridegroom comes out of the bridechamber, then may they fast and pray." Since logion 75 implies that no gnostic leaves the bridechamber, this means that no gnostic will ever fast or pray.

---

[1] Here and 17:7.

[2] See the discussion of this verse on pp. 90-91.

[3] *The Secret Sayings of Jesus*, p. 132.

There are a number of factors which suggest that 2 Clement is refuting conceptions similar to those found in the Gospel of Thomas. First, these are the only two pieces of literature in Christian circles that combine the three elements of charity, prayer and fasting. Second, they both use these same terms in a diametrically opposed way. In reference to prayer, the Gospel of Thomas states that "if you pray, you will be condemned;" 2 Clement asserts the reverse: "prayer ... rescues from death." Further, the Gospel of Thomas suggests that "If you fast, you will beget for yourselves a sin ... and if you give alms, you will do harm to your spirits." While 2 Clement asserts the opposite: "Charity ... is a good thing ... for charity lightens sin" and "fasting is better than prayer." For 2 Clement it is at the last judgment that "men's secret and overt actions will be made clear"; according to the Gospel of Thomas 4, gnosis reveals all secrets.

If the relationship of these two writings is not simply coincidental, it becomes intelligible why 2 Clement puts this verse in the context of the last judgment.[1] Since some deny the value of charity, fasting and prayer because they claim that there is no last judgment, 2 Clement stresses the urgency of fasting, prayer and charity precisely because there *is* a last judgment. This interpretation gains further support from the fact that we have already had occasion to observe contact between 2 Clement and the Gospel of Thomas and we also know that 2 Clement is dealing with enthusiasts who deny a future judgment.[2] Such a polemical argument would explain the present position of these words in 2 Clement 16, as well as being congruent with the nature of the opponents. This appears to be a more plausible possibility than the one which suggests that 2 Clement is here dependent upon Tobit 12:8, where one finds a similar combination of the terms fasting, prayer and charity. Yet the differences between the two accounts are clear: in 2 Clement it is prayer which "rescues from death"; in Tobit

---

[1] Should it be that 2 Clement is not directly opposing any such gnostic tradition, this examination does indicate that the three elements of fasting, charity and prayer are definitely linked up with eschatology, either positively or negatively. In 2 Clement one must observe fasting, prayer and charity because of the last judgment and it is for this reason that prayer can lighten the load of sin. What our author must have in mind here is the image of scales at the last judgment. If one has been faithful in prayer, then this rests heavy on the one side of the scale and lightens the other side, namely that of sin. The Gospel of Thomas shows how Jewish and early Christian practice is reinterpreted in an atmosphere of realized eschatology.

[2] See pp. 75-76 and 98-103.

12:9 it is almsgiving which "delivers from death." In 2 Clement it is love which "covers a multitude of sins;"[1] in Tobit it is almsgiving which "will purge away every sin." While it is possible that the book of Tobit may have exercised some influence upon 2 Clement, the earlier suggestion concerning the relationship with the Gospel of Thomas is the more attractive.

d) 2 Clement 17: the day of judgment

2 Clement proceeds to define even more closely what will happen at the last judgment: "For the Lord said, 'I am coming to gather together all peoples, clans and tongues.' This refers to the day of his appearing, when he will come to redeem us, each according to his deeds."[2] On this last day the unbelievers (weak Christians, not pagans) "will be surprised to see the sovereignty of the world given to Jesus ...." They will be surprised precisely because they denied this eschatological function of Jesus. This carries us right back to the very beginning of 2 Clement, where our author urges his congregation: "Brothers, we ought to think of Jesus Christ as we do of God—as the 'judge of the living and the dead.' And we ought not to belittle our salvation. For when we belittle Him, we hope to get but little ...." But at the last day, asserts the preacher, they will learn that he is the judge of the living and the dead because he will judge every work of theirs. And on that last day they will say (17:5): "Alas (Οὐαί) for us, for you really existed, and we neither recognized it nor believed, and we did not obey the presbyters who preached to us our salvation." The salvation which the presbyters proclaimed was one with a vivid future dimension, whereas some in the congregation felt that they were so grasped by the spirit that they recognized only a realized eschatology which had as its result a libertinistic attitude. This latter fact is immediately confirmed in 17:6: "He refers to that day of judgment when

---

[1] See the previous discussion of this phrase on pp. 91-92.

[2] The first quotation, as has already been noted, stems from Is. 66:18. Throughout 2 Clement 17 we note the important role which Isaiah 66 plays. The concept ἡ ἡμέρα τῆς ἐπιφανείας has been discussed in connection with chapter 12, where it also occurs. "Each according to his deeds" is a thought which appears frequently in the Old Testament (Ps. 61:33; Prov. 24:12; Job. 34:11; Jer. 17:10; 39:19) and is then taken over by the New Testament (Mt. 16:27; Rom. 2:6; 2 Cor. 5:10; Gal. 6:7; Eph. 6:8; Col. 3:24, 25; Rev. 2:23; 20:12; 22:12).

men will see those who were ungodly among us and παραλογισαμένους τὰς ἐντολὰς Ἰησοῦ Χριστοῦ."

Verse 7 refers to the blessings of those who have been obedient. A number of key words used in 2 Clement are taken up again and put in this eschatological framework. ὑπομένω is not only used here, but also in 11:5. What is there urged, "Rather must we patiently hold out in hope so that we may also gain our reward," is here fulfilled. The tortures which the upright have patiently endured (17:7) are the same which Jesus endured (1:2). The righteous will see those who have "denied Jesus in word and act" (17:7) punished. Here again a theme which was discussed at the beginning of the ethical section (3:1) is taken up again and put into an eschatological context. It is now said that those persons who deny Jesus will be punished with "dreadful torments and undying fire ...." And the last sentence of 2 Clement 17, " 'There is hope for him who δεδουλευκότι θεῷ ἐξ ὅλης καρδίας,' " takes up themes which have also occurred before, namely, δουλεύω[1] and ἐξ ὅλης καρδίας.[2] We see, then, how 2 Clement takes up previous themes and puts them into an eschatological context, adding the specific sanctions of blessings and curses to what has been said earlier.

The preacher's stress on converting and admonishing one another in verses 1 and 2, and in more frequent worship attendance in verse 3, is directly related to this central theme of the last judgment. Let us examine verse 1: "For if we have a commandment[3] to do this, too—to draw men away from idols and instruct them—how much more is it wrong for the soul which already knows God to perish?" The exact meaning of εἰ γὰρ ἐντολὰς ἔχομεν is not altogether clear. Lightfoot[4] suggests that 2 Clement has Mt. 28:19-20 in mind. But there is no significant support for such an assertion. One must remember that the opening verses of chapter 17 are related to what has been said in chapters 1 and 2. In light of this it might very well be that our writer is referring to 2 Clem. 2:4ff.: "And another Scripture says, 'I did not come to call the righteous, but sinners.' This means that those perishing must be saved." 2 Clement can say this because both before

---

[1] 2 Clem. 6:1; 11:1 (twice).

[2] 2 Clem. 3:4; 8:2; 17:1.

[3] Richardson, *Early Christian Fathers*, p. 200, translates "we have been commanded," but this is somewhat too free.

[4] *Apostolic Fathers*, p. 253; Graham, *The Apostolic Fathers*, p. 129, seemingly follows Lightfoot at this point.

(1:6) and after (3:1) he has asserted that those who now have accepted Christianity were up to that point also perishing—worshiping idols, viz., dead gods and works of men. According to 17:1 the missionary command includes not only the negative aspect of drawing men away from idols, but also the positive aspect of instructing (κατηχεῖν) them. In reference to our verse, Beyer understands the meaning of κατηχέω to refer specifically to "der Unterricht vor der Taufe ...."[1] This may be a further confirmation that we are dealing with a hymnic confession related to baptism in chapter 1.

While our preacher recognizes this missionary responsibility, he moves beyond it to his own church situation: "how much more is it wrong for the soul which already knows God to perish? Consequently we must help one another and bring back those weak in goodness, so that we may all be saved ...." There is no guaranteed salvation, as the phrase "he ... saved us" (1:7) could imply. Rather, we must keep His commands. Therefore, all have a responsibility to help those who are weak for the sake of the total community "so that we may all be saved" at the last judgment. To achieve this end he advises: ἐπιστρέψωμεν ἀλλήλους καὶ νουθετήσωμεν.[2] These two verbs are found together again in 19:2.

νουθετέω in the New Testament is, very often, as Behm states, "Aufgabe und Funktion des Seelsorgers ...."[3] The context in which the word often appears in the New Testament may assist our understanding of its function in 2 Clement. In 2 Thessalonians there is a relationship between pastoral instruction and congregational responsibility similar to that in 2 Clement. In 2 Th. 3:14ff. Paul teaches that if "any one refuses to obey what we say in this letter, note that man, and have nothing to do with him, that he may be ashamed. Do not look on him as an enemy, but warn him as a brother." This same relationship is expressed in 1 Th. 5:12 and 14: "But we beseech you, brethren, to respect those who labor among you and are over you in the Lord and admonish you (νουθετοῦντας) .... And we exhort you, brethren, admon-

---

[1] *TWNT*, III, p. 639.

[2] See Rom. 15:14; 1 Th. 5:14; Col. 3:16. ἐπιστρέφω occurs alone in 16:1, but in the two other occurrences (17:2; 19:2), ἐπιστρέφω is linked with νουθετέω. One should also take note of the following terms which our author uses in a summary fashion in the opening of chapter 17: ἐντολή - 3:4; 4:5; 6:7; 8:4; 17:1,3,6; πράσσω - 4:5; 8:2; 10:5; 17:1; ἀπόλλυμι - 1:4; 2:5,7; 15:1; 17:11.

[3] *TWNT*, IV, p. 1015.

ish (νουθετεῖτε) the idle, encourage the fainthearted, help the weak, be patient with them all." In 1 Cor. 4:14, Paul uses the term νουθετέω in a polemical context: "I do not write this to make you ashamed, but to admonish you as my beloved children." In Tit. 1:11 and Acts 20:31 it is used in a context combating heretics. Acts 20:31 is introduced by verse 29: "I know that after my departure fierce wolves will come in among you, not sparing the flock." Verse 31 continues, "Therefore be alert, remembering that for three years I did not cease night or day to admonish every one with tears." Behm sees clearly that some of these texts, notably Tit. 3:10, are dealing with a "*Versuch, dem Häretiker das Verkehrte seiner Haltung begreiflich zu machen* ...."[1]

The use of the verb νουθετέω in 2 Clement is also related to the exercise of authority against "heretics." If it is felt that the word "heretic" is too strong, one need only remember the warning against those who "persist in teaching evil to innocent souls" in 2 Clem. 10:5. These persons, together with their followers, constitute a definite threat to the authority of the presbyters. This is clear from 17:5 where reference is made to those who "did not obey the presbyters who preached to us our salvation." What is unique to 2 Clement is that it places this whole discussion in the context of "the day of judgment," which serves to strengthen the urgency of the presbyter's warnings and exhortations, as well as his own authority.

The preacher's concern about congregational worship attendance is also discussed in an eschatological context. "Rather should we strive to come here more often and advance in the Lord's commands, so that 'with a common mind' we may all be gathered together to gain life. For the Lord said, 'I am coming to gather together all peoples, clans and tongues.' This refers to the day of his appearing, when he will come to redeem us, each according to his deeds" (17:3c-4). An almost identical concern in found in Heb. 10:23-25, especially verse 25, which speaks about "not neglecting to meet together, as is the habit of some, but encouraging one another, and all the more as you see the Day drawing near." One element which is unique to 2 Clement is the close relationship between worship and "advance in the Lord's commands." Those who stay away from the community worship are probably those libertinists "who perverted the commands of Jesus Christ "(17:6). 2 Clement also stresses that there should be regular worship so that

---

[1] *Ibid.*, p. 1015.

"we may all be gathered to gain life." "Life" is still a future gift and is gained as we "advance in the Lord's commands ...."

Both Michel[1] and Moffatt[2] suggest that the warning in Hebrews is addressed to those who were involved in another religious fellowship. Moffatt understands this to be a mystery cult. This view gains some support from Heb. 13:9, "for it is well that the heart be strengthened by grace, not by foods, which have not benefited their adherents." One might make a similar argument for 2 Clement, especially in light of the reference to idols in 17:1. Yet the more likely view in light of our previous observations is that one is here dealing with libertinistic pneumatics who felt that the spiritual achievement which they had already attained put them beyond the need of the average Christian for common worship.[3]

There are two other illuminating references in the Apostolic Fathers. The first is Did. 16:2. Here, too, the exhortation to frequent meeting is set in a eschatological context. Just prior to verse 2, such key eschatological terms as "watch" and "be ready" occur, and immediately after the references to frequent meetings one learns that "in the final days multitudes of false prophets and seducers will appear." What is noteworthy is that this is the final chapter, just as 2 Clement 17, stands near the close of the eschatological section.

The second passage is from Ignatius, Eph. 5:2ff.: "If anyone is not inside the sanctuary, he lacks God's bread. And if the prayer of one or two has great avail, how much more that of the bishop and the total Church. He who fails to join in your worship shows his arrogance by the very fact of becoming a schismatic. It is written, moreover, 'God resists the proud.' Let us, then, heartily avoid resisting the bishop so that we may be subject to God." What is striking here is the way in which the attendance at congregational worship is related to not "resisting the bishop." In 2 Clement the state of affairs is very similar: attendance at worship is related to not disobeying the presbyters. Here again we seem to have another hint of the tensions between libertinistic pneumatics and the authority of the presbyters and/or bishops.

---

[1] Otto Michel, *Der Brief an die Hebräer* (Göttingen, 1966), p. 349.

[2] James Moffatt, *Epistle to the Hebrews* (Edinburgh, 1963), p. 148.

[3] For a further discussion of gnostic attitudes toward worship, see Robert Grant, *After the New Testament*, chapter 12, ("Gnostic and Christian Worship"), especially the subsection "Rejection of Conventional Worship," pp. 178ff.

In 2 Clement the exhortation to more frequent worship is connected with the phrase τὸ αὐτὸ φρονοῦντες. Although the identical terminology is not used, the same train of thought is contained in 1 Clem. 34:7, also in an eschatological context: "We too, then, should gather together for worship in concord and mutual trust, and earnestly beseech him as it were with one mouth, that we may share in his great and glorious promises." The expression τὸ αυτὸ φρονεῖν is found only in the Pauline letters[1] and is generally used by Paul in an effort to bring two diverging attitudes or points of view together. This is expressed in Rom. 12:16, "Live in harmony with one another; do not be haughty, but associate with the lowly; never be conceited." Michel appropriately comments: "V 16 ... nimmt Rücksicht auf eine ganz bestimmte Schwierigkeit im Gemeindeleben: die Eintracht des Glaubens und die Gemeinschaft untereinander sind durch das Selbstbewusstsein der Pneumatiker gefährdet ...."[2] A similar situation exists in Rom. 15:5, where the plea for a common mind follows upon the discussion of the relationship between the strong and the weak. In 2 Cor. 13:11, after Paul's lengthy and heated dispute with the Corinthians concerning their relationship to him and their internal problems, Paul concludes his "angry letter" with these words: "Finally, brethren, farewell. Mend your ways, heed my appeal, agree with one another (τὸ αὐτὸ φρονεῖτε), live in peace, and the God of love and peace will be with you." In Phil. 4:2, the goal of τὸ αὐτὸ φρονεῖν could not be clearer: "I entreat Euodia and I entreat Syntyche to agree (τὸ αὐτὸ φρονεῖν) in the Lord."

That 2 Clement not only took over the terminology from Paul, but also its specific meaning is suggested by the context of 2 Clement 17, where it is explicitly stated that there are some who did not obey the presbyters, that there are "ungodly among us and who perverted the commands of Jesus Christ" (17:6). In other words, there was a faction in this congregation who opposed the presbyters. Therefore, they are urged "to come here more often and advance in the Lord's commands, so that 'with a common mind' we may all be gathered to gain life." What is the basis for this appeal? "For the Lord said, 'I am coming to gather together all peoples, clans, and tongues.' This refers to the day of his appearing, when he will come to redeem us, each according to his deeds."

---

[1] Rom. 12:16; 15:5; 2 Cor. 13:11; Phil. 2:2; 4:2.
[2] Otto Michel, *Der Brief an die Römer* (Göttingen, 1963), p. 306.

e) *2 Clement 18: the day of judgment*

This final chapter in the eschatological section is a personal confession of the presbyter which is guided by the central theme of this section, "for I am afraid of the judgment to come." He tells his congregation, "For myself, I too am a grave sinner, and have not yet escaped temptation (πειρασμόν)." The nature of this temptation is then further defined: "I am still surrounded by the devil's devices, though I am anxious to pursue righteousness." What does our author mean with the words ἐν μέσοις τοῖς ὀργάνοις τοῦ διαβόλου? ὄργανον literally means "tool, instrument, engine." It is not used in the New Testament, but appears frequently in Philo and the LXX. In the LXX it refers either to musical instruments or military engines, as in 2 Macc. 12:27. The author of 2 Clement most likely has this military meaning in mind. "The tools of the devil" could then refer to the various devices used by the opponents of the presbyters against him. Thus, Lightfoot is quite right when he states: "The preacher finds himself ἐν ἀμφιβόλῳ, the enemy having environed him with his engines of war."[1]

This is the end of the hortatory address. What follows in chapters 19 and 20 is merely a summary, as is made clear by the words of the presbyter in 19:1, "So, my brothers and sisters, after God's truth I am reading you an exhortation to heed what was there written ...." Chapters 19 and 20 have already been discussed in the context of the general historical problems of 2 Clement in chapter one of this study. We must finally ask the question whether there is any significance in the fact that the last section of our address is an eschatological one, and whether there is any precedent for such placement.

We believe that in placing the eschatological section of 2 Clement (15-18), with its warning against those who disobey the presbyters and against those who pervert the commands of Jesus Christ, in its present position, the author was following a well known form-critical principle. Günther Bornkamm in his monograph *Die Vorgeschichte des sogenannten Zweiten Korintherbriefes*,[2] discusses the puzzling position of 2 Cor. 10-13, a section of 2 Corinthians that was not written last, but placed last by the redactor. In attempting to explain this

---

1 Lightfoot, *Apostolic Fathers*, p. 256.
2 Heidelberg, 1961.

phenomenon, Bornkamm asserts: "Wichtig ist ... dass die Ankündigung von Pseudopropheten und Irrlehren und die Warnung vor ihnen sehr häufig am Ende einzelner Schriften und Schriftabschnitte begegnet."[1] To demonstrate this principle Bornkamm cites many New Testament and other early Christian writings, among them Rom. 16:17-20; Jude 17ff.; 2 Pet. 3:2ff.; Mt. 7:15-23; and Did. 16:2ff. This last reference is a good example of how warnings against opponents are embedded in an eschatological context. What Bornkamm has shown is that in early Christian paraenesis and preaching, warnings against various kinds of opponents often are found at the end of a writing in connection with eschatological references. This characteristic may also have had some influence upon the formation of 2 Clement.

4. SUMMARY

It may be helpful to summarize in broad strokes some of the observations we have made concerning the intention of 2 Clement. As we have already observed, the writer himself devotes the final two chapters (19 and 20) of his address to such a summary.

Basic to the discourse is a hymnic confession which describes the redeeming work of Jesus Christ. This credo, however, has been misinterpreted in a libertinistic and gnosticizing direction by some in the congregation. That the preacher and his congregation live in such a gnosticizing environment is suggested not only by the presence of such terms as "rest," "Father of truth," "Name," "spiritual church" and the concept of a pre-existent church, but also by the references in 2 Clement 6, 9, 12 and 16 which are closely related to the Gospel of Thomas. The primary characteristic of this group's false teaching (10:5) is that they carried the pendulum too far in the direction of a realized eschatology. It is an eschatological misunderstanding which sees baptism as the essence and completion of salvation. The central purpose of 2 Clement is to correct this eschatological misinterpretation, together with its false understanding of the present and future life of the Christian. To accomplish this the writer must remind and exhort his congregation on the following matters: that it is crucial to keep baptism and its seal undefiled, or otherwise there will be no eternal life; that the flesh must be kept ethically pure, since it shares in the

---

[1] Bornkamm, *Vorgeschichte*, p. 25.

spirit; that there will be a future resurrection in the flesh; that one must repent, do the will of the Father, and keep his commands, or otherwise there will be no eternal life; that the church is the wandering people of God moving toward its heavenly home and that the Christian is only a temporary sojourner on the earth; and, finally, that it is wrong to oppose the presbyters. This eschatological corrective, which the preacher hopes will result in a renewed ethical seriousness, is then reinforced and sharpened in the last section of the discourse, with the sanctions of blessing and curses, along with the stress on the final day of judgment. In his attempt to deal with this situation, the author of 2 Clement carried the pendulum too far in the direction of the futurity of salvation. Perhaps he felt that only such an intense stress on the themes of future judgment and reward could bring the enthusiasts of his congregation to their correct senses.

The distinctive intention of 2 Clement may be further clarified by a comparison with Paul. Such a comparison can be instructive at a number of points, as long as one does not arbitrarily establish Paul as a norm and then simply consider the Apostolic Fathers as a deviation from this Pauline norm. Therefore, such a comparison with Paul is intended only to illuminate the differences between these two early Christian authors.

The striking thing is that the theology of 2 Clement seems devoid of any present Christological significance. The author's initial intention as expressed in 1:1, "We ought to think of Jesus Christ as we do of God—as the 'judge of the living and dead,' " leads him to an eschatology which for all practical purposes has no present significance, other than viewing the present as a preparation for future salvation. Jesus Christ as the future judge of the world is the one who puts into effect the various rewards and punishments. This, in fact, is the basic goal of the eschatology of 2 Clement: that the righteous will be rewarded and that the wicked will be destroyed. We have here an eschatology which is primarily man-centered and which supports a doctrine of retribution.[1]

---

[1] For a further discussion of this theme with relation to the synoptic gospels, see G. Bornkamm, *Der Lohngedanke im Neuen Testament* (Göttingen, 1961); for Paul, H. Braun, *Gerichtsgedanke und Rechtfertigungslehre bei Paulus* (Göttingen, 1961); and for 2 Peter, E. Käsemann, "An Apologia for Primitive Christian Eschatology" in *Essays on New Testament Themes*, pp. 169-95.

In distinct contrast to Paul, Jesus Christ is for 2 Clement no longer the one who brought about the turn of the ages, but simply the one through whom God "disclosed to us the truth and the heavenly life ...." One can attain this heavenly life if certain things are performed, such as practicing self-control, all of which can be described in chapter 19 as εὐσέβεια, as religiosity. We see that there is no longer any link with justification and that the Christian life is not seen as a life under the sign of the cross and resurrection, as it is in Paul. In fact, in chapter 9 the resurrection of Jesus Christ is an event which affects only himself, in contradistinction to Romans 6. But could it be that the aspect of "dying and rising with Christ" had already been so misinterpreted that our author had no alternative? In a real sense chapter 9 is a demonstration of the divorce of Christology and eschatology; the only link between the two is that eschatology can be corrected (resurrection in *the flesh*) by a reference to the life of the earthly Jesus. The whole point of chapter 9 and its reference to the resurrection is to give a further basis for the doctrine of rewards and punishments, because it is "in this very flesh (that we) will receive our reward." One may legitimately ask whether, according to chapter 9, Jesus has any soteriological function at all?

It is no longer the man who lives in the light of the cross, but the man who pursues ἀρετή, virtue, who is important. It is this latter man who gains for himself the promised prize. Instead of the obedience of faith nurtured by the Spirit, a *nova lex*, a new Christian morality appears which in essence is little different from that which was practiced in Hellenistic Judaism. That is why it is those "who perverted the commands of Jesus Christ" who will be "a spectacle to all flesh" (17:6).[1] Thus, our writer never stresses baptism as a saving event, but merely as the beginning of the road to virtue. Therefore, the seal must be kept pure and certain moral actions must be performed so that one may receive his final reward in the kingdom. While both the position of the "false teachers" and 2 Clement contain correct insights, it is their exclusive character which leads to distortion: the former along the paths of gnosticism, the latter in the direction of a legalism characteristic of the third century Western church.

---

[1] One is again reminded of a proximity to 4 Maccabees. Not only is there here a discussion of self-control, judgment and rewards and εὐσέβεια, but also a discussion of brotherly love (13:26,27), the "contest" (11:20; 17:15,16) and such similar sounding thoughts as, "For on that day virtue, proving them through endurance, set before them the prize of victory in incorruption in everlasting life" (17:12).

THE BACKGROUND OF 2 CLEM. 1:4-8

The human situation before Christ is described in this hymnic confession by terminology which for the most part has no parallel in the New Testament or the Apostolic Fathers. These terms include: ἀμαύρωσις; ἀχλύς; νέφος; πλάνη; ἀπώλεια; πηρός; οὐκ ὄντας; θάνατος. From what kind of a religious milieu are these terms derived?

The first assertion made concerning man's condition before Christ is this: πηροὶ ὄντες τῇ διανοίᾳ. This is the only occurrence of πηρός in either the New Testament or the Apostolic Fathers. However, Philo does use the term frequently, as in Leg All III 109. In this reference it is not the mind but the sense which is blind.[1] For 2 Clement, as we shall see, it is not the reasoning faculty which confers sight, but Jesus Christ. An even closer parallel can be found in Lucian, Am. 46: πηροὶ οἱ τῆς διανοίας λογίσμοι.

The next assertion continues as follows: προσκυνοῦντες λίθους καὶ ξύλα καὶ χρυσὸν καὶ ἄργυρον καὶ χαλκόν, ἔργα ἀνθρώπων. It may have been influenced by the old Greek of Is. 60:17, Wisd. 13:10ff., or Rev. 9:20 (Dan. 5:23). The most likely influence in terms of context and language appears to be Wisdom 13.

Next we hear: ὁ βίος ἡμῶν ὅλος ἄλλο οὐδὲν ἦν εἰ μὴ θάνατος. In other words ὁ βίος was not ζωή but θάνατος. What is obviously meant is a spiritual death, a concept which has its parallels in the New Testament, paricularly in the Johannine literature, as for example in 1 Jn. 3:14: ἡμεῖς οἴδαμεν ὅτι μεταβεβήκαμεν ἐκ τοῦ θανάτου εἰς τὴν ζωήν, ὅτι ἀγαπῶμεν τοὺς ἀδελφούς· ὁ μὴ ἀγαπῶν μένει ἐν τῷ θανάτῳ. A similar thought is found in Rom. 8:6: τὸ γὰρ φρόνημα τῆς σαρκὸς θάνατος, τὸ δὲ φρόνημα τοῦ πνεύματος ζωὴ καὶ εἰρήνη.

Such an understanding of θάνατος is very widespread in Hellenistic Judaism. As examples we may refer to the Corpus Hermeticum[2] and

---

[1] However, Philo can also assert that the mind is blind, although not using the term πηρός. One of the clearest examples is Cher 58 59.

[2] Our understanding of the relationship of the Corpus Hermeticum to Hellenistic Judaism is influenced by C. H. Dodd's, *The Bible and the Greeks* (London, 1954). Translation is by F. C. Grant, in Robert M. Grant, *Gnosticism*.

to Philo. Corp. Herm. 7:2, as we shall see below, shows many similarities with 2 Clement 1. For our present purposes we will refer to
merely one line: "But first you must tear off the tunic which you
wear, the fixture of corruption, the dark vestment, *the living death*
(τὸν ζῶντα θάνατον) ...." In Philo this conception of a living death is
found often. In Post 45 we read: τῷ μὲν δὴ Κάιν ὁ τὸν θάνατον
δεχόμενός ἐστιν οἰκεῖος ἀεὶ τὸν πρὸς ἀρετὴν βίον θνῄσκοντι.... τὴν
γὰρ ἀληθῆ ζωὴν ὁ σπουδαῖος κεκάρπωται. Similar assertions can be
found in Agr 98; Heres 290; and Spec Leg I 345.

The next phrase contains two words which are (with one exception,
ἀχλύς, Acts 13:11) without parallel in either the New Testament or
the Apostolic Fathers: ἀμαύρωσις and ἀχλύς. The larger context reads:
ἀμαύρωσιν οὖν περικείμενοι καὶ τοιαύτης ἀχλύος γέμοντες ἐν τῇ ὁράσει ... . ἀμαύρωσις means a "darkening" or "dimness." While ἀμαύρωσις does not appear in the LXX, Theodotion has ἀμαύρωσιν in Amos
5:26 for כִּיּוּן צַלְמֵיכֶם. The verb ἀμαυροῦν is used in a similar sense in
Wisd. 4:12, βασκανία γὰρ φαυλότητος ἀμαυροῖ τὰ καλά. This word
also appears in Corp. Herm. 3:4, χρόνων ἀμαύρωσιν. A thought not
unrelated to our context is found in GT 18:15: "Through Him
(Jesus Christ) He (the Father) enlightened those who were in *darkness*
because of Oblivion."

Philo uses ἀχλύς in a manner exactly parallel. Not only does he use
the word ἀχλύς in the same fashion, but the whole context of Cher
56-62 is similar. ἀχλύς appears in the following context: "This Eve
or sense from the very moment of coming into being through each
of her parts as through orifices poured multitudinous light into the
Mind, and purging and dispersing the mist (τὴν ἀχλύν) set it as it were
in the place of a master, able to see in luminous clearness the natures
of things bodily." Already here we can note the general correspondence
in thought. In 2 Clement we read: πηροὶ ὄντες τῇ διανοίᾳ.... τὸ φῶς
γὰρ ἡμῖν ἐχαρίσατο .... It is precisely this light which disperses the
mist, both in Philo and 2 Clement.

Further, in regard to the mind in Cher 58-59, we learn, "It was blind,
incapable, not in the common meaning of blindness as applied to
those whom we observe to have lost their eyesight, for they though
deprived of one sense have the others more abundantly. No, the Mind
was docked of all its powers of sense-perception, thus truly power-
less. ... And thus all bodily objects were wrapped in profound darkness and none of them could come to the light." The obvious similarity
in thought-world is clear.

ἀχλύς also appears in Philo, Quod Deus 130, again in a context dealing with the mind's depravity. "But the leprosy which changes into a single white appearance, represents involuntary error, when the mind is throughout reft of reasoning power, and not a germ is left of what might grow into understanding, and thus, as men in a mist and profound darkness (ὥσπερ οἱ ἐν ἀχλύι καὶ σκότῳ βαθεῖ μηδὲν ὁρᾷ τῶν πρακτέων), it sees nothing of what it should do, but, like a blind man tripping over every obstacle since he cannot see before him, it is subject to constant slips and repeated falls in which the will has no part."

Dio Chrysostom (12.36) also uses the word in a sense similar to 2 Clement. Speaking of certain men who "have shown themselves wiser than all wisdom," he asserts that "they also methinks have hung before their eyes a certain deep darkness and mist (πρὸ τῶν ὀφθαλμῶν σκότος πολὺ προβαλόμενοι καὶ ἀχλύν) like that which, according to Homer, kept the god from being recognized when he was caught; these men, then, despise all things divine, and having set up the image of one single female divinity, depraved and monstrous ... to which they gave the name of Pleasure ...." The aspect of false worship is, of course, also found in 2 Clement 1.

In the next phrase of our confession we find the word νέφος, a cloud, used here as a symbol of darkness. This word appears in Philo, Vita Mos I 176: "... but a thick black cloud (νέφος) covered the whole heaven ...." The contexts, however, are quite different. The idea that idolatry is a cloud which obscures man's perception of God's will, which is central for 2 Clement, is totally absent.

It is interesting to note that while νέφος does not occur in the New Testament (except for the very different use in Heb. 12:1) nor in other early Christian literature, it does appear frequently in the old Greek, and there almost wholly in the Wisdom tradition (especially Job, Proverbs and Ecclesiastes). A rather exact parallel appears in Job 22:14, although the reference here is to God and not man: νέφη ἀποκρυφὴ αὐτοῦ, καὶ οὐκ ὁραθήσεται.... Just prior to this man is described in verse 11: "your light is darkened, so that you cannot see ...."

Our confession continues to describe man's situation before the coming of Christ by stating that he saw much πλάνην καὶ ἀπώλειαν in us. πλάνη has the general meaning of wandering from the path of truth, or the error, delusion, deceit to which one is subject. It is used in the Acts of Thomas very frequently.[1] We will examine one of these

---

[1] 31, 38, 67, 80, 156.

references. In section 80, Judas speaks of Jesus: σὺ εἶ ὁ ἐπουράνιος λόγος τοῦ πατρός· σὺ εἶ τὸ ἀπόκρυφον φῶς τοῦ λογισμοῦ, ὁ τὴν ὁδὸν ὑποδεικνύων τῆς ἀληθείας, διώκτα τοῦ σκότους καὶ τῆς πλάνης ἐξαλειπτά. Similarly, in 2 Clement, because Jesus is the light-giver, man can put off the cloud and the error which surround and are in him. The Corp. Herm. also offers some close parallels, especially 13:1 and 1:19: ὁ δὲ ἀγαπήσας τὸ ἐκ πλάνης ἔρωτος σῶμα, οὗτος μένει ἐν τῷ σκότει πλανώμενος, αἰσθητῶς πάσχων τὰ τοῦ θανάτου.

A verbal form of πλάνη is found in Philo, Quod Det 22, which reveals a number of similarities to 2 Clement 1: "Those who say so are themselves, too, in some sort astray (πεπλανημένοι), owing to their inability to see clearly the right way in matters generally. For had they not been smitten with partial blindness of the soul's eye, they would ...." In Spec Leg I 15 there is a direct connection between the worship of false gods and error, a theme also found in our hymnic confession: "Well indeed and aptly does he call the acceptance of the heavenly bodies as gods a going astray (πλάνον) or wandering." πλάνη is also common in gnostic literature and is found, for example, in GT 17:15. When one begins with 17:12, one sees that πλάνη is an unguided wandering which is the logical consequence of an existence in foggy darkness. This same order of events is found in 2 Clement 1.

There are a number of passages in the Testament of the Twelve Patriarchs, Qumran and the New Testament which speak of a dualism involving a "prince of error." This is really not the point in 2 Clement. While there is a dualism present, it is much more accurately described as a dualism of this world and the heavenly world or the coming world. The closest parallels to our passage from the New Testament are found in Titus and 2 Peter. Tit. 3:3ff. is indeed interesting: "For we ourselves were once foolish, disobedient, led astray (πλανώμενοι), slaves to various passions and pleasures, passing our days in malice and envy, hated by men and hating one another; but when the goodness and loving kindness of God our Savior appeared, he saved us." Here we have a pattern similar to that in 2 Clement 1. First, the human situation before Christ is described, then the situation after his appearance—he saved men from this condition of error. Similarly in 2 Pet. 2:18 the phrase "those who live in error" describes the human condition outside of Christ.

Coordinate with πλάνη is the term ἀπώλεια, meaning "destruction" or "ruin". While 1 Tim. 6:9, 2 Pet. 3:16 and Heb. 10:39 use ἀπώλεια in a somewhat similar manner, the predominant New Testament usage seems to be eschatological: it speaks of that judgment which is to come in the future to a given person because of his bad acts, or it refers to a coming of eternal destruction. 2 Clement's usage is obviously different since it describes the situation of the author's congregation before the Christ event. It is describing a past, not a future, situation. Similar usages can be found in Corp. Herm. 12:16, and in the old Greek of Is. 57:14 (note connection with idolatry), Wisd. 1:12-13 and 5:6-7.

The final assertion of the hymnic confession concerning man's condition before Christ gave him light and saved him, is as follows: ἐκάλεσεν γὰρ ἡμᾶς οὐκ ὄντας καὶ ἠθέλησεν ἐκ μὴ ὄντος εἶναι ἡμᾶς. Without going into the numerous parallels in Hellenistic Judaism,[1] we will concentrate on only two. The first and closest is from Philo, Spec Leg IV 187 : τὰ γὰρ μὴ ὄντα ἐκάλεσεν εἰς τὸ εἶναι .... It is most probable that it was this realm of Hellenistic Judaism, of which Philo is one representative, which influenced 2 Clement. The second passage we wish to consider is Rom. 4:17: ἐπίστευσεν θεοῦ ... καλοῦντος τὰ μὴ ὄντα ὡς ὄντα. Michel correctly observes: "Die anschliessenden Partizipien klingen bekenntnisartig und liturgisch." With specific reference to 2 Clem. 1:8, he continues: "Wichtig ist die liturgische Verwendung dieser alten Formel auf die Berufung der Christen."[2] Michel's observation also supports our categorization of 2 Clem. 1:4-8 as a whole.[3]

What is meant by φῶς in the phrase τὸ φῶς γὰρ ἡμῖν ἐχαρίσατο ? The concept of light is common to both the Old Testament and the Greek philosophers, although in different ways. However, after the time of Alexander the concept of light underwent a transformation both in Hellenism and in Hellenistic Judaism.[4] This transformation in the meaning of φῶς in the Hellenistic period is well described by Bultmann: "Wohl bleibt insofern der alte Sinn, als 'Licht' auch hier das Heil bezeichnet und 'Dunkel', 'Finsternis' das Unheil. Aber der Sinn von Heil und Unheil hat sich gewandelt. Das Heil ist nicht mehr

---

[1] Philo, Op 81; Vita Mos II 100; Heres 36; Migr 183; Clem. Hom. III 32; Hermas, Vis. 1 and Mand. 1; see also 1 Cor. 1:28.

[2] Michel, *Römerbrief*, p. 124, including n. 5.

[3] See pp. 103-107.

[4] For a full discussion of the term see G. P. Wetter, *Phos* (Uppsala, 1915); Martin Dibelius, "Die Vorstellung vom göttlichen Licht," *DL* 36 (1915), col. 1469-83; and R. Bultmann, "Zur Geschichte der Lichtsymbolik im Altertum" *Phil* 97 (1948), pp. 1-36.

das Zurechtkommen und Wohlergehen innerhalb der Sphäre des weltlichen Lebens, nicht mehr dieses Leben selbst im hellen Tageslicht,
nicht mehr die Erhelltheit des weltlichen Daseins im Sich-Verstehen;
sondern das Heil ist ein überweltliches Gut, primär gedacht als die
individuelle Unsterblichkeit, ἀθανασία, ἀφθαρσία."[1] Bultmann suggests that in this period φῶς must be understood as a "Kraftsubstanz."
It is only in this way that it can be understood in 2 Clement 1. It is
the φῶς which pulls man out of his dark and misty condition and
permits him to see again (ἀνεβλέψαμεν). Because Jesus Christ has given
men φῶς and because he has called them as sons, they can put off
the cloud which surrounded them. It is precisely because they have
been given "light" and because "they can see again" that it can be
said: ἀποθέμενοι ἐκεῖνο ὃ περικείμεθα νέφος τῇ αὐτοῦ θελήσει.
Wetter's summary of the use of φῶς in Hellenistic literature is also
applicable to 2 Clement: "So ist denn das Licht überall in der hellenis-
tischen Frömmigkeit als das errettende Prinzip gedacht, der Ausfluss
der Gottheit, wodurch die Menschen zum Heil verholfen werden."[2]

We have already noted, and will continue to note, a certain similarity
between 2 Clement and the Gospel of Truth. Related to our discussion
of light, the following references in the Gospel of Truth are of interest.
In 30:15ff. we read: "And blessed is He who has opened the eyes
of the blind.... Many received Light and turned towards Him.... Light
spoke through His mouth, and His voice engendered Life." The
relation of "light" and "life" is quite common in much of the gnostic
literature. Very often, too, the trio φῶς, ζωή and πνεῦμα appears
together. While these three terms do not appear together in 2 Clement,
nevertheless, ζωή and πνεῦμα appear not only frequently (ζωή — 5:5;
8:4,6; 14:5; 17:3; 19:1; 20:5; πνεῦμα—9:5; 14:3,4; 20:4), but also
together—14:4ff. and 20:4ff.

In order to understand the Christological statement τὸ φῶς γὰρ ἡμῖν
ἐχαρίσατο, we must also take into account the other statements concerning the function of Jesus Christ in 2 Clement. In addition to the
assertions already considered in chapter 14, we must note two more.
In chapter 3, the relation of Christ to the "Father of truth" is clearly
indicated: ... ἀλλὰ ἔγνωμεν δι᾽ αὐτοῦ τὸν πατέρα τῆς ἀληθείας· τίς ἡ
γνῶσις ἡ πρὸς αὐτόν, ἢ τὸ μὴ ἀρνεῖσθαι δι᾽ οὗ ἔγνωμεν αὐτον;
Christ is the one who brings γνῶσις concerning the Father. The doxo-

---

[1] Bultmann, "Lichtsymbolik," p. 24.
[2] Wetter, Phos, p. 74.

logy in chapter 20:5 is also revealing. Here we read: Τῷ μόνῳ θεῷ ἀοράτῳ, πατρὶ τῆς ἀληθείας, τῷ ἐξαποστείλαντι ἡμῖν τὸν σωτῆρα καὶ ἀρχηγὸν τῆς ἀφθαρσίας, δι' οὗ καὶ ἐφανέρωσεν ἡμῖν τὴν ἀλήθειαν καὶ τὴν ἐπουράνιον ζωήν, αὐτῷ ἡ δόξα εἰς τοὺς αἰῶνας τῶν αἰώνων. God is described as "invisible," "the Father of truth," titles which are common in the gnostic literature. God "sent" the "Saviour and prince of immortality." The function of this one sent by God is to reveal "the truth and the heavenly life."

We are here dealing with a definite pattern which is also presupposed in chapters 1, 2 and 14. The pattern takes different forms in 2 Clement, Gal. 4:4ff., Rom. 8:3ff., Jn. 3:16ff., 1 Jn. 4:9, Wisd. 9:10ff., and Philo, but there is one common element, viz., that God sends a divine agent of salvation from the heavenly to the earthly realm. The dualism which is presupposed in these texts comes to vivid expression in 2 Clem. 6:3. That 2 Clement is influenced by these New Testament passages is doubtful since there it is always God's Son who is sent. This is not the case in 2 Clement where it is the σωτήρ and the ἀρχηγός who is sent. However, that which lies behind both the New Testament and 2 Clement is a tradition which flows from the realm of Hellenistic Judaism, specifically its speculation about "wisdom" and the "logos." It is this tradition which then feeds into later gnosticism and is there amplified.

We have already discussed the Philonic and gnostic conception of τόπος. In connection with this theme, either directly or as a background, Philo speaks of God's "giving or sending" the logos, angels, etc. In Somn I 69 God sends (ἀποστέλλει) λόγοι who act as "physicians of the soul and completely heal its infirmities ...." Jewish-Hellenistic texts outside of Philo which are of importance here include Tobit. In Tobit 12:14 (B,A) the angel states: καὶ νῦν ἀπέστειλέν με ὁ θεὸς ἰάσασθαί σε .... Remarkable similarities to Tobit can be found in Joseph and Asenath,[1] which is also of great importance for our understanding of 2 Clement. Here, too, there is an angel, a messenger from heaven, who brings light with him: Καὶ ὡς ἐπαύσατο Ἀσενὲθ ἐξομολογουμένη τῷ κυρίῳ ἰδοὺ ἀνέτειλεν ὁ ἑωσφόρος ἀστὴρ ἐκ τοῦ οὐρανοῦ κατὰ ἀνατολάς, καὶ εἶδεν αὐτὸν Ἀσενὲθ καὶ ἐχάρη καὶ εἶπεν· ἄρα ἐπήκουσέ μου κύριος ὁ θεός, διότι ὁ ἀστὴρ οὗτος ἄγγελος καὶ κήρυξ ἐστὶ φωτὸς τῆς μεγάλης ἡμέρας. Καὶ ἰδοὺ πλησίον τοῦ

---

[1] Chapter 14; Greek text according to Philonenko, *Joseph et Aseneth*, pp. 176ff., unless otherwise stated.

ἐωσφόρου ἐσχίσθη ὁ οὐρανὸς καὶ ἐφάνη φῶς ἀνεκλάλητον. Toward the end of the chapter we hear the angel say: καὶ λαλήσω σοι τὰ ῥήματα τὰ πρὸς σὲ ἀποσταλέντα [παρὰ κυρίου]. In chapter fifteen Asenath speaks to the angel: Εὐλογητὸς κύριος ὁ θεός, ὁ ἐξαποστείλας σε τοῦ ῥύασθαί με ἐκ τοῦ σκότους καὶ ἀναγαγεῖν με εἰς τὸ φῶς, καὶ εὐλογημένον τὸ ὄνομα αὐτοῦ εἰς τὸν αἰῶνα. After all is said and done, Asenath says: καὶ ἰδοὺ νῦν πορεύεται πάλιν εἰς τὸν οὐρανὸν πρὸς τὸν τόπον αὐτοῦ.[1] This same motif of a divine agent coming down from heaven is found in the prayer of Solomon in Wisd. 9:10: ἐξαπόστειλον αὐτὴν (σοφία) ἐξ ἁγίων οὐρανῶν καὶ ἀπὸ θρόνου δόξης σου πέμψον αὐτήν.... It is this background in speculative Hellenistic Judaism which assists us in understanding the doxology in 2 Clem. 20:5.[2]

Having gained some further insight into the phrase τὸ φῶς γὰρ ἡμῖν ἐχαρίσατο, we must briefly examine a verb related to our discussion of φῶς, viz., ἀναβλέπω, which means "to regain sight," especially of those who were formerly blind, either physically or spiritually. Prior to receiving light, men were blind; but since Jesus Christ has given them light, they can assert: ἀνεβλέψαμεν ἀποθέμενοι,[3] ἐκεῖνο ὃ περικείμεθα νέφος τῇ αὐτοῦ θελήσει. Because Jesus Christ has given them light, they can see again. A close relationship between φῶς and ἀναβλέπω exists in the Corpus Hermeticum. In Corp. Herm. 7.2, we hear of the gates of knowledge: "There is the shining light (φῶς), pure from darkness ...." But before one can reach this "haven of safety," the chapter continues in a confessional style not dissimilar to 2 Clement 1, "you must tear off from around you this tunic which you wear—this fabric of ignorance, this support of wickedness, this bondage of corruption, this cloak of darkness, this living death, this sensate corpse .... Such is the hateful tunic with which you have clothed yourself; it holds you down in a strangle-grip tight to itself, so that you may not look upwards (μὴ ἀναβλέψας) and behold the beauty of the Truth and

---

[1] Chapter 17; Greek text based upon P. Battifol, "Le Livre de la Prière d'Aseneth," in *Studia Patristica*, I-II (Paris, 1889-1890), p. 67.

[2] See the important articles by Eduard Schweizer, "Zum religionsgeschichtlichen Hintergrund der 'Sendungs-Formel' Gal 4,4f; Röm 8,3f; Joh 3,16f; 1 Joh 4,9", *ZNW* 57 (1966), pp. 199-210; and Dieter Georgi, "Der vorpaulinische Hymnus Phil 2, 6-11" in *Zeit und Geschichte* (Tübingen, 1964), ed. Erich Dinkler, pp. 263-93.

[3] ἀποτίθεσθαι is common in the paraenetic sections of the New Testament: Rom. 13:12; Col. 3:8ff.; Eph. 4:22,25; Jas. 1:21; 1 Pet. 2:1; Heb. 12:1. In a number of these texts, the context is clearly baptismal.

the Good that abides in it ...." The difference between 2 Clement and
Corp. Herm. 7 is that in 2 Clement God sends Jesus Christ to reveal
the truth (20:5) and to give the light (1:4). Because this has happened,
the mist and the cloud surrounding man can be thrown off and he can
see again.

The verb προσαγορεύω can be translated in various ways, and it
has been translated diversely in 2 Clement 1. Although Richardson's[1]
translation "as a Father he called us sons" is correct, it can be misleading. For this reason Goodspeed's translation is to be preferred,
since he best captures the intent of this hymnic statement: "as a
Father he has acknowledged us as sons ...."[2] What does this mean?
Insight into this verse can be gained from Gal. 3:26: Πάντες γὰρ υἱοὶ
θεοῦ ἐστε διὰ τῆς πίστεως ἐν Χριστῷ ᾽Ιησοῦ. Schlier[3] and Oepke[4] are
correct in insisting that ἐν Χριστῷ ᾽Ιησοῦ and διὰ τῆς πίστεως do
not belong together, since Paul never speaks of a πίστις ἐν Χριστῷ
᾽Ιησοῦ, but rather of a πίστις Χριστοῦ (Gal. 2:16, 20; 3:22; Rom.
3:22,26, etc.), or of a πίστις πρὸς τὸν κύριον ᾽Ιησοῦν (Philem. 5).
διὰ τῆς πίστεως takes up the ἐλθούσης τῆς πίστεως of Gal. 3:25.
"Deshalb," observes Schlier, "ist nicht der Glaubensvollzug gemeint,
sondern der eben erwähnte Glaube, der gekommen ist .... Es ist also
ein von jeder Schwankung im persönlichen Glaubensstand des Einzelnen unabhängiges Faktum, dass der mit Christus gekommene Glaube
alle in Christus Jesus zu Söhnen Gottes gemacht hat."[5] πίστις therefore means the possibility of a new existence which is given in Christ's
coming. As Paul immediately continues, it is through baptism that we
became "sons of God." If 2 Clement 1 contains a baptismal hymn, as
we have suggested, then here too, as is indicated in other parts of
2 Clement, it is in baptism that one ceases worshipping other gods,
receives "light," is "acknowledged as a son," and is "saved."

While our author accepts this statement, he is aware of a possible
"gnosticizing" interpretation in his congregation. Because of this
possible *mis*interpretation, he himself speaks of sonship in a more cautious way: δῶμεν οὖν αὐτῷ αἶνον, μὴ ἀπὸ στόματος μόνον, ἀλλὰ καὶ
ἀπὸ καρδίας, ἵνα ἡμᾶς προσδέξηται ὡς υἱούς (9:10). Just because one

---

[1] *Apostolic Fathers*, p. 193.
[2] Edgar Goodspeed, *The Apostolic Fathers* (New York, 1950), p. 85.
[3] Heinrich Schlier, *Der Brief an die Galater* (Göttingen, 1962), p. 171.
[4] Albrecht Oepke, *Der Brief des Paulus an die Galater* (Berlin, 1964), p. 88.
[5] Schlier, *Galater*, pp. 171-72.

has been acknowledged as a son does not automatically mean that one will be accepted as a son. Final acceptance as a son is dependent upon doing the will of the Father and being obedient to His law. For the author of 2 Clement it is the ethical consequence of baptism which will be of decisive importance in the eschatological judgment.

The conclusion we have reached in reference to the background of the confession in 2 Clem. 1:4-8 is that it stems from a Christian tradition which is heavily influenced by Hellenistic Judaism and a religious atmosphere which has points of contact with a developing gnosticism. Where there are parallels to the New Testament it is usually to some of the later writings, which display a similar relationship as does 2 Clement to Hellenistic Judaism and to Hellenistic culture.

2 CLEMENT 14 AND PAUL'S *ΑΝΩ ΙΕΡΟΥΣΑΛΗΜ*

FURTHER REFLECTIONS ON THE USE OF IS. 54:1

When one considers 2 Clement's doctrine of the church as portrayed in chapters 1 and 2, but especially in chapter 14, one is impressed by the striking similarity of that concept to Paul's use of the term ἄνω 'Ιερουσαλήμ in Gal. 4:26, together with its idea of pre-existence. One need only look at 2 Clem. 14:2 where the church is described as οὐ νῦν εἶναι, ἀλλὰ ἄνωθεν. ἦν γὰρ πνευματική, ὡς καὶ ὁ 'Ιησοῦς ἡμῶν, ἐφανερώθη δὲ ἐπ' ἐσχάτων τῶν ἡμερῶν, ἵνα ἡμᾶς σώσῃ.[1] This aspect of pre-existence is also assumed in 2:1: "for our Church was barren before it was given children." The similitarity between the two pieces of literature gains further significance when one considers 2 Clement's statement in 6:3, ἔστιν δὲ οὗτος ὁ αἰὼν καὶ ὁ μέλλων δύο ἐχθροί, in light of Paul's distinction between the νῦν 'Ιερουσαλήμ and the ἄνω 'Ιερουσαλήμ. A careful investigation into the setting of Isaiah 54 in the Pauline context could shed valuable light on the intention and background of 2 Clement 2 and 14.

We must examine Gal. 4:26 dealing with the ἄνω 'Ιερουσαλήμ, and verse 27 dealing with the quotation from Is. 54:1. To fully understand Paul's discussion, one must recognize the apocalyptic presuppositions of his eschatology. The apocalypticists introduced a new note into Jewish Messianic thought, viz., a cosmological dualism, which leads to the doctrine of the two aeons, this aeon and the future aeon. This development can be observed in such writings as Enoch, Baruch and IV Ezra, to name only a few. It is this same kind of aeon speculation which dominates Paul's eschatology. In Jesus' resurrection the new aeon has come, and all that is to be expected in the future is the consummation of that which has already begun. This involves the final victory over death, the last judgment which will take place at the return of the Messiah (1 Cor. 4:5; 2 Cor. 5:10), and finally, the restoration of complete sovereignty to God (1 Cor. 15:24). Paul is living in a transitional epoch in which this age and the coming age already mingle,

---

[1] See our previous discussion on pp. 160-66.

signifying that the Messianic age has dawned. With Schoeps we agree that the "mingling of the two ages constitutes the distinctive eschatological standpoint of Pauline theology."[1] In 1 Cor. 7:31 we hear that the present form of the world is passing away, and although the old aeon is still in force, it is already crumbling (1 Cor. 2:6); for upon Paul's generation the end of the ages has come (1 Cor. 10:11). It is a reality now which only awaits consummation (Rom. 8:19ff.; 2 Cor. 4:16-18). It is precisely this kind of aeon speculation which is reflected in the terms *νῦν Ἰερουσαλήμ* and *ἄνω Ἰερουσαλήμ* in Galatians 4. Schlier is correct when he says that "sicherlich ist auch für Paulus das obere Jerusalem der neue Äon."[2]

What is the background of this term *ἄνω Ἰερουσαλήμ*? Moore and others claim that it can be sufficiently explained from the Jewish tradition.[3] The biblical roots can be traced back to such writings as Ezek. 40ff.; Is. 54:11ff., 60:10-14. However, the concept of the "Jerusalem above" as presented in Galatians is more closely approximated in 4 Ezra 7:26ff.:

> For behold the days come, and it shall be when the signs which I have foretold unto thee shall come to pass, [Then shall the city that now is invisible appear, and the land which is now concealed be seen;] And whosoever is delivered from the predicted evils, the same shall see my wonders. For my Son the Messiah shall be revealed, together with those who are with him, and shall rejoice the survivors four hundred years.

Also, 1 Enoch 90:28-29:

> And I stood up to see till they folded up that old house; and carried off all the pillars, and all the beams and ornaments of the house were at the same time folded up with it, and they carried it off and laid it in a place in the south of the land. And I saw till the Lord of sheep brought up a new house greater and loftier than that first, and set it up in the place of the first which had been folded up: all its pillars were new, and its ornaments were new and larger than those of the first, the old one which He had taken away, and all the sheep were within it.

Even more explicit is the Book of Elijah, chapter 10:

---

[1] H. J. Schoeps, *Paul* (Philadelphia, 1961), p. 99.

[2] Schlier, *Galater*, p. 223.

[3] He holds that the "whole conception is Jewish. Jerusalem is to be the seat of the theocracy in the future as in the past. It is, indeed, a new Jerusalem which comes down from heaven in place of the old ...." G. F. Moore, *Judaism* (Cambridge, 1958), II, p. 342.

> Elias sprach: Ich sehe, wie eine schöne, prächtig grosse Stadt vom Himmel kommt;
> es heisst ja in der Schrift: 'Jerusalem, du wieder aufgebaut wie eine Stadt, die wohl
> zusammen ist gefügt', gebaut und auch vollendet. Es wohnt ihr Volk darin ...."[1]

The basic assumption of these apocalyptic writings is that there is a
pre-existent heavenly Jerusalem which will be revealed at a given point
in history, a fact which is also expressed with great clarity in 2 Baruch
4:2-7.

When Paul states that the heavenly Jerusalem is our mother, he is
asserting that the existence of the Christian is determined by this realm.
It is the church, those who are in Christ, who receive life from the
Jerusalem above. As Schlier comments: "Für ihn ist also der neue
Äon, das himmlische Jerusalem, schon gegenwärtig in der christlichen
Kirche."[2] But what is peculiar to Paul is that this heavenly Jerusalem does not fulfill nor replace the Jerusalem that now is. Rather,
both exist next to one another as two opposing spheres. The Jerusalem
which now is, represents slavery, sin and death, while the Jerusalem
above, represented in and through the church, is the realm of freedom.
At this point one detects a different stress in 2 Clement, where the
reality of the heavenly, spiritual church in the present realm of corruption is minimized. The tension which Paul was able to maintain
was lost by many after him; either they overstressed the present
reality of the heavenly existence, or they overemphasized the futurity
of that new existence, as did 2 Clement.

With this background in mind, we can now ask why Paul at this
point introduces a quotation from Is. 54:1.[3] Is. 54:1 is a hymn of re-
joicing. The "barren one" is Jerusalem who was barren after the
destruction of the city in 586 B.C. She is now solitary, desolate and
unloved, but soon she will have more children than in the days of her
marriage, viz., from the covenant on Sinai to their separation after the
destruction of Jerusalem. In short, the "barren" wife is a figure for
Zion during the exile, the married one is the city before the exile.[4] Even
though Isaiah speaks as if the turning point was a past event, we must

---

[1] P. Riessler, *Altjüdisches Schrifttum ausserhalb der Bibel* (Darmstadt, 1966), p. 239.

[2] Schlier, *Galater*, p. 223.

[3] The quotation follows the Greek versions of the Old Testament, all of which fail
to translate the Hebrew "to rejoice or to sing."

[4] The figure of a barren wife is quite a common one in the tradition of Israel. One
need think only of the wives of the patriarchs. As Muilenberg says, *Interpreter's Bible*, V
(Nashville, 1952), p. 634, "Birth was a wonder full of mystery and was considered to be
the gift and act of God's gracious goodness."

keep in mind that the day of salvation was still a promise—a hope yet to be fulfilled. The three major elements of Isaiah 54, the hymn of praise ("Sing, O barren one ..."), the promise of salvation ("Fear not ...") and the announcement of salvation ("my steadfast love shall not depart from you ...") all have a future reference. It is interesting to note how these promissory themes of Isaiah 54 are taken up again in capsule form in 2 Clement's exegesis of Isaiah 54.[1] If our understanding of Isaiah 54 is correct, then it may have been because of this eschatological note that Paul found this passage of scripture appropriate for his description of the Jerusalem above.[2] It serves both as a description of and a proof-text for his understanding of the ἄνω 'Ιερουσαλήμ. Paul takes the married one to be the νῦν 'Ιερουσαλήμ and the desolate one (who will now bear fruit) as the pre-existent ἄνω 'Ιερουσαλήμ, the new aeon which was revealed in the death and resurrection of Jesus Christ. It is this one, the ἄνω 'Ιερουσαλήμ which is our mother. Insofar as Paul retains the original eschatological sense of the verse, which for him is now being realized, he is much more faithful to its original intent, than, for example, the rabbinical exegetical tradition, which on the whole has totally misplaced the eschatological accent.

Let us summarize our findings thus far. Paul begins with two present realities—the Jews and the Christians, the present Jerusalem and the Jerusalem above. It is Paul's intention to show to the threatened Christian community at Galatia that they really are members of the Jerusalem above, and that they cannot be members of the present Jerusalem because God has rejected it as a possibility for salvation. In short, he is telling them that they live by faith; it is through this that they became sons of God, which is true freedom, and not by works of the law, which is slavery. In order to prove this authoritatively he refers to the Genesis narrative concerning Hagar and Sarah and states that this is really an allegory referring to the present situation.

---

[1] Westermann, *Jesaja*, p. 220, confirms this promissory character in Isaiah 54 when he states: "Damit ist nun ganz klar, dass Deuterojesaja in Kap. 54 die Verheissung, die er zu verkünden hat, ausweitet: zur Verheissung der Rettung tritt die Verheissung des Segens in der besonderen Form der Mehrungsverheissung."

[2] Certainly James Smart's reflections concerning the eschatological nature of this verse would have been shared by Paul and 2 Clement. "This was Second Isaiah's vision, but it was not to have its true power and to begin its invasion of the world until the vision came out of the future and became the reality of life in human flesh and blood in Jesus Christ." *History and Theology in Second Isaiah* (Philadelphia, 1965), p. 218.

Hagar is equivalent to the old covenant and the νῦν 'Ιερουσαλήμ, and
Sarah is equivalent to the new covenant and the ἄνω 'Ιερουσαλήμ. That
the Jerusalem above has already broken in is described and supported
by the use of Is. 54:1. Finally, the allegorical treatment of Isaac and
Ishmael permits the final conclusion that it is only the sons κατὰ
πνεῦμα who receive the κληρονομία. The old Israel has been rejected
by God whereas it is now the new Christian community which is the
Israel of God.[1]

Is there any relation between Paul's exegesis in Galatians 4 and that
of Philo?[2] Philo was a proponent of allegorical exegesis, but he himself tells us that his is a mediating position between those who accept
only the literal sense and reject all allegorising and those who accept
only the allegorical sense.[3] In Congr 1ff., Philo allegorizes the Sarah-

---

[1] A few further comments must be made with reference to Gal. 4:28-31. When Paul
begins by saying "Now we, brethren, like Isaac, are children of promise," he is moving
to the next step in his allegory. Thus far the two women have represented the two communities; now he allegorizes the two sons, Isaac and Ishmael, to make the basic point
crystal clear to his readers. Paul need only mention here the word "promise" without
further development, since this has been one of the leading themes in the preceding
chapter. He quickly moves on to the theme of persecution: "But as at that time he who
was born according to the flesh persecuted him who was born according to the Spirit,
so it is now. But what does the scripture say? 'Cast out the slave and her son; for the
son of the slave shall not inherit with the son of the free woman.' " One must agree with
Schlier, *Galater*, pp. 226-27, when he states that: "Paulus denkt keineswegs an die Unruhen
und die Verwirrung, die seine judaistischen Gegner in den galatischen Gemeinden an-
richten. Deren Tätigkeit hat er 1:7 (2:4) 3:1 ganz anders gekennzeichnet. Vielmehr hat
er die Verfolgung der Christen durch die Synagoge vor Augen, wie er sie selbst betrieben
hatte (1:13,23) ...." The point of the Genesis quotation, allegorically understood, is that
the rejection of Ishmael points to a rejection of the sons of Abraham κατὰ σάρκα in favor
of κατὰ πνεῦμα. Paul's final conclusion is: "So, brethren, we are not children of the
slave but of the free woman." We would suggest that the διό refers to the preceding
scriptural arguments. "Deshalb nun, weil die Kennzeichen aus der Allegorie zutreffen,
die auf die geistliche Abstammung hinweisen, sind die Christen nicht der Magd Kinder,
sondern der Freien" (Kähler in Schlier, *Galater*, p. 228).

[2] The allegorical method which Paul employs with reference to Hagar and Sarah in
Galatians 4 has no rabbinical parallel. Speaking of Pauline exegesis in Gal. 4:21-31,
Schoeps comments that "by its wilful distortions (it) is sheer Hellenistic midrash speculation, against a rather obscure apocalyptic background." And further "... it is an utter
violation of the basic rule of rabbinical hermeneutics: 'No word of scripture must ever
lose its original sense' (Sabb. 63a)" (*Paul*, p. 238, n. 3). Certainly such a sharp differentiation between "rabbinical" and "Hellenistic" can no longer be maintained today.
See n. 3 on p. 26.

[3] Somn 1 92; Migr 89ff.

Hagar story. For Philo, as he states in the previous section, Sarah cannot become one's mother unless one is properly trained in the culture of education. There is a certain process that must be gone through, and this is represented by Hagar. The higher wisdom, Sarah, can only be attained gradually. For Paul, in contrast to Philo, there is no process needed to reach Sarah, only faith. Hagar is not a stage on the way, but that which has been rejected. Where Philo's exegesis is marked by a non-eschatological reinterpretation of historical events as symbolizing processes in the human soul, Paul's exegesis is always oriented toward τὰ ἔσχατα.

Certainly one cannot underestimate the influence of the apocalyptic tradition on Paul. It is in this realm of apocalyptic literature, viz., in the Qumran sect, that we find the closest parallel to the Pauline exegesis of Gal. 4:21-31. Without going into great detail, let us simply refer to at least two examples which show how very similarly Paul and Qumran use allegorical exegesis. In CD 6:1-11 a passage concerning the digging of the well is quoted from Num. 21:18. This is then allegorically applied to the Teacher of Righteousness: "The well is the Law, and those who dug it are the converts of Israel who went out from the land of Judah and were exiled in the land of Damascus ...." Otto Betz states: "Der Lehrer der Gerechtigkeit und Toraforscher hat nach der Damaskusschrift eine einzigartige Stellung in der Gemeinde. Auf ihn weist das Zeugnis der Tora, wie in einer allegorischen Auslegung des Brunnenliedes nachgewiesen wird (CD 6,7-11)."[1] Then, in the same way that Paul uses Is. 54:1 to support his understanding of the Jerusalem above, the Damascus Document quotes Is. 53:16 to support its understanding of the Teacher of Righteousness. One could also refer to such other passages as CD 7:14ff., or 1 QS 8:14ff. The rationale for using allegory in Qumran is very similar to that of Paul in Galatians 4. The end-time is here and the present eschatological moment is already reflected in the scripture. Therefore, the scriptures become a support for the present moment.[2]

---

[1] Otto Betz, *Offenbarung und Schriftforschung in der Qumransekte* (Tübingen, 1960), p. 23. We are not asserting a direct influence of Qumran; we are only citing a parallel from Qumran for the sake of illumination in order to more clearly show the processes involved in this type of exegesis. Because of their peculiar historical situation both Qumran and the primitive church move a step beyond the Jewish-Hellenistic synagogue in their interpretation of scripture.

[2] "Die Kunst der Allegorese wird vor allem da benötigt," says Betz, *Offenbarung*, p. 176, "wo die Notwendigkeit der Toraforschung und die grosse Bedeutung des Lehrers

An analysis of 2 Clement 2 reveals that Is. 54:1 is used in a manner similar to the way Paul uses it. The author of our discourse interprets "Rejoice, you who are barren and childless" as follows: "he (Isaiah) refers to us; for our Church was barren before it was given children." That our author is here referring to the pre-existent heavenly church is made clear from chapter 14 where he describes "the first Church, the spiritual one, which was created before the sun and the moon." In addition, he states: "The Bible, moreover, and the Apostles say that the Church is not limited to the present, but ἀλλὰ ἄνωθεν [see Gal. 4:26]. For it was spiritual, as was our Jesus, and was made manifest in the last days to save us." 2 Clement, therefore, means that the church, the pre-existent one, was barren before Jesus Christ came to call us as sons. And precisely because we have been called as sons "we must choose to belong to the Church of life in order to be saved" (14:1). All those who do the will of God the Father "shall belong to the first Church, the spiritual one ...." This seems to be very similar to what Paul means when he says that the ἄνω Ἰερουσαλήμ is our mother.

Yet there are differences. In 2 Clement the revelation of "the first Church, the spiritual one" in Jesus Christ (14:3) does not have the character of being "the first fruits" of that which is to come; rather it pulls man away from his old life and sets him on the road to ἀρετή. If he has been faithful and obedient, then and only then will he participate in the future, spiritual church. Whereas the "already—not yet" aspect of the Christian life is kept in balance by Paul, the "not yet" dominates the theology of 2 Clement. In all likelihood the writer felt compelled to stress this aspect because some in his congregation overemphasized the "already" to the exclusion of the "not yet."

Because of his situation, the author of 2 Clement is not satisfied simply to quote Is. 54:1. He proceeds to give an allegorical exegesis. Even though 2 Clement is not dependent upon a verse by verse exegesis of Isaiah 54 by Paul, as Paul never gives one, one can nevertheless see a possible Pauline influence shimmer through in 2 Clement's exegesis. In commenting upon "Shout, you who were never in labor," 2 Clement states: "this is what he (Isaiah) means: we should offer our prayers to God with sincerity, and not lose heart like women in labor." It is rather striking that ἐγκακέω appears only here in all of the

---

der Gerechtigkeit durch das Wort der Schrift belegt werden sollen." See also F. F. Bruce, *Biblical Exegesis in the Qumran Texts* (London, 1960).

Apostolic Fathers, and that in the New Testament it appears only within the Pauline letters (2 Cor. 4:1; Gal. 6:9; 2 Th. 3:13) or those of his school (Eph. 3:13), with the single exception of Lk. 18:1. Strikingly, ἐγκακέω appears in Gal. 6:9, precisely that section in which Paul is drawing the consequences of his previous theological discussion. This again gives the impression that the author of 2 Clement might have the Pauline letters in mind, especially Galatians, or that he stands in a similar exegetical tradition.

The final portion of Is. 54:1ff. which our author interprets is this: "'The desolate woman has many more children than the one with the husband,' because our people seemed to be abandoned by God. But now that we believe, we have become more numerous than those who seemed to have God." Again a number of points of contact between 2 Clement and Galatians arise. Decisive for the argument at hand in 2 Clement is this fact: "But now ... we believe." It is exactly this which is the turning point for Paul, too. In Gal. 3:25 he states: "But now that faith has come, we are no longer under a custodian; for in Christ Jesus you are all sons of God, through faith. For as many of you as were baptized into Christ have put on Christ." It is because "faith has come" that the Christians no longer belong to Hagar, the present Jerusalem, but to Sarah, the ἄνω Jerusalem. And so we would suggest that the author of 2 Clement is interpreting Isaiah 54 to say, now, because we believe "we have become more numerous than those who seemed to have God." The "we" obviously refers to the church and "those who seemed to have God" to the Jews. This is certainly how Justin interprets the quotation from Isaiah 54 at this point. Possibly the phrase τῶν δοκούντων ἔχειν θεόν in 2 Clement may be similar to the reference to the rejection of the present Jerusalem in Gal. 4:30 which Paul stresses by quoting the verse from Gen. 21:10: "Cast out the slave and her son; for the son of the slave shall not inherit with the son of the free woman."

We would conclude our discussion with the observation that there are significant points of contact between 2 Clement 2 and 14 and Paul and the Pauline school.[1] This suggestion is also strengthened by our

---

[1] One must also consider the possibility that 2 Clement stands close to the exegetical tradition of Paul's opponents in Galatia. Why does Paul argue as he does in Gal. 4:21ff. ? Could it be that he is trying to refute his opponents on their own grounds ? It is difficult to imagine that Paul would argue the way he does unless he anticipated that his opponents would understand him.

previous examination which found that in 2 Clement and Paul, Is. 54:1 is placed in the context of the "soteriologische Kontrast-Schema," a pattern found predominantly within writings belonging to Paul and the Pauline school.[1]

Let us attempt to draw together these observations. The concept of a heavenly Jerusalem which is prominent in Jewish apocalyptic circles, is taken up by Paul, together with the quotation from Is. 54:1, in Galatians 4. That he might have chosen this line of argument because of some specific element in the Galatian situation is not clear, but possible. At any rate, Paul's discussion could be easily misinterpreted in a gnosticizing direction. This might be suggested not only by the argument of the writer and the use of terms in 2 Clement 14 which have parallels in gnostic literature, but also by the reflection of Is. 54:1 in GP 107:31-36 and by the use of the term ἄνω 'Ιερουσαλήμ in Hippolytus' presentation of the gnostics: τοῦτό ἐστι, φησί, τὸ γεγραμμένον· ἐγὼ εἶπα· θεοί ἐστε καὶ υἱοὶ ὑψίστου πάντες, ἐὰν ἀπὸ τῆς Αἰγύπτου φυγεῖν σπεύδητε καὶ γένησθε πέραν τῆς 'Ερυθρᾶς θαλάσσης εἰς τὴν ἔρημον, τουτέστιν ἀπὸ τῆς κάτω μίξεως ἐπὶ τὴν ἄνω 'Ιερουσαλήμ, ἥτις ἐστὶ μήτηρ ζώντων[2].

It has become clear from this study that 2 Clement is being preached in a situation marked by a gnosticizing environment. Perhaps it is not by accident that our author takes up Is. 54:1 and a phrase such as the "spiritual church." Precisely because some had ignored the eschatological tension present in the Pauline tradition[3] and thus misinterpreted these matters, he felt compelled to take them up and to interpret them correctly for his congregation.

---

[1] See pp. 107-109

[2] Philosophumena 5.7.39.

[3] We have suggested previously, pp. 160-62, that 2 Clement 14 refers to the Pauline tradition not only with the term οἱ ἀπόστολοι, but also with the reference to the church as the "body of Christ."

BIBLIOGRAPHY

I. PRIMARY SOURCES, EDITIONS AND COLLECTIONS

Acta Apostolorum Apocrypha. Edited by R. A. Lipsius and M. Bonnet. Darmstadt, 1959.

The Apocrypha and Pseudepigrapha of the Old Testament. Edited by R. H. Charles. Oxford, 1963.

Die apostolischen Väter. Edited by Karl Bihlmeyer. Tübingen, 1956.

Biblia Hebraica. Edited by Rudolf Kittel. 7th edition. Stuttgart, 1961.

Corpus Hermeticum. Edited by A. D. Nock and A.-J. Festugière. Paris, 1960.

Evangelium Veritatis. Edited by Michel Malinine, Henri-Charles Puech and Gilles Quispel. Zürich, 1956. Includes Coptic text with translations into French, German and English. English translation used unless otherwise indicated.

The Gospel According to Thomas: Coptic Text Established and Translated. A. Guillaumont, H.-Ch. Puech, G. Quispel, W. C. Till, Y. 'Abd al Masiḥ. New York, 1959.

Joseph et Aséneth. Marc Philonenko. Leiden, 1968.

"Le Livre de la Prière d'Aseneth" in *Studia Patristica* I-II. Edited by M. Battifol. Paris, 1889-90.

Novum Testamentum Graece. Edited by Eberhard Nestle. 24th ed. rev. by Erwin Nestle and Kurt Aland. Stuttgart, 1960.

Patrologia graeca. Edited by Jacques Paul Migne. Paris, 1857-66.

Patrologia latina. Edited by Jacques Paul Migne. Paris, 1878-90.

De Resurrectione (Epistula ad Rheginum). Edited by Michel Malinine, Henri-Charles Puech, Gilles Quispel, and Walter Till. Zürich, 1963.

Septuaginta. Auctoritate Academiae Litterarum Gottingensis editum. Göttingen, 1931—. This edition used where available.

Septuaginta. Edited by Alfred Rahlfs. 6th edition. Stuttgart, 1959. This edition used only where Göttingen edition is incomplete.

II. TRANSLATIONS

The Ante-Nicene Fathers. Edited by Alexander Roberts and James Donaldson. Grand Rapids, n.d.

The Apostolic Fathers. Edgar J. Goodspeed. New York, 1950. English translation of the Shepherd of Hermas is from this volume.

Bible. The Oxford Annotated Bible with the Apocrypha: Revised Standard Version. Edited by Herbert G. May and Bruce M. Metzger. New York, 1965.

Early Christian Fathers. Edited by Cyril C. Richardson. Philadelphia, 1953. With the exception of the Shepherd of Hermas, all English translations from the Apostolic Fathers are from this volume.

The Essene Writings from Qumran. A. Dupont-Sommer. Cleveland, 1962.

The Gospel of Philip. R. McL. Wilson. London, 1962.

The Gospel of Thomas. Translation by William R. Schoedel in *The Secret Sayings of Jesus* edited by Robert M. Grant. New York, 1960.

The Gospel of Truth. Translated by W. W. Isenberg in *Gnosticism,* edited by Robert
    M. Grant. New York, 1961. When this translation is used it is so indicated by the
    use of the name Isenberg in brackets. Note listing under primary sources.
Loeb Classical Library. Cambridge, Mass., 1912—.
New Testament Apocrypha. Edited by Edgar Hennecke, Wilhelm Schneemelcher and
    R. McL. Wilson. Philadelphia, 1963.

III. GENERAL WORKS

Altaner, Berthold. *Patrologie.* Freiburg, 1963.
Andresen, Carl. "Zum Formular frühchristlicher Gemeindebriefe," *ZNW* 56 (1965),
    pp. 233-59.
Arai, Sasagu. *Die Christologie des Evangelium Veritatis.* Leiden, 1964.
Aschermann, Hartmut. *Die Paränetischen Formen der Testamente der 12 Patriarchen
    und ihr Nachwirken in der früchristlichen Mahnung.* Dissertation. Berlin, 1955.
Bacher, W. *Die Proöemien der alten jüdischen Homilie.* Leipzig, 1913.
Baltzer, Klaus. *Das Bundesformular.* Neukirchen, 1964. ET: *The Covenant Formulary.*
    Philadelphia, 1971.
Bardenhewer, Otto. *Geschichte der altkirchlichen Literatur.* Freiburg, 1913.
Barnard, L. W. *Studies in the Apostolic Fathers and Their Backgrounds.* Oxford, 1966.
Barnett, Albert E. *Paul Becomes a Literary Influence.* Chicago, 1941.
Barrett, C. K. *The First Epistle to the Corinthians.* New York, 1968.
Bartlet, Vernon. "The Origin and Date of 2 Clement," *ZNW* 7 (1906), pp. 123-35.
Bartsch, Hans Werner. *Gnostisches Gut und Gemeindetradition bei Ignatius von Antiochien.*
    Gütersloh, 1940.
Bauer, Walter. *Aufsätze und Kleine Schriften.* Tübingen, 1967.
——. *Aus der Frühzeit des Christentums.* Tübingen, 1963.
——. *Johannes.* Tübingen, 1912.
——. *Rechtglaübigkeit und Ketzerei im ältesten Christentum.* Tübingen, 1964. ET: *Ortho-
    doxy and Heresy in Earliest Christianity.* Philadelphia, 1971.
——. *Der Wortgottesdienst der ältesten Christen.* Tübingen, 1930.
Bauer, W., Arndt, W.F. and Gingrich, F. W. *A Greek-English Lexicon of the New Testa-
    ment.* Chicago, 1963.
Beckmann, Joachim. *Quellen zur Geschichte des christlichen Gottesdienstes.* Gütersloh,
    1956.
Bellinzoni, A. J. *The Sayings of Jesus in the Writings of Justin Martyr.* Leiden, 1967.
Benoit, A. *Le Baptême chrétien au deuxième Siècle.* Paris, 1953.
Betz, Hans Dieter. "Orthodoxy and Heresy in Primitive Christianity," *Int* 19 (1965),
    pp. 299-311.
Betz, Otto. *Offenbarung und Schriftforschung in der Qumransekte.* Tübingen, 1960.
Beumer, Johannes. "Die altchristliche Idee einer präexistierenden Kirche und ihre
    theologische Auswertung," *Wissenschaft und Weisheit* 9 (1942), pp. 13-22.
Beyschlag, Karlmann. *Clemens Romanus und der Frühkatholizismus.* Tübingen, 1966.
Bianchi, Ugo (ed.). *The Origins of Gnosticism.* Leiden, 1967.
Bietenhard, Hans. *Die himmlische Welt im Urchristentum und Spätjudentum.* Tübingen,
    1951.

Black, Matthew. "The Christological Use of the Old Testament in the New Testament," *NTS* 18 (1971), pp. 1-14.

Blass, F., Debrunner, A. and Funk, Robert W. *A Greek Grammar of the New Testament and Other Early Christian Literature*. Chicago, 1962.

Bloch, Renée. "Midrash," *Dictionnaire de la Bible, Supplément*, 5. Paris, 1957, cols. 1263-81.

Bonhöffer, Adolf. *Epiktet und das Neue Testament*. Geissen, 1911.

Bonsirven, J. *Exégèse Rabbinique et Exégèse Paulinienne*. Paris, 1939.

Borgen, Peder. *Bread from Heaven*. Leiden, 1965.

Bornkamm, Günther. "Der Auferstandene und der Irdische. Mt. 28,16-20," *Zeit und Geschichte*. Ed. Erich Dinkler. Tübingen, 1964, pp. 171-91. ET: "The Risen Lord and the Earthly Jesus: Matthew 28.16-20," *The Future of our Religious Past*. Ed. James M. Robinson. New York, 1971, pp. 203-29.

——. "Das Bekenntnis im Hebräerbrief," *Studien zu Antike und Urchristentum* II. München, 1959, pp. 188-203.

——. "Formen und Gattungen II. Im NT," *RGG*[3] II, cols. 999-1005.

——. "The History of the Origin of the So-called Second Letter to the Corinthians," *The Authorship and Integrity of the New Testament*. Ed. Kurt Aland, et. al. London, 1965, pp. 73-81.

——. "Homologia. Zur Geschichte eines politischen Begriffes," *Hermes* 71 (1936), pp. 377-93. Now also in *Geschichte und Glaube* 1 (München, 1968), pp. 140-56.

——. *Der Lohngedanke im Neuen Testament*. Göttingen, 1961.

——. *Die Vorgeschichte des sogenannten Zweiten Korintherbriefes*. Heidelberg, 1961.

——. "Vorjohanneische Tradition oder nachjohanneische Bearbeitung in der eucharistischen Rede Johannes 6?" *Geschichte und Glaube*, 2. München, 1971, pp. 51-64.

Bousset, Wilhelm. *Hauptprobleme der Gnosis*. Göttingen, 1907.

——. *Die jüdische Apokalyptik*. Berlin, 1903.

——. *Jüdisch-christlicher Schulbetrieb in Alexandria und Rom*. Göttingen, 1915.

——. *Kyrios Christos*. Göttingen, 1965. ET: Nashville, 1970.

——. *Die Religion des Judentums im Späthellenistischen Zeitalter*. Tübingen, 1966.

Bowker, J. W. "Speeches in Acts: A Study in Proem and Yellammedenu Form," *NTS* 14 (1967), pp. 96-111.

——. *The Targums and Rabbinic Literature*. Cambridge, 1969.

Box, G. H. *The Apocalypse of Abraham*. London, 1919.

Brandenburger, Egon. *Adam und Christus*. Neukirchen, 1962.

Braun, Herbert. *Gerichtsgedanke und Rechtfertigungslehre bei Paulus*. Göttingen, 1961.

Broneer, Oscar. "Paul and the Pagan Cults at Isthmia," *HTR* 64 (1971), pp. 169-87.

Brown, Raymond E. "Does the New Testament Call Jesus God?" *TS* 26 (1965), pp. 545-73. Now also in *Jesus God and Man*. Milwaukee, 1967, pp. 1-38.

Bruce, F. F. *Biblical Exegesis in the Qumran Texts*. London, 1960.

Buchanan, G. W. *To the Hebrews*. New York, 1972.

Bultmann, Rudolf. *Die drei Johannesbriefe*. Göttingen, 1967. ET: *The Johannine Epistles*. Philadelphia, 1973.

——. "Zur Geschichte der Lichtsymbolik im Altertum," *Phil* 97 (1948), pp. 1-36.

——. *The Gospel of John*. Oxford, 1971.

——. *The History of the Synoptic Tradition*, New York, 1963.

——. *Der Stil der paulinischen Predigt und die kynisch-stoische Diatribe*. Göttingen, 1910.

Burchard, Christoph. *Untersuchungen zu Joseph und Aseneth*. Tübingen, 1965.

von Campenhausen, Hans. *Die Entstehung der christlichen Bibel*. Tübingen, 1968. ET: *The Formation of the Christian Bible*. Philadelphia, 1972.

——. *Aus der Frühzeit des Christentums*. Tübingen, 1963.

——. *Die Idee des Martyriums in der alten Kirche*. Göttingen, 1964.

——. *Kirchliches Amt und geistliche Vollmacht*. Tübingen, 1963. ET: *Ecclesiastical Authority and Spiritual Power in the Church of the First Three Centuries*. Stanford, 1969.

——. *Tradition und Leben*. Tübingen, 1960. ET: *Tradition and Life in the Church*. Philadelphia, 1968.

——. and Dinkler, E., *et. al.* (eds.). *Die Religion in Geschichte und Gegenwart*. 6 vols. 3rd edition. Tübingen, 1957.

Cancik, Hildegard. *Untersuchungen zu Senecas epistulae morales*. Hildesheim, 1967.

Capelle, W. and Marrou, H. I. "Diatribe," *Reallexikon für Antike und Christentum*, 3. Ed. Albert Hauck. Leipzig, 1896, cols. 990-1009.

Chavasse, C. *The Bride of Christ*. London, 1940.

Clark, Donald L. *Rhetoric in Greco-Roman Education*. New York, 1957.

Cohn, Leopoldus, and Wendland, Paulus. *Philonis Alexandrini*. 6 vols. Berlin, 1962.

Conzelmann, Hans. *Der erste Brief an die Korinther*, Göttingen, 1969.

——. *An Outline of the Theology of the New Testament*. New York, 1969.

Cope, Edward M. *The Rhetoric of Aristotle with a commentary*. Cambridge, 1877.

Crafer, T. W. *Second Epistle of Clement to the Corinthians*. London, 1921.

Creed, J. M. *The Gospel According to St. Luke*. London, 1960.

Cross, F. L. (ed.). *The Jung Codex*. London, 1955.

Cullmann, Oscar. *Early Christian Worship*. London, 1962.

——. *Immortality of the Soul or Resurrection of the Dead?* London, 1962.

Dahl, M. E. *The Resurrection of the Body*. London, 1962.

Dahl, Nils A. "Christ, Creation and the Church," *The Background of the New Testament and Its Eschatology*. Ed. W. D. Davies. Cambridge, 1964, pp. 422-43.

——. "Formgeschichtliche Beobachtungen zur Christusverkündigung in der Gemeindepredigt," *Neutestamentlichen Studien für Rudolf Bultmann*. Ed. W. Eltester. Berlin. 1954, pp. 3-9.

Dalbert, P. *Die Theologie der hellenistisch-jüdischen Missionsliteratur unter Ausschluss von Philo und Josephus*. Hamburg, 1954.

Daniélou, Jean. *From Shadows to Reality*. Westminster, Maryland, 1960.

——. *The Theology of Jewish Christianity*. London, 1964.

Daube, David. "Rabbinic Methods of Interpretation and Hellenistic Rhetoric," *HUCA* 22 (1949), pp. 239-64.

Davies, W. D. *The Setting of the Sermon on the Mount*. Cambridge, 1964.

Deichgräber, Reinhard. *Gotteshymnus und Christushymnus in der frühen Christenheit*. Göttingen, 1967.

Deissmann, Adolf. *Bible Studies*. Edinburgh, 1928.

——. *Light from the Ancient East*. Grand Rapids, 1965.

Delling, Gerhard. *Worship in the New Testament*. Philadelphia, 1962.

Dibelius, Martin. *Der Brief des Jakobus*. Göttingen, 1964. ET: *The Pastoral Epistles*. Philadelphia, 1972.

——. "Zur Formgeschichte des Neuen Testaments (ausserhalb der Evangelien)," *ThRu* NF 3 (1931), pp. 207-42.

——. *Geschichte der urchristlichen Literatur*. Berlin, 1926.

——. *Die Pastoralbriefe*. Tübingen, 1955.

——. "Die Vorstellung vom göttlichen Licht," *DL* 36 (1915), cols. 1469-83.

——. *From Tradition to Gospel*. New York, n.d.

Dinkler, Erich. *Signum Crucis*. Tübingen, 1967.

——. (ed.). *Zeit und Geschichte*. Tübingen, 1964. ET: *The Future of our Religious Past*. Ed. James M. Robinson. New York, 1971.

Di Pauli, Andreas. "Zum sogennanten 2. Korintherbrief des Clemens Romanus," *ZNW* 4 (1903), pp. 321-29.

Dix, G. "The Ministry in the Early Church," *The Apostolic Ministry*, Ed. K. E. Kirk. London, 1947, pp. 183-303.

——. "The Seal in the Second Century," *Theology* 51 (1948), pp. 7-12.

Dodd, C. H. *According to the Scriptures*. London, 1961.

——. *The Apostolic Preaching and Its Developments*. New York, 1962.

——. *The Bible and the Greeks*. London, 1954.

Doeve, J. W. *Jewish Hermeneutics in the Synoptic Gospels and Acts*. Assen, 1954.

Donfried, K. P. "The Theology of 2 Clement," *HTR* 66 (1973), pp. 487-501.

Doresse, Jean. *Les Livres secrets des gnostiques d'Égypte*. Paris, 1958. ET: *The Secret Books of the Egyptian Gnostics*. New York, 1960.

Dorries, Herman (ed.). *Aufsätze zur Gnosis*. Göttingen, 1967.

Doty, William G. "The Concept of Genre in Literary Analysis," *Proceedings of the Society of Biblical Literature*, vol. 2, 1972, pp. 413-48.

Duhm, Andreas. *Der Gottesdienst im ältesten Christentum*. Tübingen, 1928.

Ehrhard, Albert. *Überlieferung und Bestand der hagiographischen und homiletischen Literatur der griechischen Kirche von den Anfängen bis zum Ende des 16 Jahrhunderts*. Leipzig, 1937-43.

Elbogen, Ismar. *Der jüdische Gottesdienst in seiner geschichtlichen Entwicklung*. 1913.

——. "Gottesdienst III. Synagogaler Gottesdienst," *RGG*[3] II. cols, 1756-61.

Ellis, E. Earle. "Midrash, Targum, and New Testament Quotations." *Neotestamentica et Semitica*. Ed. E. Earle Ellis and Max Wilcox. Edinburgh, 1969, pp. 61-69.

——. *Paul's Use of the Old Testament*. Edinburgh, 1957.

Eltester, Walther (ed.). *Judentum Urchristentum Kirche: Festschrift für Joachim Jeremias* Berlin, 1964.

——. (ed.). *Neutestamentliche Studien für Rudolf Bultmann*. Berlin, 1957.

Exler, Francis. *The Form of the Ancient Greek Letter: A Study in Greek Epistolography*. Washington, D. C., 1923.

van Eysinga, G. A. van den Bergh. *La littérature chrétienne primitive*. Paris, 1926.

Fascher, Erich. "Briefliteratur, urchristliche," *RGG*[3] I., cols. 1412-15.

Fischel, Henry A. "Graeco-Roman Rhetoric and the Study of Midrash." Unpublished.

——. "Story and History: Observations on Graeco-Roman Rhetoric and Pharisaism," *American Oriental Society, Middle West Branch, Semi-Centennial Volume*. Ed. Denis Sinor. Bloomington, 1969.

Fischer, Joseph A. *Die apostolischen Väter*. Darmstadt, 1964.

Flesseman-van Leer, E. *Tradition and Scripture in the Early Church*. Assen, 1954.

Freed, Edwin D. *Old Testament Quotations in the Gospel of John*. Leiden, 1965.

Friedländer, Ludwig. *Darstellungen aus der Sittengeschichte Roms*, II. Leipzig, 1922.

Friedländer, Moriz. *Der vorchristliche jüdische Gnosticismus*, Göttingen, 1898.

Fuller, Reginald H. *A Critical Introduction to the New Testament*. London, 1966.

Funk, F. X. "Der sogennante zweite Klemensbrief," *ThQ* 84 (1902), pp. 349-64.

——. "Der sogennante zweite Klemensbrief," *Kirchengeschichtliche Abhandlungen und Untersuchungen* 3 (1907), pp. 272-75.

Funk, Robert. "The Apostolic Parousia: Form and Significance," *Christian History and Interpretation: Studies Presented to John Knox*. Ed. W. R. Farmer. Cambridge, 1967, pp. 249-68.

——. "The Form and Structure of II and III John," *JBL* 86 (1967), pp. 424-30.

——. *Language, Hermeneutic and Word of God*. New York, 1966.

Furnish, Victor Paul. *Paul's Exhortation in the Context of his Letters and Thought*. Unpublished Ph.D. dissertation. Yale, 1960.

Gärtner, Bertil. *The Theology of the Gospel of Thomas*. London, 1961.

Gardiner, E. Norman. *Greek Athletic Sports and Festivals*. London, 1910.

von Gebhardt, O. "Zur Textkritik der neuen Clemensstücke," *ZKG* I (1877), pp. 305-10.

Georgi, Dieter. *Die Gegner des Paulus im 2. Korintherbrief*. Neukirchen, 1964.

——. "Der vorpaulinische Hymnus Phil 2, 6-11," *Zeit und Geschichte*. Ed. Erich Dinkler. Tübingen, 1964, pp. 263-93.

Gerhardson, Birger. *Memory and Manuscript*. Lund, 1961.

Gerke, Friedrich. *Die Stellung des 1. Clemensbriefes innerhalb der Entwicklung der altchristlichen Gemeindeverfassung und des Kirchenrechts*. Leipzig, 1931.

Glaue, Paul. *Die Vorlesung heiliger Schriften im Gottesdienste*. Berlin, 1907.

Goodenough, Erwin R. *By Light, Light: The Mystic Gospel of Hellenistic Judaism*. New Haven, 1935.

Goodspeed, Edgar. *The Apostolic Fathers*. New York, 1950.

——. *Index Apologeticus*. Leipzig, 1912.

——. *Index Patristicus*. Leipzig, 1907.

Graham, Holt H. "Second Clement," *The Apostolic Fathers*, II. Ed. Robert M. Grant and Holt H. Graham. New York, 1965, pp. 109-38.

Grant, Frederick. *The Gospels: their Origin and Growth*. New York, 1957.

Grant, Robert. *After the New Testament*. Philadelphia, 1967.

——. *The Apostolic Fathers*, I. New York, 1964.

——. "Eusebius and His Church History," *Understanding the Sacred Text*. Ed. John Reumann. Valley Forge, 1972, pp. 233-47.

——. *Miracle and Natural Law in Graeco-Roman and Early Christian Thought*. Amsterdam, 1952.

——. and Freedman, David N. *The Secret Sayings of Jesus*. Garden City, 1960.

——. and Graham, Holt. *The Apostolic Fathers*, II. New York, 1965.

Grässer, Erich. "Der Hebräerbrief 1938-1963," *ThRu* 30 (1964), pp. 138-236.

Gray, George B. *The Forms of Hebrew Poetry*. 1915.

Haenchen, Ernst. *Die Botschaft des Thomas-Evangeliums*. Berlin, 1961.

——. *Der Weg Jesu*. Berlin. 1966.

Hagemann. "Über den zweiten Brief des Clemens von Rom," *ThQ* 43 (1861) pp. 509-31.

Hahn, Ferdinand. "Jakobus 5.7-11," *Göttinger Predigtmeditationen* 18 (1963/64), pp. 376-86.

von Harnack, Adolf. *Die Chronologie der altchristlichen Literatur bis Eusebius*, II, 1. Leipzig, 1897.

——. *Geschichte der altchristlichen Literatur bis Eusebius*. Leipzig, 1893.

——. *Das Schreiben der römischen Kirche an die Korinthische aus der zeit Domitians (I. Clemensbrief)*. Leipzig, 1929.

——. "Über das Alter der Bezeichnung 'Die Bücher' ('Die Bibel') für die Heiligen Schrift in der Kirche," *Zentralblatt fur Bibliothekswesen* 45 (1928), pp. 337-42.

——. "Über den sogenannten zweiten Brief des Clemens an die Korinther," *ZKG* I (1877), pp. 264-83; 329-64.

——. "Zum Ursprung des sogenannten zweiten Klemensbriefes," *ZNW* 6 (1905), pp. 67-71.

Harnack, Theodosius. *Der christliche Gemeindegottesdienst im apostolischen und altkatholischen Zeitalter*. Erlangen, 1854.

Harris, Rendel. "The Authorship of the So-called Second Epistle of Clement," *ZNW* 23 (1924), pp. 193-200.

Hatch, Edwin, and Redpath, Henry A. *A Concordance to the Septuagint*. 2 vols. Graz, 1954.

Heinemann, Isaak. *Philons Griechische und Jüdische Bildung*. Hildesheim, 1962.

Heinrici, Georg. *Die valentinianische Gnosis und die heilige Schrift*. Berlin, 1871.

Hennecke, Edgar. *Neutestamentliche Apokryphen*. Tübingen, 1924.

Hilgenfeld, Adolf. *Die apostolische Väter*. Halle, 1853.

——. *Die Ketzergeschichte des Urchristentums*. Darmstadt, 1963.

Hofius, Ottfried. *Katapausis: Die Vorstellung vom endzeitlichen Ruheort im Hebräerbrief*. Tübingen, 1970.

Hoh, Josef. *Die kirchliche Busse im 2. Jahrhundert*. Breslau, 1932.

Hornschuh, Manfred. *Studien zur Epistula Apostolorum*. Berlin, 1965.

Hummel, Reinhart. *Die Auseinandersetzung zwischen Kirche und Judentum im Matthäusevangelium*. München, 1963.

Hunzinger, Claus-Hunno. "Unbekannte Gleichnisse Jesu aus dem Thomas-Evangelium," *Judentum Urchristentum Kirche*. Ed. Walther Eltester. Berlin, 1964, pp. 209-20.

Hurd, John C., Jr. *The Origin of I Corinthians*. London, 1965.

——. "Concerning the Structure of 1 Thessalonians," *Society of Biblical Literature annual meeting papers*. 1972.

James, Montague Rhodes. *The Apocryphal New Testament*. Oxford, 1963.

Jeremias, Joachim. "Chiasmus in den Paulusbriefen," ZNW 49 (1958), pp. 145-56.

——. "The Last Supper," *ExpT* 64 (1952), pp. 91-92.

——. *Unbekannte Jesusworte*. Gütersloh, 1963. ET: *Unknown Sayings of Jesus*. New York, 1957.

Jonas, Hans. *Gnosis und Spätantiker Geist*. 2 vols. Göttingen, 1964.

Jordan, Hermann. *Geschichte der altchristlichen Literatur*. Leipzig, 1911.

Jülicher, Adolf. *Die Gleichnisreden Jesu*. Darmstadt, 1963.

Käsemann, Ernst. "An Apologia for Primitive Christian Eschatology," *Essays on New Testament Themes*. London, 1964, pp. 169-95.

——. *New Testament Questions of Today*. Philadelphia, 1969.

——. *Das wandernde Gottesvolk*. Göttingen, 1961.

Kamlah, Ehrhard. "Bekenntnis III. Im NT," *RGG*³ I, cols. 991-93.

——. *Die Form der katalogischer Paränese im Neuen Testament*. Tübingen, 1964.

Karris, Robert J. *The Function and Sitz im Leben of the Paraenetic Elements of the Pastoral Epistles*. Unpublished Th.D. dissertation. Harvard, 1971.

Katz, P. "The Early Christian Use of Codices Instead of Rolls," *JTS* 46 (1945), pp.63-65.

Kautzch, E. *Die Apokryphen und Pseudepigraphen des Alten Testaments*. 2 vols. Darmstadt, 1962.

Kelly, J. N. D. *The Pastoral Epistles*. New York, 1963.

Kennedy, George. *The Art of Persuasion in Greece*. Princeton, 1963.

Kilpatrick, G. D. "The Last Supper," *ExpT* 64 (1952), pp. 4-8.

Kirk, Kenneth E. (ed.). *The Apostolic Ministry*. London, 1962.

Kittel, Gerhard. *Theologisches Wörterbuch zum Neuen Testament*. 8 vols. Stuttgart, 1933-.
    ET: *Theological Dictionary of the New Testament*. Grand Rapids, 1964-.

Klauser, Theodor (ed.). *Reallexikon für Antike und Christentum*. 6 vols. Stuttgart, 1950.

Klein, Franz-Nobert. *Die Lichtterminologie bei Philon von Alexandrien und in den Hermetischen Schriften*. Leiden, 1962.

Klein, Günther. *Der älteste christliche Katechismus und die jüdischen propaganda Literatur*. Berlin, 1909.

Klein, Günther. *Die zwölf Apostel*. Göttingen, 1961.

Kleinert, Paul. *Zur christlichen Kultus und Kultusgeschichte*. Berlin, 1889.

Klevinghaus, J. *Die theologische Stellung der apostolischen Väter zur alttestamentlichen Offenbarung*. Gütersloh, 1948.

Klijn, A. F. *The Acts of Thomas*. Leiden, 1962.

Klostermann, Erich. *Apocrypha II*. Berlin. 1929.

Knoch, Otto. *Eigenart und Bedeutung der Eschatologie im theologischen Aufriss des ersten Clemensbriefes*. Bonn, 1964.

Knopf, Rudolf. "Die Anagnose zum zweiten Clemensbrief," *ZNW* 3 (1902), pp. 266-79.

——. *Der erste Clemensbrief*. Leipzig, 1899.

——. *Die Lehre der zwölf Apostel. Die zwei Clemensbriefe*. Tübingen, 1920.

——. *Das nachapostolische Zeitalter*. Tübingen, 1905.

Köster, Helmut. "Die ausserkanonischen Herrenworte," *ZNW* 48 (1957), pp. 220-37.

——. "*ΓΝΩΜΑΙ ΔΙΑΦΟΡΟΙ*: The Origin and Nature of Diversification in the History of Early Christianity," *HTR* 58 (1965), pp. 279-318.

——. *Synoptische Überlieferung bei den apostolischen Vätern*. Berlin, 1957.

Koskenniemi, Heikki. *Studien zur Idee und Phraseologie des griechischen Briefes bis 400 n. Chr.* Helsinki, 1956.

Kraft, Robert. *The Didache and Barnabas*. New York, 1965.

Krause, Johann H. *Die Gymnastik und Agonistik der Hellenen*. Leipzig, 1841.

——. *Die Pythien, Nemeen, und Isthmien*. Leipzig, 1841.

Kretschmar, Georg. "Auferstehung des Fleisches," *Leben Angesichts des Todes*, Helmut Thielicke zum 60. Geburtstag, (Tübingen, 1968), pp. 101-37.

Krüger, Gustav. "Bemerkungen zum zweiten Klemensbrief." *Studies in Early Christianity*. Ed. S. J. Case. New York, 1928, pp. 419-39.

——. "Zu II Klem. 14.2," *ZNW* 31 (1932), pp. 204-205.

Kümmel, W. G. *Introduction to the New Testament*. Nashville, 1966.

Kuhn, K. G. "The Lord's Supper and the Communal Meal at Qumran," *The Scrolls and the New Testament*. Ed. Krister Stendahl. London, 1958, pp. 65-93.

Lampe, G. W. H. *A Patristic Greek Lexicon*. Oxford, 1961.

——. *The Seal of the Spirit*. London, 1967.

Langerbeck, Hermann. *Aufsätze zur Gnosis*. Ed. Hermann Dörries. Göttingen, 1967.

Lawson, John. *A Theological and Historical Introduction to the Apostolic Fathers*. New York, 1961.

LeDéaut, Roger. "Apropos a Definition of Midrash," *Int* 25 (1971), pp. 259-82.

Leipoldt, Johannes. *Der Gottesdienst der ältesten Kirche jüdisch? griechish? christlich?* Leipzig, 1937.

——, and Schenke, H. *Koptisch-gnostische Schriften aus den Papyrus-Codices von Nag-Hamadi.* Hamburg, 1960.

Leisegang, Ionnes. *Philonis Alexandrini,* vol. 7. Berlin, 1963.

Lerle, Ernst. *Die Predigt im Neuen Testament.* Berlin, 1957.

Liddell, H. G. and Scott, R. *A Greek-English Lexicon.* London, 1961.

Lieberman, Saul. *Hellenism in Jewish Palestine.* New York, 1950.

Lietzmann, Hans. *Messe und Herrenmahl.* Berlin, 1955.

Lightfoot, J. B. *The Apostolic Fathers.* London, 1890.

Lindars, Barnabas. *New Testament Apologetic.* London, 1961.

Lührmann, Dieter. "Epiphaneia," *Tradition und Glaube.* Ed. G. Jeremias, H-W. Kuhn and H. Stegemann. Göttingen, 1971, pp. 185-99.

——. *Die Redaction der Logienquelle.* Neukirchen, 1969.

Lütgert, W. *Amt und Geist im Kampf.* Gütersloh, 1911.

Lund, N. W. *Chiasmus in the New Testament: A Study in Formgeschichte.* Chapel Hill, 1942.

Malherbe, Abraham J. "1 Thessalonians as a Paraenetic Letter." *Society of Biblical Literature annual meeting papers,* 1972.

Mann, Jacob. *The Bible as Read and Preached in the Old Synagogue,* I. New York, 1971.

Marmorstein, A. "The Background of the Haggadah," *HUCA* 6 (1929), pp. 141-204.

Martyn, J. Louis. *History and Theology in the Fourth Gospel.* New York, 1968.

Marxsen, Willi. *Introduction to the New Testament.* Philadelphia, 1968.

Maybaum, Sigmund. *Die ältesten Phasen in der Entwicklung der jüdischen Predigt.* Berlin, 1901.

——. *Jüdische Homiletik.* Berlin, 1890.

Meinhold, Peter. "Schweigende Bischöfe," *Festgabe Joseph Lortz.* Ed. Erwin Iserloh and Peter Manns. Baden-Baden, 1958, pp. 467-90.

Michaelis, Wilhelm. "Zeichen, Siegel, Kreuz," *TZ* 12 (1956), pp. 505-26.

Michel, Otto. *Der Brief an die Hebräer.* Göttingen, 1966.

——. *Der Brief an die Römer.* Göttingen, 1963.

Miller, Merrill P. "Targum, Midrash and the Use of the Old Testament in the New Testament," *JSJ* 2 (1971), pp. 29-82.

Mitton, C. Leslie. *The Formation of the Pauline Corpus of Letters.* London, 1955.

Moffatt, James. *Epistle to the Hebrews.* Edinburgh, 1963.

Moore, George Foot. *Judaism.* 3 vols. Cambridge, Mass., 1958.

Moore, L. V. *The Use of the Gospel Material in Pre-Catholic Christian Literature.* Unpublished Ph.D. dissertation. University of Chicago, 1929.

Morris, Leon. *The New Testament and the Jewish Lectionaries.* London, 1964.

Moule, C. F. D. *Worship in the New Testament.* Richmond, 1962.

Moulton, James Hope, and Milligan, George. *The Vocabulary of the Greek Testament.* London, 1963.

Moulton, W. F., and Geden, A. S. *A Concordance to the Greek Testament.* Edinburgh, 1963.

Mounce, Robert H. *The Essential Nature of New Testament Preaching.* Grand Rapids, 1960.

Mowry, Lucetta. "The Early Circulation of Paul's Letters," *JBL* 63 (1944), pp. 73-86.

Mueller, Karl. *Die Forderung der Ehelosigkeit für alle Getauften in der alten Kirche.* Tübingen, 1927.

Mueller, K. F., and Blankenburg, W. *Leiturgia.* 3 vols. Kassel, 1954.

Nauck, Wolfgang. "Die Tradition und Komposition der Areopagrede," *ZTK* 53 (1956) pp. 11-52.

Neufeld, Vernon H. *The Earliest Christian Confessions.* Grand Rapids, 1963.

Neusner, Jacob. *Rabbinic Traditions about the Pharisees before 70.* 3 vols. Leiden, 1971.

——. "Types and Forms in Ancient Jewish Literature: Some Comparisons," *HR* 11 (1972), pp. 354-90.

The New Testament in the Apostolic Fathers, by a Committee of the Oxford Society of Historical Theology, Oxford, 1905.

Nickelsburg, George W. *Resurrection, Immortality, and Eternal Life in Intertestamental Judaism.* Cambridge, Mass., 1972.

Niebergall, Alfred. "Predigt I. Geschichte der Predigt," *RGG*[3] V, cols. 515-30.

Nilsson, Martin P. *Die hellenistische Schule.* München, 1955.

Nock, Arthur Darby. *Early Gentile Christianity and Its Hellenistic Background.* New York, 1964.

Norden, Eduard. *Agnostos Theos.* Darmstadt, 1956.

——. *Die Antike Kunstprosa.* 2 vols. Darmstadt, 1958.

Oepke, Albrecht. *Der Brief des Paulus an die Galater.* Berlin, 1964.

——. *Die Missionspredigt des apostels Paulus.* Leipzig, 1920.

Oesterley, W. O. E. *The Jewish Background of the Christian Liturgy.* Oxford, 1925.

——, and Box, G. H. *The Religion and Worship of the Synagogue.* London, 1911.

Opitz, Helmut. *Ursprünge frühkatholischer Pneumatologie.* Berlin, 1960.

Orbe, Antonio. "Cristo y la Iglesia en su Matrimonio anterior a los siglos," *Estudios Ecclesiasticus* 29 (1955), pp. 299-344.

Oulton, J. E. L. "Second Century Teaching on Holy Baptism," *Theology* 50 (1947), pp. 86-91.

Peel, Malcolm Lee. *The Epistle to Rheginos.* London, 1969.

Pernveden, Lage. *The Concept of the Church in the Shepherd of Hermas.* Lund, 1966.

Perrin, Norman. *Rediscovering the Teaching of Jesus.* New York, 1967.

Peterson, Erik. *Frühkirche, Judentum und Gnosis.* Freiburg, 1959.

Peterson, Norman R., Jr. "So-called Gnostic Type Gospels and the Question of the 'Genre Gospel,'" *Society of Biblical Literature annual meeting papers,* 1970.

Pfitzner, Victor. *Paul and the Agon Motif.* Leiden, 1967.

Pfleiderer, Otto. *Das Urchristentum, seine Schriften und Lehren.* Berlin, 1902.

Plümacher, Eckhard. *Lukas als hellenistischer Schriftsteller.* Göttingen, 1972.

Plumpe, J. C. *Mater Ecclesia.* Washington, 1943.

Poschmann, Bernhard. *Paenitentia Secunda.* Bonn, 1940.

Praetorius, W. "Die Bedeutung der beiden Klemensbriefe für die älteste Geschichte der kirchlichen Praxis," *ZKG* 33 (1912), pp. 347-63; 501-28.

Procksch, Otto. *Das Bekenntnis im Alten Testament.* Leipzig, 1936.

Puech, H. C., and Quispel, Gilles. "Le quatrième écrit gnostique du Codex Jung," *VC* 9 (1955), pp. 94-102.

Quacquarelli, Antonio. *Retorica E Liturgia Antenicena.* Rome, 1960.

Quasten, Johannes. *Patrology.* 3 vols. Utrecht, 1962.

Quispel, Gilles. "Christliche Gnosis und jüdische Heterodoxie," *EvTh* 14 (1954), pp. 474-84.

——. "Gnosticism and the New Testament," *VC* 19 (1965), pp. 65-85.

——. "The Gospel of Thomas and the New Testament," *VC* 11 (1957), pp. 189-207.

——. "The Jung Codex and its Significance," *The Jung Codex*. Ed. F. L. Cross. London, 1955, pp. 35-78.

——. *Makarius, Das Thomasevangelium und das Lied von der Perle*. Leiden, 1967.

——. "The Original Doctrine of Valentine," *VC* 1 (1947), pp. 43-73.

von Rad, Gerhard. "Es ist noch eine Ruhe vorhanden dem Volk Gottes," *Gesammelte Studien zum Alten Testament*. München, 1961, pp. 101-108.

Rahn, Helmut. *Morphologie der antiken Literatur*. Darmstadt, 1969.

Reicke, B. "A Synopsis of Early Christian Preaching," *The Root of the Vine*. Ed. Anton Fridrichesen. London, 1953, pp. 128-60.

——. and Rost, Leonhard. *Biblisch-Historisches Handwörterbuch*. 3 vols. Göttingen, 1962.

Resch, Alfred. *Agrapha*. Darmstadt, 1967.

Richter, Georg. "Zur Formgeschichte und literarischen Einheit von John 6,31-58," *ZNW* 60 (1969), pp. 21-55.

Riesenfeld, Harald. "Gottesdienst IV. Im NT," *RGG*³ II, cols. 1761-63.

Riessler, Paul. *Altjüdisches Schrifttum ausserhalb der Bibel*. Darmstadt, 1966.

Ringgren, Helmer. *The Faith of Qumran*. Philadelphia, 1963.

Roberts, C. H. "The Codex," *Proceedings of the British Academy* 40 (1954), pp. 169-204.

Robinson, James M. "The Coptic Gnostic Library Today," *NTS* 14 (1968) pp. 356-401.

——. "Kerygma and History in the New Testament," *The Bible in Modern Scholarship*. Ed. J. Phillip Hyatt. Nashville, 1965, pp. 114-50.

——. "*ΛΟΓΟΙ ΣΟΦΩΝ*. Zur Gattung der Spruchquelle Q," *Zeit und Geschichte*. Ed. Erich Dinkler. Tübingen, 1964, pp. 77-96. ET: *Logoi Sophon: on the Gattung of Q*," *The Future of our Religious Past*. Ed. James M. Robinson. New York, 1971, pp. 84-130.

Robinson, John A. T. *The Body*. London, 1961.

Roller, Otto. *Das Formular der paulinischen Briefe*. Stuttgart, 1933.

Ropes, James Hardy. *Die Sprüche Jesu, die in den kanonischen Evangelien nicht überliefert sind*. Leipzig, 1896.

Rowley, H. H. *The Relevance of Apocalyptic*. London, 1963.

Russell, D. S. *The Method and Message of Jewish Apocalyptic*. Philadelphia, 1964.

Sanders, E. P. *The Tendencies of the Synoptic Tradition*. Cambridge, 1969.

Sanders, Jack T. *The New Testament Christological Hymns*. Cambridge, 1971.

Sanders, Louis. *L'Héllenisme de Saint Clément de Rome et le paulinisme*. Louvain, 1943.

Sataki, Akira. *Die Gemeindeordnung in der Johannesapokalypse*. Neukirchen, 1966.

Schenke, Hans-Martin. *Die Herkunft des sogenannten Evangelium Veritatis*. Göttingen, 1959.

Schian, M. "Geschichte der christliche Predigt," *Realencyklopädie für protestantische Theologie und Kirche* XV, Leipzig (1904), pp. 627ff.; XXIV (1913), pp. 335ff.

Schille, Gottfried. *Frühchristliche Hymnen*. Berlin, 1965.

——. "Katechese und Taufliturgie," *ZNW* 51 (1960), pp. 112-31.

——. "Zur urchristlichen Tauflehre. Stylistische Beobachtungen am Barnabasbrief," *ZNW* 49 (1958), pp. 31-52.

Schlier, Heinrich. *Der Brief an die Galater*. Göttingen, 1962.

——. *Christus und die Kirche im Epheserbriefe*. Tübingen, 1930.

——. *Religionsgeschichtliche Untersuchungen zu den Ignatiusbriefen*. Berlin, 1929.

Schmidtke, Alfred. *Neue Fragmente und Untersuchungen zu den judenchristlichen Evangelien.* Leipzig, 1911.

Schmithals, Walter. *Die Gnosis in Korinth.* Göttingen, 1959. ET: *Gnosticism in Corinth.* Nashville, 1971.

——. *The Office of Apostle in the Early Church.* Nashville, 1969.

Schnackenburg, Rudolf. *Die Johannesbriefe.* Freiburg, 1965.

Schneemelcher, Wilhelm. *Bibliographia Patristica.* Berlin, 1956—.

——. *Neutestamentliche Apokryphen,* II. Tübingen, 1964. ET: *New Testament Apocrypha.* 2 vols. Philadelphia, 1963-65.

Schoedel, William R. "Naassene Themes in the Coptic Gospel of Thomas," *VC* 14 (1960), pp. 225-34.

Schoeps, Hans Joachim. *Paul.* Philadelphia, 1961.

——. *Theologie und Geschichte des Judenchristentums.* Tübingen, 1949.

——. *Urgemeinde Judenchristentum Gnosis.* Tübingen, 1956.

Scholem, Gershom. *Major Trends in Jewish Mysticism.* New York, 1961.

Scholer, David M. *Nag Hammadi Bibliography 1948-1969.* Leiden, 1971.

Schrage, Wolfgang. *Das Verhältnis des Thomas-Evangeliums zur synoptischen Tradition.* Berlin, 1964.

Schrenk, G. "Urchristliche Missions-Predigt im 1 Jh.," *Festgabe für Th. Wurm.* Ed. M. Loiser. 1948, pp. 51-66.

von Schubert, H. "Der sog. zweite Clemensbrief, eine Gemeindepredigt." *Neutestamentliche Apokryphen.* Ed. Edgar Hennecke. Tübingen, 1924, pp. 588-95.

Schubert, Paul. *Form and Function of the Pauline Thanksgivings.* Berlin, 1939.

Schürmann, Heinz. *Das Lukasevangelium,* I. Freiburg, 1969.

Schüssler, W. "Ist der zweite Klemensbrief ein einheitliches Ganzes," *ZKG* 28 (1907), pp. 1-13.

Schwegler, Albert. *Das nachapostolischen Zeitalter.* Tübingen, 1846.

Schweizer, Eduard. "Concerning the Speeches in Acts," *Studies in Luke-Acts.* Ed. L. E. Keck and J. L. Martyn. Nashville, 1966, pp. 208-16.

——. "Zum religionsgeschichtlichen Hintergrund der 'Sendungs-Formel' Gal 4,4f; Röm 8,3f; Joh 3,16f; 1 Joh 4,9," *ZNW* 57 (1966), pp. 199-210.

Sedgwick, W. B. "The Origin of the Sermon," *HibJ* 45 (1947), pp. 158-64.

Seeberg, Alfred. *Die Didache des Judentums und der Urchristenheit.* Leipzig, 1908.

——. *Der Kathechismus der Urchristenheit.* München, 1966.

Seitz, O. J. F. "Relationship of the Shepherd of Hermas to the Epistle of James," *JBL* 63 (1944), pp. 131-40.

——. "Antecedents and Signification of the Term *ΔΙΨΥΧΟΣ,*" *JBL* 66 (1947), pp. 211-19.

Silberman, Lou H. "A Midrash on Midrash." Unpublished paper distributed to members of seminar on Jewish Exegesis, 1971 annual meeting of *Studiorum Novi Testamenti Societas.*

Simonin, H. D. "Le 'doute' d'après les Pères Apostoliques," *Vie Spirituelle* 51 (1937), pp. 165-78.

Smart, James. *History and Theology in Second Isaiah.* Philadelphia, 1965.

Smith, Morton. *Tannaitic Parallels to the Gospels.* Philadelphia, 1968.

von Soden, Hans. "Sakrament und Ethik bei Paulus," *Urchristentum und Geschichte,* I. Ed. H. von Campenhausen. Tübingen, 1951, pp. 239-75.

Sowers, Sidney G. *The Hermeneutics of Philo and Hebrews*. Richmond, 1965.

Stein, E. "Die homiletische Peroratio im Midrasch," *HUCA* 8 (1931/32), pp. 353-71.

Stendahl, Krister. "Matthew," *Peake's Commentary on the Bible*. Ed. Matthew Black and H. H. Rowley. London, 1962, pp. 769-98.

——. *The School of St. Matthew*. Philadelphia, 1968.

Stengel, Paul. *Die griechischen Kultusaltertümer*. München, 1898.

Strack, Hermann, and Billerbeck, Paul. *Kommentar zum Neuen Testament aus Talmud und Midrash*. 6 vols. München, 1926.

Streeter, B. H. *The Primitive Church*. London, 1929.

Swete, Henry Barclay. *The Holy Spirit in the Ancient Church*. Grand Rapids, 1966.

——. *The Holy Spirit in the New Testament*. Grand Rapids, 1964.

Taylor, C. "The Homily of Pseudo-Clement," *The Journal of Philosophy* 28 (1901), pp. 195-208.

Tcherikover, Victor. *Hellenistic Civilization and the Jews*. Philadelphia, 1966.

Teeple, Howard M. "The Origin of the Son of Man Christology," *JBL* 84 (1965), pp. 213-50.

Thraede, Klaus. *Grundzüge griechisch-römischer Brieftopik*. München, 1970.

Thyen, Hartwig. *Der Stil der Jüdisch-Hellenistischen Homilie*. Göttingen, 1955.

Till, Walter C. *Die gnostischen Schriften des koptischen Papyrus Beroliniensis 8502*. Berlin, 1955.

Torrance, T. F. *The Doctrine of Grace in the Apostolic Fathers*. Edinburgh, 1948.

Towner, W. Sibley. "Form Criticism of Rabbinic Literature," *Society of Biblical Literature annual meeting papers*, 1971.

Turner, H. E. W. *The Pattern of Christian Truth*. London, 1954.

——, and Montefiore, Hugh. *Thomas and the Evangelists*. London, 1962.

van Unnik, W. C. *Newly Discovered Gnostic Writings*. London, 1960.

——. "Die Rücksicht auf die Reaktion der Nicht-Christen," *Judentum Urchristentum Kirche*. Ed. W. Eltester. Berlin, 1964, pp. 221-34.

——. "Studies over de zogenaamde eerste Brief van Clemens. I. Het litteraire genre," *Mededelingen der Koninklijke Nederlandse Akademie van Wetenschappen, Afd. Letterkunde*. Nieuwe Reeks 33 (1970), pp. 151-204.

Urner, Hans. *Die ausserbiblische Lesung im christlichen Gottesdienst*. Göttingen, 1952.

Usher, Stephen. "Oratory," *Greek and Latin Literature*. Ed. John Higginbotham. London, 1969, pp. 342-89.

Vielhauer, Philipp. *Aufsätze zum Neuen Testament*. München, 1965.

Vögtle, Anton. *Die Tugend- und Lasterkataloge im Neuen Testament*. Münster, 1936.

Völker, Walther. *Quellen zur Geschichte der christlichen Gnosis*. Tübingen, 1932.

Völter, Daniel. *Die älteste Predigt aus Rom*. Leiden, 1908.

Wehofer, Thomas. *Untersuchungen zur altchristlichen Epistolographie*. Vienna, 1901.

Weiss, Johannes. "Beiträge zur paulinischen Rhetorik," *Theologische Studien*, (B. Weiss dargebracht). Göttingen, 1897.

Wendland, Paul. "Philo und die kynisch-stoische Diatribe," in P. Wendland and O. Kern, *Beiträge zu Geschichte der griechischen Philosophie und Religion*. Berlin, 1895.

——. *Die urchristlichen Literaturformen*. Tübingen, 1912.

Westermann, Claus. "Bekenntnis II. Im AT und im Judentum," *RGG*[3] I, cols. 989-91.

——. *Das Buch Jesaja*. Göttingen, 1966.

Wetter, G. P. "Eine gnostische Formel im 4. Evangleium," *ZNW* 18 (1917/18), pp. 49-63.

——. *Phos*. Uppsala, 1915.

White, J. S. *The Form and Structure of the Official Petition*. Missoula, 1972.

Wilckens, Ulrich. *Die Missionsreden der Apostelgeschichte*. Neukirchen, 1963.

——. *Weisheit und Torheit*. Tübingen, 1959.

Wilson, R. McL. "The Early History of the Exegesis of Gen 1, 26," *Studia Patristica*, II (Oxford, 1957), pp. 420-37.

——. (ed.). *The Gospel of Philip*. London, 1962.

——. "Gnostic Origins," *VC* 9 (1955), pp. 193-212.

——. "Gnostic Origins Again," *VC* 11 (1957), pp. 93-110.

——. *The Gnostic Problem*. London, 1964.

——. *Studies in the Gospel of Thomas*. London, 1960.

Windisch, Hans. "Das Christentum des zweiten Klemensbriefes," *Harnack-Ehrung*, *Beitrage zur Kirchengeschichte*. Leipzig, 1921, pp. 119-34.

——. "Julius Cassianus und die Clemenshomilie," *ZNW* 25 (1926), pp. 258-62.

——. *Taufe und Sünde im ältesten Christentum bis auf Origenes*. Tübingen, 1908.

Wissowa, George (ed.). *Paulys Real-Encyclopaedie der Classischen Altertumswissenschaft*. Stuttgart, 1893.

Wright, Addison G. *The Literary Genre Midrash*. New York, 1967.

Wocher. *Der brief des Clemens und des Polykarp*. Tübingen, 1830.

Wright, A. G. *The Literary Genre Midrash*. New York, 1967.

Wright, Leon E. *Alterations of the Words of Jesus as Quoted in the Literature of the Second Century*. Cambridge, Mass., 1952.

Wuellner, Wilhelm. "Haggadic Homily Genre in 1 Conrinthians 1-3," *JBL* 89 (1970), pp. 199-204.

Wustmann, Georg. *Die Heilsbedeutung Christi bei den apostolischen Vätern*. Gütersloh, 1905.

Ziegler, Adolf. *Neue Studien zum ersten Klemensbrief*. München, 1958.

Zunz, Leopold. *Die gottesdienstlichen Vorträge der Juden historisch entwickelt*. Hildesheim, 1966.

I. TEXTUAL INDEXES

1. OLD TESTAMENT

2. JEWISH WRITINGS

3. NEW TESTAMENT

4. EARLY CHRISTIAN LITERATURE

5. GNOSTIC WRITINGS

6. CLASSICAL AND HELLENISTIC AUTHORS

II. INDEX OF GREEK WORDS

λίθος 105, 182
λόγισμος 185
λόγος 46, 49, 51, 58, 65, 74, 80, 149, 151, 185, 188
λύκος 69
λυπέω 41
λύω 90

μακάριος 41
ματοιότης 53, 87
μέγας 102, 122, 141, 188
μελετάω 137
μέλλω 71, 102, 120, 123, 124, 142, 192
μέλος 139
μεμβράνα 94
μένω 182
μεσίτης 102
μέσος 69
μεταβαίνω 182
μεταβολή 140
μεταλαμβάνω 115, 125, 126
μετανοέω 13, 34, 40, 41, 88, 90, 104, 115, 122, 129, 130, 132
μετάνοια 13, 40, 57, 90, 116, 131
μηδείς 39, 98, 155
μημονεύω 34
μήτηρ 74, 200
μικρός 37, 38, 98, 115, 120, 124
μίξεως 200
μισέω 78
μισθός 10, 38, 78, 100, 113
μοιχάω 114, 115, 124
μόνος 34, 51, 188
Μωσῆς 81

ναός 145
νεκρός 37, 98, 99, 100, 106, 143
νέφος 105, 106, 182, 184, 187, 189
νηστεία 170
νουθεσία 18
νουθετέω 13, 18, 34, 35, 36, 174, 175
νῦν 162, 163, 192, 193, 195
νυνί 39, 107, 108, 109
Νῶε 51

ξένος 101, 120
ξύλον 52, 105, 182

ὁδός 102, 120, 185
ὁδούς 64, 65
οἶδα 2, 38, 64, 66, 86, 98, 147, 182
οἰκεῖος 183
οἰκέτης 71
οἶκος 53
οἴομαι 34, 88
ὀλιγοχρόνιος 120, 124
ὅλος 134
ὁμιλέω 26, 27
ὁμιλία 22, 25, 26, 27
ὅμοιος 138
ὁμολογέω 60, 64, 87, 106, 113
ὄμφαξ 52
ὄνομα 53, 60, 64, 65, 86, 87, 154, 155, 189
ὅρασις 38, 51, 92, 105, 183
ὁράω 65, 92, 184
ὀργάνον 178
ὀργή 14
ὅσιος 38, 120
ὅσος 38
οὐαί 86, 87
οὐδέποτε 64, 66, 67
οὐδείς 101
οὐρανός 60, 63, 64, 65, 74, 89, 90, 122, 188, 189
οὕτως 37, 82, 98, 99, 105
ὀφείλω 38, 114
ὄφελος 83
ὀφθαλμός 86, 184

πάλαι 52
πάλιν 81, 189
παραβάσις 103
παράκλησις 46, 89
παράκλητος 131
παρακούω 61, 113
παραλογίζομαι 173
παραπόλλυμαι 89
πάρειμι 54
παρεισφέρω 116
παρεπίδημος 120
παρέχω 14, 122
παρθένος 122
παρίστημι 52
παροικέω 119, 120
παροικία 118, 119

III. INDEX OF SUBJECTS

IV. INDEX OF MODERN AUTHORS